101 WINE REGIONS

101 WINE REGIONS

A tour of the best and most uplifting wine regions in the world

Roger Barlow & Mark Rowlinson

PaRragon

Bath · New York · Singapore · Hong Kong · Cologne · Delhi · Melbourne

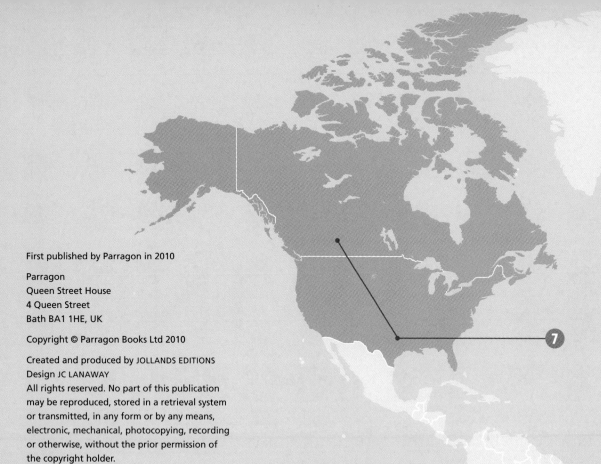

First published by Parragon in 2010

Parragon
Queen Street House
4 Queen Street
Bath BA1 1HE, UK

Copyright © Parragon Books Ltd 2010

Created and produced by JOLLANDS EDITIONS
Design JC LANAWAY

ISBN 978-1-4075-5561-4

Printed in Malaysia

RECOMMENDED WINES

The wines recommended in this book
have been chosen to represent a cross
section of those that are generally
available throughout the wine world.
They are all good examples of their
kind, ranging from value-for-money
wines to the ultimate. The
recommendations are not vintage-
specific, but are of wines that show
consistency year after year.

Wine is bought in a variety of ways
– through supermarkets, specialist wine
merchants, mail order, direct from the
winemaker, at airports and so on. In
order to find a local stockist of a
particular wine, a useful search engine
is wine-searcher.com.

The wines have been categorized by average
price according to the following scheme:

 Everyday drinking wine with
regional characteristics: up to £7.50.

 Well-made wine to be enjoyed with
family and friends: £7.50 to £15.

 Fine wine that would grace a
special occasion: £15 to £50.

 The finest expression of a region,
with a price to match: over £50.

Key to wine

 Red

 Rosé

 White

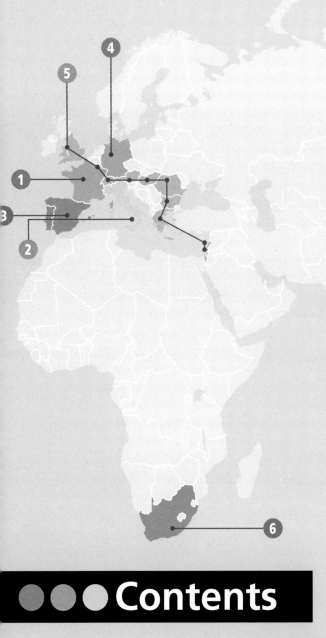

●●○ Contents

●●●● Introduction

When you buy a bottle of wine its label should tell you which region it comes from, though this may be as vague as 'Australia' or as precise as 'Château Grillet', as grape-specific as 'Beaujolais' or as multi-faceted as 'Napa Valley'. Each wine region is characterized by its geography and its climate, and many are legally defined 'appellations' – areas authorized to produce particular wines and classified as AOCs, AVAs, DOCs and so on, according to each country's wine laws.

There are thousands of wine regions, big and small, throughout the world and even more subregions and appellations. In this book, 101 of the most significant are described, while others are noted on the detailed maps that accompany each entry. A concluding section covers other wine-producing countries that are beginning to make names for themselves.

The regions selected have been chosen because they offer quality wines whose individual characters are largely derived from 'terroir': the unique combination of soil, sun and weather that influences each vineyard. Most of the wines are

ABOVE LEFT AND RIGHT
Vines are grown in many dramatic locations, whether the Hill of Hermitage above the Rhône Valley in France or the Elgin region of South Africa. Geology is an immense factor in the resultant wines.

BELOW AND OPPOSITE
Overseeing the journey from harvest to table is the business of the winemaker. Those at Château Haut-Brion (harvest) and Cape Mentelle (decanter) are among the most fastidious.

prominent in export markets, though a few are only to be found locally. The producer may be anything from a giant, multinational company to the owner of just a few rows of vines. It is impossible to mention all the best producers of every single wine, but the authors have personal experience of all the specific wines listed and are happy to recommend them as good, representative examples.

However happy the marriage of sun, soil, climate and grape varieties, to be good a wine needs something extra: the human influence of vine grower and winemaker. That there are so many first-rate wines to be found today is a tribute to the wisdom, skill and dedication of individuals and teams who are determined to make the very best wine they can.

Throughout, the aim has been to provide a greater understanding of what is in the glass and how it got there, in order to enhance the enjoyment that wine can give. After all, as Ernest Hemingway remarked, 'Wine is one of the most civilized things in the world.'

From Vine to Wine

It is often said that the best wines are made in the vineyard, not in the cellar. Unless you have high quality grapes with which to work you cannot make quality wine. The modern vineyard is scrupulously maintained with this in mind.

There are many types of vine, but only one, *Vitis vinifera*, that makes quality table wine. Left alone it will produce abundant quantities of indifferent grapes. By taming it, through pruning, the vine grower allows the soil, climate and aspect in which it grows to add their unique stamp: that expression is often referred to as terroir.

Vines will grow almost anywhere, but only when the fruit is able to achieve full ripeness can it give the necessary levels of sugar and acidity to make good wine. Each variety requires different ideal conditions. Some grapes are more tolerant than others, but it is the marriage of the correct grape variety to the three elements (soil, climate and aspect) that is essential for the growing of perfectly ripened grapes.

Before a wine is made, the winemaker has to decide what sort it will be: red, pink, white or sparkling. All grape juice is white. The colour of red or pink wines comes from the pigmentation of the skin of the fruit. This dictates how the juice is to be obtained and whether the subsequent fermentation is made in contact with the skins. During fermentation, the sugar in the fruit is converted into alcohol by the action of yeasts that are naturally present on the grapes and in the air (cultured yeasts can also be used). At that point the wine is made. But before it reaches the bottle it may be necessary to age it, either in stainless steel or concrete tanks to preserve freshness, or in wooden barrels (usually made of oak) to allow it to develop further. Wines have traditionally been bottled with a cork closure, allowing gradual ageing over many years, but increasingly the screw cap is used to retain youthful fruit while eliminating the possibility of cork taint. Plastic 'corks' are also used.

The application of science and new technologies has improved much of the world's winemaking, but tradition still plays a part. After all, many great winemaking families go back for generations, bringing a wealth of incomparable accumulated experience to bear. However, there is one ingredient that can add a touch of magic – the skill of the winemaker. The best wines cannot be made in factories. It is the human element that adds the extra dimension.

Vintages

The quality of a vintage is determined by the weather. Historically, there were huge variations between vintages, from great to downright appalling, but – while great vintages still occur – the general quality level has increased dramatically thanks to the development of modern technology. The generally more predictable weather patterns in parts of the southern hemisphere give wines with less vintage variation.

PRUNING & TRAINING

These critical processes control yields, provide grapes with ideal access to sunlight and create a structure which will serve the vine well for a life of perhaps a hundred years.

FLOWERING

Successful pollination is vital to the outcome of the vintage. During the ten to fourteen days of flowering poor weather can severely deplete – or even completely destroy – the crop.

SPRAYING

Fungal diseases and rots are a serious threat to healthy vines. Spraying with a copper-based fungicide is the traditional means of control, with levels closely monitored in organic viticulture.

GREEN HARVEST

Green harvest or vendange verte is the removal of bunches of immature grapes to restrict overproduction and to ensure that the remaining grapes receive all the energy that the vine can supply.

CANOPY MANAGEMENT

Vines are trained according to their variety and the prevailing climate. Canopy management ensures maximum exposure to the sun in cool climates and shade in hot climates.

HARVESTING

Ideally, harvesting takes place when the grapes are at their maximum ripeness, but much can depend on the weather. Mechanical harvesting is common, but hand picking produces the finest wines.

GRAPE SELECTION

Grape selection should be carried out in the vineyard, quickly rejecting any bunches of grapes that are less than satisfactory. The more rigorous the selection the better the resulting wine.

FERMENTATION

Another critical process, in which the speed and temperature must be carefully controlled to ensure perfect conversion of sugars to alcohol and the preservation of flavours and scents.

BARREL OR TANK AGEING

Before bottling, wines are stored in wooden barrels or in glass, stainless steel or concrete tanks. New wooden barrels allow gentle oxidation, while tanks preserve a wine's freshness.

RACKING

Wines stored in barrel are 'racked' into clean barrels to leave behind the larger deposits of lees. Racking brings the additional benefit of exposure to the air, softening the wine gently.

BOTTLING

Most quality wines are bottled by their producer. There is much well-informed debate about what sort of closure to use: the traditional cork, a synthetic cork or screw cap.

BOTTLE AGEING

Good wines benefit from several (or many) years of development in bottle. But storage conditions are crucial, for light, vibration, temperature variations and dryness can ruin a good wine.

Grape varieties

The heart and soul of a wine is the grapes from which it is made. They give the wine its individual character, flavours, nose and longevity, and are dependent principally on the soil, climate and exposure to the sun of the vineyard in which the grapes have been grown – terroir.

More than 3,000 years ago the Phoenicians planted vines as they colonized the lands around the Mediterranean. The Greeks followed in their footsteps, and by the time of the Roman Empire important vineyards had been established across Europe. But vines would not grow just anywhere; the climate and terrain dictated the terms. Gradually growers learnt which vines did best under which conditions, beginning the process of selection that eventually led to the breeding of the great grape varieties.

In the 19th century, when European settlers began to establish commercial vineyards in other continents, it was inevitable that they should choose vines from the best vineyards in their homelands. Thus, Cabernet Sauvignon, Merlot, Pinot Noir, Syrah, Chardonnay, Sauvignon Blanc and Riesling have been grown very successfully throughout the world. These are truly international varieties. There is a danger, however, that they might be planted everywhere, to the detriment, or even extinction, of local grape varieties. Fortunately many dedicated growers have made strenuous efforts to save local grapes and wines, while other enthusiasts seek to make wine from, say, Spanish varieties in California or Italian varieties in New Zealand.

Varietal wines, made from a single variety of grape, are produced in ever-increasing numbers. But many great wines, such as those produced at most of the famous châteaux of Bordeaux and almost all Châteauneuf-du-Pape, are blended from several varieties. Winemakers with vivid imaginations are today producing some unlikely, but very attractive, wines from all manner of grape varieties.

RIGHT An ideal wine glass is clear and balloon-shaped, so that the wine may be swirled within it to help aerate it and to concentrate the aromas.

Cabernet Sauvignon
COLOUR Red.
DESCRIPTION Blackcurrant, eucalyptus or mint flavour. Tannic.
FINEST EXPRESSION Haut-Médoc, Pessac-Léognan, California.
ENJOY WITH red meats, game, Cheddar cheese.
SERVE AT 17–18°C/63–64°F.

Sangiovese
COLOUR Red.
DESCRIPTION Sour cherries with bright acidity.
FINEST EXPRESSION Chianti and Brunello.
ENJOY WITH well-seasoned red meat dishes.
SERVE AT 16–17°C/61–63°F.

Riesling
COLOUR White.
DESCRIPTION Green apples turning to petrol.
FINEST EXPRESSION Mosel, Rheingau, Pfalz.
ENJOY WITH fish, pork or as an aperitif.
SERVE AT 11–12°C/52–54°F.

Merlot
COLOUR Red.
DESCRIPTION Spicy plums or dark red fruits often with earthy notes. Tannic.
FINEST EXPRESSION Pomerol, St-Émilion.
ENJOY WITH red meats, game.
SERVE AT 17–18°C/63–64°F.

Syrah/Shiraz
COLOUR Red.
DESCRIPTION Syrah: black fruit with spice, bacon fat. Shiraz: spicy but tending towards blackcurrant.
FINEST EXPRESSION Syrah: Côte Rôtie, Hermitage. Shiraz: Australia.
ENJOY WITH rich casseroles.
SERVE AT 17–18°C/63–64°F.

Pinot Noir
COLOUR Red.
DESCRIPTION Red or black berry fruit.
FINEST EXPRESSION Côte d'Or red Burgundy, Oregon.
ENJOY WITH game, boeuf bourguignon.
SERVE AT 16–17°C/61–63°F.

Zinfandel
COLOUR Red.
DESCRIPTION Black fruits, berries and spice, often rustic.
FINEST EXPRESSION California.
ENJOY WITH winter casseroles and chargrilled meats.
SERVE AT 17–18°C/63–64°F.

Tempranillo
COLOUR Red.
DESCRIPTION Red and black berries with vanilla and animal notes in age.
FINEST EXPRESSION Rioja, Ribera del Duero (as Tinto Fino).
ENJOY WITH roast lamb.
SERVE AT 17–18°C/63–64°F.

Nebbiolo
COLOUR Red.
DESCRIPTION Tar and roses, perfumed but tannic.
FINEST EXPRESSION Barolo, Barbaresco.
ENJOY WITH game, wild boar, oxtail.
SERVE AT 16–17°C/61–63°F.

Gamay
COLOUR Red.
DESCRIPTION Red and black fruit, often black cherry, even banana.
FINEST EXPRESSION Beaujolais.
ENJOY WITH casseroles, poultry or white meats.
SERVE AT 14–15°C/57–59°F.

Chardonnay
COLOUR White.
DESCRIPTION From floral to peach perfume, generally with oak nuances.
FINEST EXPRESSION Côte de Beaune white Burgundy, Chablis, California.
ENJOY WITH fine fish or poultry.
SERVE AT 14°C/57°F.

Sauvignon Blanc
COLOUR White.
DESCRIPTION Either grassy, nettles, gooseberry or more tropical.
FINEST EXPRESSION Sancerre, Pouilly Fumé, New Zealand.
ENJOY WITH goat's cheese, asparagus.
SERVE AT 12–13°C/54–55°F.

Chenin Blanc
COLOUR White.
DESCRIPTION Bright apple fruit, good acidity.
FINEST EXPRESSION Loire Valley, Vouvray, Bonnezeaux.
ENJOY WITH pork, black pudding (demi-sec), terrines.
SERVE AT 14°C.

Muscat
COLOUR White.
DESCRIPTION Intensely grapey, fruit salad.
FINEST EXPRESSION Alsace (dry), Muscat de Beaumes de Venise.
ENJOY WITH asparagus (dry) or fruit-based desserts (sweet).
SERVE AT 11–12°C/52–54°F.

Gewürztraminer
COLOUR White.
DESCRIPTION Lychee, tropical fruits with spice notes.
FINEST EXPRESSION Alsace, Alto Adige.
ENJOY WITH oriental dishes or soft cheeses (late-harvest).
SERVE AT 12–13°C/54–55°F.

Sémillon
COLOUR White.
DESCRIPTION Lemony, sometimes honeyed.
FINEST EXPRESSION Hunter Valley.
ENJOY WITH seafood (young), poultry and white meats (aged), terrines (sweet).
SERVE AT 12–13°C/54–55°F.

Viognier
COLOUR White.
DESCRIPTION Intense perfumes of apricot/peach blossom and dried fruits.
FINEST EXPRESSION Condrieu.
ENJOY WITH fish soup, tapenade, foie gras.
SERVE AT 12–13°C/54–55°F.

Pinot Gris/Pinot Grigio
COLOUR White.
DESCRIPTION Fruity with nuances of pear and smoke.
FINEST EXPRESSION Alsace, (as Pinot Grigio) Italy.
ENJOY WITH white meat and mushroom dishes.
SERVE AT 12–13°C/54–55°F.

●●● Regions 1–25

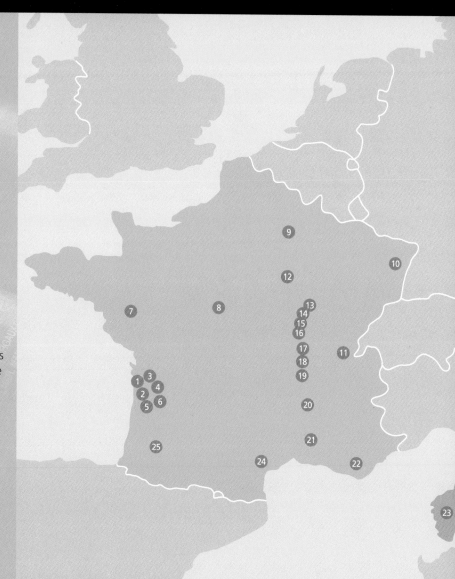

●●● France

Wine lies at the heart of French culture, and has done so for centuries: it is as central to French life as the country's incomparable gastronomy. Just as famous chefs have striven diligently to perfect their prized dishes, so French winemakers have passed down their secrets through the generations, to create the great Champagnes, Burgundies and Bordeaux that remain the pinnacles of wine.

And it is at every level, from the humblest to the most aristocratic, that French winemaking has made great strides in recent years. There are good or great wines being produced in every wine-growing department, and in the classic regions bad vintages are now almost unheard of. Quality, not quantity, is the driver – spurred on, no doubt, by competition from rising standards the world over, and the New World in particular.

The diversity of wine produced in France is remarkable, its accomplishment astonishing. Yet none of this would be possible without the magical conjunction of geography, soils and climate that gives France that something extra.

Bordeaux

More great wine is produced in Bordeaux than anywhere else in the world. These sublime wines are of such excellence that winemakers across the globe have striven to emulate them but have rarely equalled them. The vast majority of the finest wines are red, although small quantities of fabulous Sauternes and Barsac are made – the benchmarks against which all dessert wines pretending to greatness must be measured. And a handful of Graves and Pessac-Léognan châteaux produce one of the world's great dry white wines, in similarly minuscule quantities.

However, these magnificent wines are the tip of the iceberg. The extensive Bordeaux vineyards produce vast quantities of lesser appellations, such as Bordeaux and Bordeaux Supérieur, Bourg, Blaye, Fronsac and so on. Improved vineyard practices and winemaking techniques have ensured higher performance throughout the region. This is particularly noticeable in some of the shippers' blends, from the likes of Sichel and Dourthe.

FRENCH WINE CLASSIFICATION

France introduced its much-imitated Appellation d'Origine Contrôlée classification system in 1920.

Appellation d'Origine Contrôlée (AOC/AC): Wines of specific geographic origin with strict regulations concerning grape varieties and their ripeness, yields and growing and production methods.

Vin Délimité de Qualité Supérieure (VDQS): Lesser wines, often awaiting elevation to AC status.

Vins de pays (VdP): Ordinary 'country wines' produced in over 150 specific locations.

Vin de table (VdT): Basic 'table wine' of no specific origin, vintage or grape variety.

BELOW *The perfect proportions of Palmer's elegant château are a reflection of the qualities of its superb wine: delicate yet strong, sensual yet direct.*

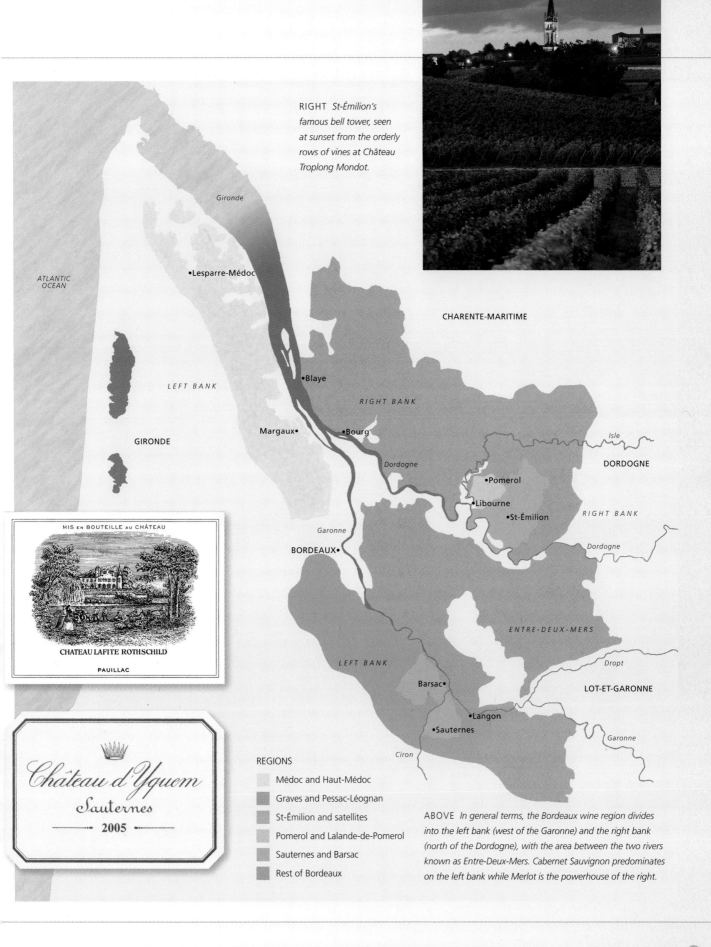

RIGHT *St-Émilion's famous bell tower, seen at sunset from the orderly rows of vines at Château Troplong Mondot.*

ATLANTIC OCEAN

Gironde

•Lesparre-Médoc

LEFT BANK

GIRONDE

CHARENTE-MARITIME

•Blaye

RIGHT BANK

Margaux•
•Bourg

Dordogne

BORDEAUX•

Garonne

•Pomerol

•Libourne

•St-Émilion

DORDOGNE

RIGHT BANK

Dordogne

Isle

ENTRE-DEUX-MERS

LEFT BANK

Dropt

Barsac•

LOT-ET-GARONNE

•Langon

•Sauternes

Garonne

Ciron

MIS EN BOUTEILLE AU CHÂTEAU

CHATEAU LAFITE ROTHSCHILD

PAUILLAC

Château d'Yquem

Sauternes

2005

REGIONS

Médoc and Haut-Médoc

Graves and Pessac-Léognan

St-Émilion and satellites

Pomerol and Lalande-de-Pomerol

Sauternes and Barsac

Rest of Bordeaux

ABOVE *In general terms, the Bordeaux wine region divides into the left bank (west of the Garonne) and the right bank (north of the Dordogne), with the area between the two rivers known as Entre-Deux-Mers. Cabernet Sauvignon predominates on the left bank while Merlot is the powerhouse of the right.*

BORDEAUX

Médoc

Lafite-Rothschild, Latour, Mouton-Rothschild and Margaux have been the leading châteaux of this star-studded peninsula north of the city of Bordeaux for at least a century and a half. Visitors driving through the quiet villages marvel at the architecture of these and many other fairy-tale castles. Yet the Médoc is unusual in lacking the hills that distinguish most other great wine regions.

In fact the area is almost totally flat. Yet the faintest of curves and changes of elevation create numerous individual microclimates giving rise to a wealth of subtly varying styles, especially since the wines of the Médoc are blended from several different grape varieties. This is red wine country, with Cabernet Sauvignon (the dominant variety), together with Merlot, being the basis of the blends. Petit Verdot, Malbec – or Cot, as it is also known here – and Cabernet Franc are found in the Médoc too, but are used very much as a chef would use herbs and spices, to complement a dish rather than dominate it. Each property has its own individual style but, since each year's weather patterns contribute enormously to the overall development and final ripeness of the grapes, there is much vintage variation.

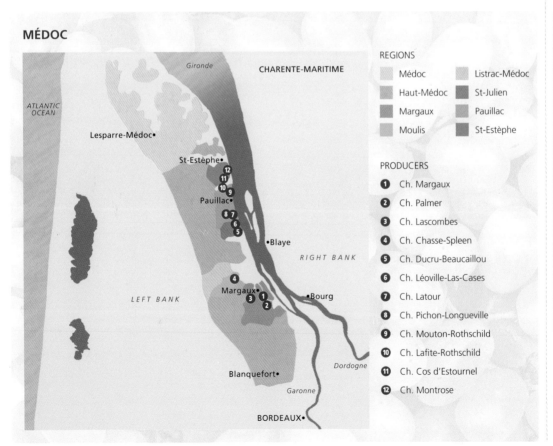

MÉDOC

REGIONS

Médoc	Listrac-Médoc
Haut-Médoc	St-Julien
Margaux	Pauillac
Moulis	St-Estèphe

PRODUCERS

1 Ch. Margaux
2 Ch. Palmer
3 Ch. Lascombes
4 Ch. Chasse-Spleen
5 Ch. Ducru-Beaucaillou
6 Ch. Léoville-Las-Cases
7 Ch. Latour
8 Ch. Pichon-Longueville
9 Ch. Mouton-Rothschild
10 Ch. Lafite-Rothschild
11 Ch. Cos d'Estournel
12 Ch. Montrose

Super seconds

The term 'super second' applies to a select group of Bordeaux's most highly regarded second-growth châteaux, whose quality and consistency are such that they can be considered almost on a par with the first growths. The group includes châteaux Rauzan-Ségla (Margaux); Ducru-Beaucaillou and Léoville-Las-Cases (St-Julien); Pichon-Longueville (formerly Baron de Pichon-Longueville) and Pichon Lalande Comtesse de Lalande (Pauillac); and Cos d'Estournel and Montrose (St-Estèphe). Just to complicate matters, Château Palmer (Margaux) – a third growth – is also usually included in this group.

LEFT *Although far from hilly, the vineyards of the Médoc slope very gently towards the Gironde Estuary, assisting drainage. The best vineyards enjoy the best drainage.*

Crus classés and crus bourgeois

From the late 18th century the brokers of Bordeaux were classifying wines according to their price, but in 1855, on the instructions of Napoleon III, they prepared a formal classification for the Great Exhibition in Paris, based on relative quality as reflected in the prices achieved at that time. The leading châteaux were divided into five ranks – known as *crus* or 'growths' – and this listing of five *crus classés* ('classed growths') is still in use today, unchanged apart from the elevation of Château Mouton-Rothschild from second to first growth in 1973.

In 1932 another list was compiled – the *crus bourgeois*. It was re-evaluated in 2003 when it at last gained official recognition, but claims of bias in selection and subsequent court hearings led to the system being annulled: wines currently bear this status subject to a taste test every vintage.

Perfect growing conditions

The Médoc is split into two main areas, one paradoxically called the Médoc and the other the Haut-Médoc, the latter producing the superior wines. Although varied, the soils are alluvial, with gravel giving good drainage. The exposed stones reflect precious sunlight by day and retain the heat to assist ripening through the evening, with vines being trained low to the ground to maximize the effect. Cabernet Sauvignon vines thrive in these soils, putting down deep roots that assist the older vines to give majestic fruit, full of differing nuances dependent on exactly where they have been grown.

Both the Gironde Estuary and the Atlantic Ocean greatly influence the local weather: the renowned estates of Margaux, St-Julien, Pauillac and St-Estèphe are all within spitting distance of the river, which helps protect them from excessive winter cold. Estuarine breezes reduce the risk of frost when the vines send out their first shoots after budburst, and they moderate the higher temperatures of summer, allowing the vines to ripen more gently and develop greater flavours within the fruit. Autumn and winter rains are expected, but rain in late summer can damage the harvest as it causes the development of rot in the crop. Bad weather of any sort at the time of flowering can lead to *coulure*, dropping of flowers or new berries.

ABOVE *Money from the French insurance giant AXA has helped restore the turreted château of 'super second' Pichon-Longueville. It is partially surrounded by the vines of premier cru Château Latour, its own vineyard lying on the other side of a minor road.*

Margaux

Travelling north from Bordeaux up the Médoc, the first of the great appellations encountered is Margaux, home to the fabulous Châteaux Margaux, Palmer and Lascombes. The warmest of the Médoc appellations, it gives wines with heady perfumes and great elegance, together with a restrained power. It is the largest of the top appellations, with the highest number of châteaux in the 1855 classification. Not all the properties justify the high prices charged today, but when they are good they are very, very good. Rauzan-Ségla is a consistently good performer, as has been Malescot St-Exupéry in recent years. Château Margaux is without doubt the pick of the crop. With its high proportion of Cabernet Sauvignon, it simply exudes black fruit and often shows mineral notes and touches of liquorice. At the lower end of the price scale, Château d'Angludet is always a good glass, and it is worth searching out the small but delicious Château Pontac Lynch.

St-Julien

Beyond Margaux, the appellations of Moulis and Listrac are noted for their impressive crus bourgeois such as Châteaux Chasse-Spleen and Cissac. Although there are no first growths in St-Julien, it possesses some sensational second growths. Château Léoville-Las-Cases, whose walled vineyard (*grand clos*) is entered via an arch topped by the lion of Las Cases, is one of the greatest, alongside Château Ducru-Beaucaillou. Both of these super seconds produce stunning and long-lived wines. The patchwork of slightly varying soils and exposures leads to variety in St-Julien production, but in general the wines are well structured and deeply coloured and – after a few years' cellaring to allow flavours to come together and tannins to soften – they offer rich, velvety fruit with layers of complexity. Château Gruaud-Larose is also a consistent high performer.

FAR LEFT *Wines maturing in barrel in the extensive second-year chai at Château Margaux. The upright barrels are about to be filled with wine from the first-year chai.*

LEFT *Gold features prominently on the labels of a number of Margaux classed growths, including Margaux (pictured), Palmer, Brane-Cantenac and d'Issan.*

Château d'Angludet, Margaux. Medium bodied with elegant, chewy fruit and finely grained tannins.

Château Pontac Lynch, Margaux. Supple with bright, ripe fruit and a refined finish.

Château Chasse-Spleen, Moulis. Often with cherry notes among ripe fruits, it has a good tannic structure that generally necessitates a few years in bottle.

Château Léoville-Las-Cases, St-Julien. One of the greatest Médoc wines, combining power and finesse with great complexity.

Château Gloria, St-Julien. Well structured and black fruit-dominated, often with notes of spice.

Clos du Marquis, St-Julien. The second wine of Léoville-Las-Cases, with all the class but showing through more in youth.

Pauillac

Bordering on St-Julien is the commune of Pauillac, with its collection of three first-growth properties: Châteaux Lafite-Rothschild, Latour and Mouton-Rothschild. They have become synonymous the world over with wine perfection and are real blockbusters, with great concentration and longevity, exuding blackcurrant-style fruit together with mineral notes such as pencil shavings. In youth they can seem tannic, but after a decade or so in bottle the great vintages are quite majestic. Even the second wines – for not every grape makes its way to be labelled as the main wine – offer great intensity and power. Wines made in the state-of-the-art winery of Pauillac's terrific super second Château Pichon-Longueville are fashioned to live for decades.

St-Estèphe

The last of the great appellations of the Haut-Médoc is St-Estèphe, which has a greater variation of soils. Parcels of limestone soil give wines that can be very tannic in youth, and some of the smaller properties are now planting Merlot as the main variety to give fuller, more rounded wines. The standard bearers are undoubtedly Château Cos d'Estournel and Château Montrose, but a host of smaller properties offer good value (for Bordeaux), such as Châteaux Phélan Ségur, Haut-Marbuzet and Valrose. Giving a general style is harder here because of the number of variables, but they are normally deeply coloured, with power and structure that rely on a few years' bottle age for the tannins to melt and harmonize with the fruit and other more complex flavours.

BELOW LEFT *Vines surrounding the pigeonnier at Château Latour, beyond which the land slopes gently down towards the Gironde Estuary.*

BELOW *One of the Médoc's more unconventional buildings is the orientally-styled chai at Château Cos d'Estournel. The château's second wine, Les Pagodes de Cos, is named after it.*

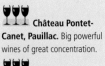 **Château Pontet-Canet, Pauillac.** Big powerful wines of great concentration.

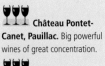 **Les Forts de Latour, Pauillac.** The second wine of Château Latour, generally a little lighter but displaying great style.

Château Phélan Ségur, St-Estèphe. Well made, offering early drinking opportunities.

Château Valrose Cuvée Aliénor, St-Estèphe. Merlot-dominated with soft ripe black fruits and ripe tannins.

Château Caronne-Ste-Gemme, Haut-Médoc. Well-made, stylish red for early drinking.

Château Coufran, Haut-Médoc. Good value, with a higher percentage of Merlot giving soft ripe fruits and well integrated oak.

Médoc

So far, all the vineyards have been in the Haut-Médoc, but soon after St-Estèphe you enter the appellation of Médoc, where vineyards become more scattered among fields of other crops and pasture. The cooler climate here is less suited to Cabernet Sauvignon, which may not always ripen fully, giving the wines a slightly green edge. Properties closer to the estuary fare best, and recently Merlot has been on the increase. It ripens a good two weeks earlier than Cabernet and gives softer, riper wines. In general, these wines offer good value for money and, while they will never overtake the quality of their southerly cousins, they still possess style and drinkability. Reliable examples include Châteaux La Tour-de-By and Patache d'Aux.

LA PLACE DE BORDEAUX

Almost none of the big-name wines is for sale at the cellar door. They are, instead, sold through the 'Place', a sort of broking house where the traders, known as *négociants*, buy wine direct from the châteaux for distribution around the world. Some of these wines are sold *en primeur* – that is, in late spring following the vintage – while the wines remain in cask, often unblended, for a further 12 to 18 months before being bottled. This provides much needed cash flow for the châteaux and offers purchasers keener prices. *En primeur* tastings take place in late March at which approximate blends are put forward; the subsequent tasting notes of respected journalists are eagerly awaited by potential buyers.

BORDEAUX
Graves and Pessac-Léognan

The Graves region has a long history of wine production and it is thought that the Romans were the first to plant here. Despite the problems of later centuries, such as the 19th-century phylloxera epidemic that devastated the whole of the Bordeaux region's vineyards, the Graves continues to enjoy a great reputation for producing some of the finest wines to be found in Bordeaux.

Chiefly known for its powerful and well-structured red blends, led by Cabernet Sauvignon together with the other Médoc varieties, Graves is also the source of some of France's greatest dry white wines, from Sémillon and Sauvignon Blanc grapes. Additionally, there is a small quantity of sweet white wine, Graves Supérieures.

In the north, where the gravel content of the soil is higher, wines of greater quality are made. This area, which became an appellation in its own right in 1987, is known as Pessac-Léognan. Here all the great châteaux of the Graves are found, such as Domaine de Chevalier, Château Pape Clément and Château Haut-Brion, the only Graves wine included in

BELOW *Château La Mission-Haut-Brion makes one of the grandest of all Bordeaux reds. That great dry white, Château Laville Haut-Brion, is made in the same chai, although the grapes are grown in a separate vineyard.*

GRAVES AND PESSAC-LÉOGNAN

REGIONS

- Graves
- Pessac-Léognan

PRODUCERS
1. Ch. Haut-Brion
2. Ch. Pape Clément
3. Ch. Carbonnieux
4. Ch. Smith-Haute-Lafitte
5. Domaine de Chevalier

BORDEAUX
Talence• •Pessac
Cadaujac•
•Léognan
•Martillac
Portets•
•La Brède
•St Morillon •Podensac
Cérons•
Barsac•
LEFT BANK
Langon•
•Sauternes
Ciron
Dordogne
ENTRE-DEUX-MERS
Garonne
Dropt
Garonne

LEFT *The villages of Talence and Pessac are now suburbs of Bordeaux, surrounded by urban sprawl. Only the great vineyards, such as Haut-Brion and La Mission-Haut-Brion, are able to repel the advance of the bulldozers.*

Château Carbonnieux Blanc, Pessac-Léognan. Delicious peachy fruit with citric notes and minerality. Good value.

Domaine de Chevalier, Pessac-Léognan. Open with ripe cherry fruit and smoke and spice notes.

Clémentin du Pape Clément, Pessac-Léognan. Excellent second wine of Pape Clément. More forward with ripe, chewy fruit and telltale smokiness.

Clos Floridène, Graves. Richly flavoured yet fresh, with apricot and pear fruit.

Château de Fieuzal, Pessac-Léognan. Strongly built with black fruits dominant and tannins that melt with age.

Château Smith-Haut-Lafitte, Pessac-Léognan. Deep black fruit with mineral aromas and ripe tannins.

'[I] drank a sort of French wine called Ho Bryen that hath a good and most particular taste.'

SAMUEL PEPYS 1663

Graves
The Graves takes its name from the gravel littering the topsoil, over a subsoil of sand and clay. The different stones making up the gravel affect the exact nature of the wines.

---

the 1855 classification (with first growth status). Additional Graves châteaux were granted the right to classed growth status in 1959. The region produces around 33 million bottles of wine a year, with around a quarter of these coming from Pessac-Léognan.

Red wines

Accounting for around 75 per cent of production, the red wines have good ripe fruit aromas in youth together with notes of wood smoke. Their tannins can be a little obvious at first but as the wines age they soften and integrate perfectly behind the more gamey aromas that have developed in bottle. Towards the southern end of the Graves appellation, the soils have less gravel; here, more recent plantings of Merlot have increased in percentage in the blends, yielding a softer style.

White wines

Graves white wines come in two styles. In Pessac-Léognan they tend to be barrel fermented, with Sauvignon Blanc dominant and sometimes alone. Full flavoured and well rounded, they have delicious fresh fruit aromas, occasionally slightly tropical. They also have the capacity to age, becoming gloriously honeyed after a few years. The lighter, tank-fermented wines are fruitier still and crisper on the palate. Generally made for young drinking, they are especially good with oysters from the nearby Bassin d'Arcachon – one of Bordeaux's gastronomic delights.

BORDEAUX

St-Émilion

On an escarpment above the right bank of the Dordogne sits one of France's most beautiful and most photographed wine towns, St-Émilion. From its hilltop, dominated by a bell tower, St-Émilion looks out over one of the country's most evocative roofscapes to a sea of vineyards. Vines stretch as far as the eye can see and, closer at hand, are planted right up to St-Émilion's medieval walls.

Official classification

All the wines of St-Émilion, no less famous than those of the Médoc, share a single appellation. They were first classified in 1955, the list being revised every ten years. In 2006, 61 châteaux were classified Grand Cru Classé, of which 13 are Premier Grand Cru Classé B and two are Premier Grand Cru Classé A. To add confusion to the mix, the classification 'Grand Cru' is awarded annually to many other wines of lesser status, subject to minimum alcohol levels, yield restrictions and tasting tests.

St-Émilion *graves* and *côtes*

The predominantly limestone and clay soil is ideal territory for the Merlot grape, the main constituent of the blends here. Cabernet Franc is also widely planted. Merlot gives St-Émilion its softer edge, with the wines coming to maturity a little earlier than those of the Médoc. However, a parcel of sandier ground on the western side of the appellation is known as the *graves* because here, around the wonderful properties of Châteaux Cheval Blanc and Figeac, there is gravel, allowing Cabernet Franc (and, in the latter's case, Cabernet Sauvignon) to be prominent in the blend. Château Cheval Blanc is one of the two A-classed châteaux. Although its wine can be delicious in youth, it has the backbone to last for a couple of decades or more.

Production at the other A-classed château, Ausone, on the clay/limestone *côtes* (hillsides) of St-Émilion, is tiny but incredibly high in quality. In youth the wine is more tannic, but great vintages are tipped to last for fifty years or more. Have patience! The rich, concentrated fruit, with wonderful layers of complexity and sweet spices, make this one of Bordeaux's greatest wines.

At a lower level, the less rare workhorse wines show good quality and make for delicious young drinking. The best can have good concentration, with plenty of ripe fruit and soft tannins.

LEFT *St-Émilion, with its vineyards, is a UNESCO World Heritage Site. Its greatest treasure, its wine, is mostly matured and stored in a network of cellars and caves beneath the houses and streets.*

LEFT *The predominance of Cabernet Franc in Château Figeac is a major contributory factor to the wine's longevity.*

St-Émilion satellites
As well as the main appellation, there are four satellite regions, St-Georges, Puisseguin, Montagne and Lussac, all suffixed 'St-Émilion'. The wines are not as rounded as those of the main appellation and this is often reflected in their prices.

ST-ÉMILION

Isle

RIGHT BANK

Dordogne

Fronsac•
Libourne•

•Lalande-de-Pomerol
•Lussac

St-Georges•
•Puisseguin

①
②
③ •St-Émilion
④⑤

Castillon-la-Bataille•

Dordogne

ENTRE-DEUX-MERS

REGIONS

St-Émilion
St-Georges-St-Émilion
Puisseguin-St-Émilion
Montague-St-Émilion
Lussac-St-Émilion

PRODUCERS

① Ch. Cheval Blanc
② Ch. Figeac
③ Ch. Angélus
④ Ch. Ausone
⑤ Ch. Troplong Mondot

ABOVE *St-Émilion is further inland than the Médoc and further from the ameliorating effects of the Gironde Estuary and the Atlantic Ocean – just far enough to prevent the guaranteed ripening of Cabernet Sauvignon grapes.*

'The Pearl of the Gironde'

HOW ST-ÉMILION
LIKES TO DESCRIBE ITSELF

Château Canon-la-Gaffelière, St-Émilion Grand Cru Classé. One of the most consistent performers, with big fruit and structure.

Château Sansonnet, St-Émilion Grand Cru. Stylish, moderately priced and on the up. Great fruit with spicy notes.

Château Rolland-Maillet, St-Émilion Grand Cru. From a property of Michel Rolland – the Merlot guru – concentrated and fruity in youth but with ageing potential.

Château Troplong Mondot, St-Émilion Grand Cru Classé. Broadly flavoured and concentrated, packed with spicy fruit.

Le Carillon de l'Angélus, St-Émilion. The second wine of superstar Château l'Angélus. Big fruit, big structure and great concentration in top years.

BORDEAUX

Pomerol

Pomerol is one of the smallest appellations of Bordeaux, with an aura of mystique about it. There are few of the wonderful buildings that bejewel the Médoc – many properties are farmhouses. The great names here produce a fraction of the quantity of wine made by those in the Médoc, but the quality is such that they are highly sought after, and their availability is consequently limited.

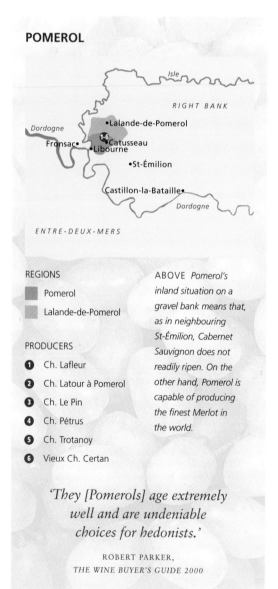

POMEROL

Isle

RIGHT BANK

Dordogne
•Lalande-de-Pomerol
Fronsac• ①-⑥ •Catusseau
•Libourne

•St-Émilion

Castillon-la-Bataille•
Dordogne

ENTRE-DEUX-MERS

REGIONS

■ Pomerol

■ Lalande-de-Pomerol

PRODUCERS

❶ Ch. Lafleur

❷ Ch. Latour à Pomerol

❸ Ch. Le Pin

❹ Ch. Pétrus

❺ Ch. Trotanoy

❻ Vieux Ch. Certan

ABOVE *Pomerol's inland situation on a gravel bank means that, as in neighbouring St-Émilion, Cabernet Sauvignon does not readily ripen. On the other hand, Pomerol is capable of producing the finest Merlot in the world.*

'They [Pomerols] age extremely well and are undeniable choices for hedonists.'

ROBERT PARKER,
THE WINE BUYER'S GUIDE 2000

There is no classification to use as a benchmark of how the properties have fared over the past few years, so the consumer needs to know the quality of each château before buying. That said, when these wines are on form they are quite magnificent, delivering loads of opulent, sweet fruit wrapped in an overcoat of velvety tannins that will charm any palate.

The finest wines

Soils vary through the appellation but the greatest wines are made in the iron-rich clay soil known as *crasse de fer*, on a plateau to the north of the village of Catusseau (there is no village of Pomerol), where Châteaux Pétrus, Le Pin, Latour à Pomerol and Lafleur are found. To the west of this plateau

Extreme measures
In 1991, when a late spring frost occurred, it was rumoured that a helicopter hovered over the Pétrus vineyards to keep the air moving and protect the burgeoning shoots from certain death.

RIGHT *Wine has been made at Vieux Château Certan since at least 1785, when it was known as Sertan.*

BELOW *The heavy clay vineyard at Château Pétrus is planted mostly with Merlot grapes, producing one of the world's most expensive wines.*

GRAND VIN DE BORDEAUX

Château

La Croix du Casse

2002

Pomerol

Appellation Pomerol Contrôlée

13% vol   750 ml

SCF CHÂTEAU LA CROIX DU CASSE 33 POMEROL (GIRONDE)
MIS EN BOUTEILLE AU CHÂTEAU

PRODUCT OF FRANCE

the soil becomes sandier and the wines are slightly lighter but not necessarily of lesser quality, as demonstrated at Clos René. South of the plateau the soil contains more gravel, as at Château Cheval Blanc in neighbouring St-Émilion. This imparts a slightly tougher style to the wines. Merlot is the customary basis of the appellation, but sometimes a higher proportion of Cabernet Franc is grown, as at Château La Conseillante. While many Pomerols retain the ability to age gracefully for many years, they generally become ready for drinking earlier than the wines of the Médoc.

The overall standard here is high and the great majority of the wines are excellent, albeit at high prices. Great winemaking can be very labour intensive, as at the great Château Le Pin,

where the 2 ha/5 acres of vines produce only around five hundred cases of the most sublime, sweet-fruited ambrosia imaginable.

Lalande-de-Pomerol

Across the little River Barbanne, prices become more affordable in the appellation of Lalande-de-Pomerol. Here, there is a greater area under vine and although the wines do not have the breeding of those of Pomerol, they still offer the delightful open fruit delivered by the Merlot grape, sometimes with a slightly rustic edge.

Vieux Château Certan, Pomerol. Always impressive with good concentration and complexity behind the delicious fruit.

Château Trotanoy, Pomerol. Dominated by sweet fruit, this can be a chunkier style that in good vintages will reward patience.

Château La Croix du Casse, Pomerol. Luscious, black cherry fruit with ripe tannins. Generally approachable in youth.

Château Bertineau St-Vincent, Lalande-de-Pomerol. Open, forward and fruity for younger drinking.

BORDEAUX

Sauternes and Barsac

Sauternes is the birthplace of some of the greatest sweet white wines in the world, such as Château d'Yquem and Château Rieussec, which can age for decades, delivering mouthfuls of succulently fresh, intensely flavoured wine. They are the product of *Botrytis cinerea* ('noble rot'), a fungus that in some years attacks the grapes and dehydrates them, leaving them looking ugly and shrivelled but concentrating their sugar, acidity and flavour.

Selective harvesting

Warm autumn days give way to evening mists, lasting until early morning, thanks to the proximity of the Ciron River. This encourages the fungus to grow on the grape skins and gradually perform its act of concentration. Botrytis does not form evenly through the bunches, and to make the greatest wines it is necessary for pickers to pass through the vineyards repeatedly, perhaps as many as ten times, with harvests sometimes lasting until late October or early November. The grapes are picked berry by berry when they are at the perfect stage of development and, such is the concentration, the fruit of one vine makes only a single glass of Sauternes at the great estates. It is inevitable, then, that good Sauternes or Barsac cannot be produced inexpensively.

> **Risky business**
> Not all châteaux can afford to pick throughout the autumn; they may have to make fewer passes or pick the whole harvest in one go. But in some vintages the noble rot will barely appear and in others, which are more humid, it can easily turn to grey rot, wiping out the crop and leaving the châteaux with nothing to sell.

Château Climens, Barsac 1er Cru. Consistently high performer; delicious fruit and perfect balance.

Château Raymond-Lafon, Sauternes. Owned by Pierre Meslier, formerly director at Château d'Yquem, and fashioned with the same care. Great value.

Château Haut-Bergeron, Sauternes. Good value with intense, exotic fruit flavours and orange peel notes.

Château Lafaurie-Peyraguey, Sauternes 1er Cru. Rich, complex style, often with notes of peach and pineapple.

Château de Fargues, Sauternes. Always excellent, with pineapple fruit and a creamy texture beneath the fresh acidity.

Such labour-intensive methods make the wines expensive, but they more than justify their price. When the grapes are fermented the yeasts cease to operate much above 14 per cent alcohol, leaving some residual sugar in the wine and giving it a sweetness that would be sickly were it not for the balancing acidity, which imparts freshness and vibrancy.

Character and complexity

Three grapes are grown here, with Sémillon being the major player because of its affinity with the noble rot. Sauvignon Blanc imparts its crisp acidity to the wines and Muscadelle adds floral notes. The wines begin their lives fresh and clean yet remarkably rich, with notes of apricots and pineapple and hints of orange peel. As they age, which they can do for many decades, they become more honeyed and complex while retaining that fresh edge of acidity.

Around the village of Barsac, the soils have a higher limestone content and generally produce a slightly lighter style, with greater subtlety. These wines can be sold either as Barsac or Sauternes. Barsac's neighbour, Cérons, makes less intense sweet white wines, plus dry wines entitled to the Graves appellation.

As the harvest in Sauternes requires very different climatic conditions from those required to produce dry white or red wines in Bordeaux, it often happens that a bad vintage for the Médoc results in something quite spectacular in Sauternes.

RIGHT *In Bordeaux, Sauternes or Barsac is considered the perfect match for foie gras. Elsewhere it is most frequently drunk at the end of a fine meal.*

BELOW *Mists that encourage the formation of 'noble rot' roll past Château d'Yquem at harvest time.*

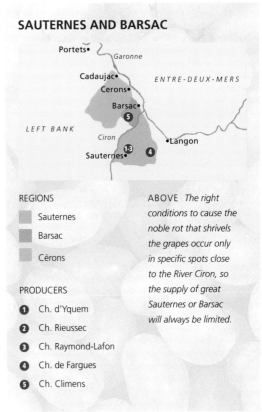

SAUTERNES AND BARSAC

Portets•
Garonne
Cadaujac•
ENTRE-DEUX-MERS
Cerons•
Barsac•
5
LEFT BANK
Ciron
1-3
•Langon
4
Sauternes•

REGIONS

- Sauternes
- Barsac
- Cérons

PRODUCERS

1. Ch. d'Yquem
2. Ch. Rieussec
3. Ch. Raymond-Lafon
4. Ch. de Fargues
5. Ch. Climens

ABOVE *The right conditions to cause the noble rot that shrivels the grapes occur only in specific spots close to the River Ciron, so the supply of great Sauternes or Barsac will always be limited.*

BORDEAUX

Rest of Bordeaux

Perhaps the best examples of the enormous improvement in winemaking techniques in Bordeaux are found in the lesser, satellite regions. There has always been considerable potential, but many of these wines did not command sufficiently high prices to justify the expense of up-to-date winemaking equipment, replanting worn-out vineyards or buying new barrels. But exciting wines are now being made, which are well worthy of exploration.

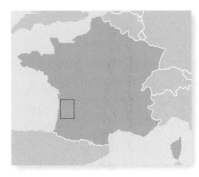

Côtes de Bourg and Premières Côtes de Blaye

Across the estuary from the great châteaux of the Médoc lie the vineyards of Bourg and Blaye. Merlot-based, these red wines offer great value for money, and long ago they often fetched prices above those of the Médoc. Bourg wines are generally well rounded with plenty of soft, ripe fruit, while those of the Premières Côtes de Blaye can have more elegance. The newly recreated appellation of Blaye offers particularly good value from lower yielding vines giving greater intensity of fruit.

Fronsac and Canon-Fronsac

Diminutive Fronsac and even smaller Canon-Fronsac were held in high regard in the 19th century. Although they are not at the same level as their neighbour Pomerol, the wines are made from the same grapes: Merlot and Cabernet Franc. Look out for Château La Vieille Cure and Michel Rolland's Château Fontenil.

Côtes de Castillon and Côtes de Francs

Both of these areas close to St-Émilion produce excellent wines, especially where limestone is plentiful in the clay. Merlot predominates, alongside Cabernet Franc, giving well-built reds with good intensity of cherry fruit, especially from hillside vineyards. The harder to find Côtes de Francs wines have more structure. Sweeter whites are also made.

LEFT *Most of the satellite regions of Bordeaux enjoy prettier countryside than the Médoc. Here the church of St-Michel-de-Fronsac overlooks the vineyard of Château Canon.*

Château du Grand Pierre, Premières Côtes de Blaye. Great value claret showing more complexity than expected for the price.

Château Fontenil, Fronsac. Concentrated, with delicious fruit and good backbone.

Château d'Aiguilhe, Côtes de Castillon. Stylish wine with concentrated black fruit.

Château Bonnet, Entre-Deux-Mers. Classy, fresh and zesty with a bright, clean and fruity finish.

Château Reynon, Sauvignon Blanc. Great value, with crisp, grassy fruit backed by minerality.

REST OF BORDEAUX

CHARENTE-MARITIME

RIGHT BANK

•Blaye

Margaux•   •Bourg

Dordogne

LEFT BANK   •Libourne
                    •St-Émilion   DORDOGNE

BORDEAUX•   Dordogne

Garonne   ENTRE-DEUX-MERS

REGIONS
- Côtes de Bourg
- Côtes and Premières Côtes de Blaye
- Fronsac and Canon-Fronsac
- Côtes de Castillon
- Bordeaux Côtes de Francs
- Entre-Deux-Mers
- Premières Côtes de Bordeaux
- Cadillac
- Loupiac
- Ste-Croix-du-Mont
- Bordeaux

Barsac•
Ciron
•Langon
•Sauternes   Dropt

Garonne

LEFT Huge quantities of wine are produced in the outlying regions of Bordeaux. In general, quality is higher in the named appellations, but simple, generic Bordeaux from a reputable source can offer affordable and pleasurable everyday drinking.

BELOW Labels from three wines representing the excellent value for money allied to state-of-the-art winemaking that is setting new benchmarks in Bordeaux.

CHATEAU
D'AIGUILHE
Comtes von Neipper
2006

CHATEAU
BONNET
ENTRE-DEUX-MERS
MIS EN BOUTEILLE AU CHATEAU
2008
SAUVIGNON BLANC
SÉMILLON - MUSCADELLE
ANDRÉ LURTON
CULTURE D'EXCEPTION

CHATEAU
DU
GRAND PIERRE
MERLOT
GRAND VIN DE BORDEAUX
PREMIÈRES CÔTES DE BLAYE

Entre-Deux-Mers and Premières Côtes de Bordeaux

Between the Dordogne and Garonne rivers, Entre-Deux-Mers (literally 'between two seas') had a reputation for easy-drinking, if dull, white wines and basic red Bordeaux, much of it very ordinary and charmless. Better producers, however, are now making red and white wines good for early drinking, as well as charming rosés. The Premières Côtes de Bordeaux traditionally produced sweeter white wines. They are still made, but soft reds are now coming to prominence. The best offer good value for young drinking.

Cadillac, Loupiac and Ste-Croix-du-Mont

Opposite Sauternes and Barsac, on the right bank of the Garonne, Cadillac, Loupiac and Ste-Croix-du-Mont are making interesting sweet whites that often benefit from noble rot. Though they never achieve the intensity of Sauternes, they offer an affordable alternative.

The right bank
The French often refer to the whole of the right bank of the Gironde as the Libournais, named after Libourne, the region's capital and the second wine-city of Bordeaux. Many long-established merchants have their base there, not least the right-bank specialist Jean-Pierre Moueix.

LOIRE VALLEY

Western Loire

The Loire is France's longest river. Its early stages, near its source in the Cévennes, are of no vinous significance, but once it reaches the Cher and Nièvre departments it kicks off in style with two of France's crispest white wines, Sancerre and Pouilly-Fumé. From there until it reaches the Bay of Biscay the Loire is a superbly stocked wine cellar.

Pays Nantais

Towards the mouth of the river, the Pays Nantais uses the Melon de Bourgogne to great effect for its Muscadet production. There are four appellations here but by far the biggest and best is Muscadet-Sèvre-et-Maine. The better wines are left in vat on their lees *(sur lie)* until the spring following the harvest, to develop greater depth of flavour; when they are bottled they have a gentle prickle from the carbon dioxide that was given off in fermentation. These have an underpinning minerality with crisp fruit and a dry finish, partnering seafood perfectly.

WESTERN LOIRE

REGIONS	SELECTED APPELLATIONS	Anjou-Saumur
Pays Nantais	Pay Nantais	⑥ Savennières
Anjou-Saumur	① Gros Plant du Pays Nantais	⑦ Quarts de Chaume
	② Muscadet-Côtes de Grandlieu	⑧ Bonnezeaux
	③ Muscadet	⑨ Coteaux du Layon
	④ Muscadet-Sèvre-et-Maine	⑩ Saumur-Champigny
	⑤ Muscadet-Coteaux de la Loire	⑪ Saumur

ABOVE *The Loire is a northern river. Its climate is comparatively cool. Its growing season is long. Loire wines, whatever their style, generally display an intensity of fruit flavour balanced by refreshing acidity.*

Anjou-Saumur

The Chenin Blanc grape is one of the glories of the Loire Valley, producing wines in a wide variety of styles – from crisp and fresh to rich and luscious, and even sparkling. Its natural acidity is used to great effect in the honeyed sweet wines of Anjou's Coteaux du Layon, with its two crus of Bonnezeaux and Quarts de Chaume. Here it is affected by noble rot, concentrating the sugars and flavour components to yield wines of great complexity with haunting sweetness and clean finish. The wines last for decades. Neighbouring Coteaux de l'Aubance also makes fine sweet wines.

Savennières wines can have an oily texture with complex nuances behind apple and quince flavours. The two smaller crus of the area, La Roche aux Moines and La Coulée de Serrant, make some of the finest white wines in France. Unfortunately they are seldom seen abroad.

Chenin Blanc is more widely used in the production of Anjou Blanc, offering similar flavours with a less pronounced minerality. It may have a small percentage of Sauvignon Blanc and/or Chardonnay added. Good rosés are made in Anjou, the best being the medium-dry Cabernet d'Anjou produced from Cabernet Franc and Cabernet Sauvignon. These also make good reds under the Anjou or Anjou Villages appellations and also the delicious Saumur-Champigny, with ripe red fruit with violet notes.

The chalk cliffs at St-Hilaire-St-Florent, outside Saumur, provide ideal conditions for the ageing of Crémant de Loire, the area's best sparkling wines. These are finely fruited and can be white, rosé or red. Some of the best are made by Langlois-Château and Bouvet-Ladubay. The Malvoisie grape makes charming whites in Coteaux d'Ancenis.

BELOW *The Savennières vineyard of La Roche aux Moines, overlooking the River Loire, was probably established in the 14th century. Today its 24 ha/60 acres of Chenin Blanc produce a powerful white wine of considerable personality.*

Biodynamics
Thanks to the pioneering work of Nicolas Joly, Clos de la Coulée de Serrant in Savennières is the cradle of French biodynamic viticulture, a holistic system of organic cultivation that treats the vineyard as a unified and self-nourishing organism.

Château de la Ragotière 1er Cru Sur Lie, Muscadet-Sèvre-et-Maine. Fresh and mineral with open fruit and clean dry finish.

Château de Fesles, Bonnezeaux. Rich and honeyed with citric freshness and great minerality.

Château Pierre-Bise 'Clos de Coulaine', Savennières. Richly flavoured with notes of dried fruits and stony minerality.

Domaine des Roches Neuves, Saumur-Champigny. Smoky, red-fruit palate with decent grip and fresh acidity.

Langlois-Château Crémant de Loire Brut. Fresh and lemony with a creamy mousse.

LOIRE VALLEY

Central and eastern Loire

On the north bank of the Loire, around the village of Vouvray, excavations into the chalk cliffs make excellent cellars for ageing wine. Wines are produced in a variety of styles. Dry white Vouvray has beautiful, green apple fruit with mineral backing; demi-secs are luscious, with enough sweetness to develop the fruit flavours, while the rich *moelleux* (mellow) wines are heady and honeyed. Sparkling wines, sec and demi-sec, are also made.

Chenin Blanc

Once again, Chenin Blanc reigns supreme here. It takes on the minerality of the chalk/clay soils and its acidity gives great potential for ageing still wines, up to fifty years for moelleux in great vintages. Across the river in Montlouis, the wines are similar in style yet rarely achieve Vouvray's depth and complexity. The isolated appellation of Jasnières produces a similar range of still wines, although the majority are dry with bright apple fruit and occasional notes of pineapple, accompanied by a clean, steely acidity.

Sauvignon Blanc

The other prominent white wine grape of Touraine and the eastern Loire is Sauvignon Blanc. Its wines tend to be light and fresh, with grassy, grapefruit-style fruit. Some of the best have a New Zealand style with tropical notes. They offer great value.

Quincy and Reuilly make decent Sauvignon Blanc, but the greatest vineyards are those of Sancerre and Pouilly-Fumé, making some of the world's best. Limestone soils give wines with good minerality, balancing the crisp, gooseberry and

Perfect cellars
The soft tuffeau rock close to the Loire around Vouvray is easy to carve, and has, for centuries, provided troglodytic accommodation for hermits and vine growers, and wonderful wine cellars of constant temperature.

BELOW *One of the villages that produces the best classic Sancerre is Chavignol, whose goat's cheese, Crottin de Chavignol, makes a wonderful partner for the wine.*

CENTRAL AND EASTERN LOIRE

Vouvray 'Le Mont Sec' Domaine Huet. Light, green apple fruit with mineral backbone and clean, bright acidity.

Jasnières 'Les Rosiers' Domaine Bellivière. Dry, pineapple fruit and stony background with notes of white pepper.

Touraine Sauvignon Château de la Presle. Clean, fresh gooseberry and melon fruit, with refreshing acidity.

Sancerre Blanc 'Les Collines Blanches' Domaine Hubert Brochard. Good value Sancerre: clean, fresh and with plenty of open, gooseberry-style fruit.

St-Nicolas-de-Bourgueil Domaine Frédéric Mabileau. Delicious spicy raspberry fruit with fresh acidity and light tannic clip in the end.

REGIONS

□ Touraine

□ Eastern Loire

SELECTED APPELLATIONS

Touraine

1. Bourgueil
2. St-Nicolas-de-Bourgueil
3. Chinon
4. Vouvray
5. Montlouis
6. Coteaux du Loir

7. Jasnières
8. Coteaux du Vendômois
9. Cheverney

Eastern Loire

10. Reuilly
11. Quincy
12. Menetou-Salon
13. Sancerre
14. Pouilly-Fumé

ABOVE *In addition to the appellations marked here, there are fresh Sauvignons Blancs (and a little red) from the Coteaux du Giennois. A much higher tributary of the Loire, the Allier, is home to the wines of St-Pourçain-sur-Sioule.*

nettle fruit on the palate. Parcels of silex soils impart a flintier style to some wines, as seen in some of the cuvées of the late Didier Dagueneau. A few producers are making more tropical styles, occasionally vinifying the wines in oak casks rather than the normal stainless steel tanks. Coteaux du Giennois is an emerging appellation producing Sancerre-like Sauvignon Blanc and reds from Pinot Noir and Gamay.

Red and rosé wines

Good rosé and red wines are made in Sancerre from Pinot Noir, but perhaps the best reds of the eastern half of the Loire Valley are the Cabernet Francs of Chinon, Bourgueil and St-Nicolas-de-Bourgueil. These have bright red and black fruit characters, with a light tannic background and savoury notes in the finish – excellent food partners.

NORTH-EAST FRANCE

Champagne

Champagne is the world's most famous and luxurious sparkling wine. It is a universal symbol of celebration, wealth, joy and – sadly – ostentation. But Champagne is more than a wine: it is a region. In fact, its vineyards are the most northerly in France, where the cool climate and chalky soils produce grapes with high levels of acidity, essential for making the best sparkling wine.

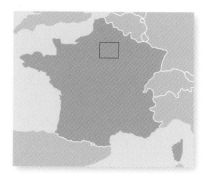

Grape varieties

Three grape varieties are used for Champagne. Chardonnay is grown mainly in the Côtes des Blancs, around the town of Avize, and is the only white grape used, giving freshness to the wines. Pinot Noir imparts depth and fruit flavours and grows best in the Montagne de Reims. Pinot Meunier is slightly more rustic and develops later, thus avoiding the risk of frost, yet ripens earlier. Its largest plantings are in the Vallée de la Marne. The Côte de Sézanne produces Chardonnay with less finesse, and the Aube, with a high proportion of Pinot Noir, lacks the overall quality of the regions further north.

Refermentation

The still white wines produced from these varieties are quite austere, with high acidity when first vinified. It is the second fermentation that transforms them: the production method captures the bubbles within the wine, giving it that delightful sparkle, exciting to the palate.

The wines are blended according to the requirements of each individual house, maintaining a constant style for the consumer. This involves the addition of small quantities of reserve wines from previous years. (Krug is blended from as many as 50 different reserve wines.) These blends are then bottled with a mixture of wine, sugar and yeast (*liqueur de*

'Three be the things I shall never attain: envy, content and sufficient champagne.'

DOROTHY PARKER

Moët & Chandon Brut Impérial N/V. The world's best-selling Champagne, of consistent quality.

Bollinger Special Cuvée N/V. A richer style of Champagne, with some base wines aged in oak barrels.

Pol Roger Cuvée Sir Winston Churchill Vintage. A good proportion of Pinot Noir gives the full and robust style so loved by the great man.

Mumm – Mumm de Cramant N/V. Fresh and elegant Champagne made from Chardonnay grown in the grand cru village of Cramant and produced at slightly lower pressure, giving it a creamy mouthfeel.

Laurent Perrier Cuvée Rosé Brut N/V. Delicious rosé made by skin contact rather than blending.

CHAMPAGNE

REGIONS

Montagne de Reims

Vallée de la Marne

Côtes des Blancs

Côte de Sézanne

Côte des Bar (Aube)

RIGHT *Despite Champagne vineyards being among the most northerly in Europe, their inland location ensures a sunnier and hotter ripening month of July than might be anticipated.*

•REIMS

Marne

Château-Thierry•   •Ay •Bouzy
•Épernay
•Avize   •Châlons-sur-Marne
•Vertus

•PARIS

•Sézanne   Vitry-le-François

Seine   *Aube*

Troyes•

Bar-sur-Aube•

•Bar-sur-Seine

tirage) and closed with a crown cap. The yeast ferments the sugar and the carbon dioxide given off is absorbed into the wine, producing the sparkle.

Resting, riddling and disgorgement

The wines are not yet ready, for to develop the wonderful biscuit aromas and flavours that blend so effortlessly with the fruit, they must mature in the cellars for a minimum of 15 months, but generally up to three years, to allow these characters to develop. Dead yeast cells are then extracted from the wines. This used to be done on racks called *pupitres*, on which the bottles were turned and riddled gently by hand, forcing the powdery sediment into the neck. Today, it is usually done using machines called *gyropalettes*, which are both faster and less labour intensive, although some houses still work by hand. The sediment is then frozen and, when the crown cap is removed, the pressure inside the bottle fires it out as a pellet. The bottle is topped up with a mixture of reserve wine and sugar *(liqueur d'expédition)*. A large cork is inserted into the bottle, held in place by a wire muzzle to counteract the pressure. After a couple of months, when the liqueur has integrated into the wine, it is finally ready for sale.

Champagne styles

As well as the non-vintage (sometimes known as multi-vintage) blends that account for the great majority of wines sold, there are also vintage blends: rather than displaying a constant house style, these have characteristics of the individual year of their production. Most houses also produce luxury *cuvées*, such as Pol Roger's Cuvée Sir Winston Churchill and Louis Roederer's Cristal, which are made in limited quantities and cost considerably more than the non-vintage blends. Pink or rosé Champagnes are enjoying the limelight at present and are unusual in that they are made mainly from a blend of red and white base wines. Wines that are made purely from Chardonnay can be labelled Blanc de Blancs, and those made purely from red grapes – a much smaller proportion – can be called Blanc de Noirs.

CHAMPAGNE HOUSES

The Champagne trade is dominated by the large négociant houses: they own only around 10 per cent of the vineyards, but buy grapes from thousands of small growers throughout the region. Most of these firms are located in Épernay and Reims, others in Ay, Bouzy and Vertus. Sir Winston Churchill once described Épernay's Avenue de Champagne as the most drinkable address in the world.

Black grapes, white wine
Apart from rosé, all Champagnes are 'white' even when made from black grapes. The juice has to be extracted in vertical presses to avoid tainting it with the dark skins.

BELOW *Moët & Chandon vineyards near their Château de Saran in the heart of the Côte des Blancs.*

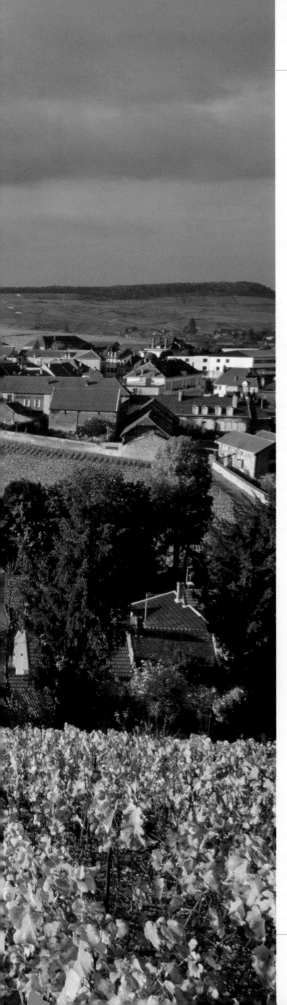

Growers' wines

Some growers do produce their own Champagnes, accounting for around 25 per cent of all sales. Because the selection of sources for their base wines is more limited, they are unable to blend out the differences between vintages. The overall quality is on the rise, however. Anselme Selosse, for example, at Champagne Jacques Selosses in Avize, produces marvellous wines that are made to express their origins, or terroir. His extremely rare Contraste Cuvée is made from Pinot Noir grown in La Côte Faron, in the grand cru village of Ay. Even more unusual is his use of a *solera* system, typical of sherry production, where a proportion of each vintage is added to a collection of previous wines. Throughout the region there are also numerous cooperative cellars producing wines of various qualities.

Protectionism

Worldwide demand for Champagne shows no sign of abating and prices for both grapes and wine are ever rising. There has been a recent increase in the area allowed for the appellation but, as time for enquiries and appeals must be given, this is not likely to be in production until 2021. With the Champagne authorities fiercely protecting the name of Champagne, saying that it can only be used on wines coming from its own unique soils, some commentators feel that this expansion is rather two-faced.

Dom Pérignon
A Benedictine monk, Dom Pierre Pérignon (1639–1715), is popularly credited with refining the production method of Champagne, although he worked on improving the region's still wines and thus regarded refermentation as a problem to be avoided.

LEFT *Some of the most expensive Champagne comes from the walled vineyard of Clos du Mesnil, owned by Krug.*

BELOW *Nine sizes of Moët & Chandon champagne bottles: quarter (18.75 cl), half (37.5 cl), bottle (75 cl), magnum (1.5 l), Jeroboam (3 l), Methuselah (6 l), Salmanazzer (9 l), Balthazar (12 l), Nebuchadnezzar (15 l).*

NORTH-EAST FRANCE

Alsace

Full of fairy-tale, centuries-old, timber-framed houses with steep, gabled roofs and bright window boxes, and storks' nests adorning every tall building, the wine villages of Alsace are exceptionally pretty. The region is noted for its gastronomy, and its wines – predominantly white – are the perfect foil. They are often described (not wholly accurately) as German wines made in a French way, which reflects the territorial history of Alsace: sometimes German, usually French.

🍷🍷 **Edelzwicker 'Terroirs des Châteaux Forts' Domaine Rolly-Gassmann.** Delicious, medium-bodied blend with fresh, spicy pear fruit and hints of lychee.

🍷🍷 **Gewurztraminer 'Jubilee' Hugel.** From Grand Cru Sporen in Riquewihr, ripe and forward with wonderful aromas of lychee, mango and roses.

🍷🍷🍷 **Pinot Gris 'Réserve Personelle' Trimbach.** Made only in the best years, it has smoky notes over fine fruit and sometimes the faintest hint of sweetness.

🍷🍷 **Riesling Grand Cru 'Rosacker' Sipp Mack.** Aromas range from floral to tropical, with good minerality on the palate.

🍷 **Pinot Blanc Cave de Turckheim.** Good value, clean, fresh and easy drinking.

🍷🍷🍷🍷 **Pinot Gris 'Clos Jebsal' Sélection de Grains Nobles Domaine Zind-Humbrecht.** Incredibly concentrated and sweet, with notes of stewed apricots and honey and lemony acidity.

LEFT AND ABOVE RIGHT
Grapes are gathered in the Schoenenberg vineyard above Riquewihr for one of Hugel's speciality late-harvest wines. Although Schoenenberg is officially a grand cru, Hugel (which does not recognize this classification) makes no mention of this fact on its wine labels.

Of the two areas of production, Bas-Rhin and Haut-Rhin, the latter is better protected by the Vosges Mountains and, having less rainfall, produces finer wines. Fifty-one vineyards have been identified as having special characteristics. Wines from them can have the status of grand cru, subject to strict conditions regarding grape varieties, yields and tasting tests. Several eminent producers (such as Hugel and Trimbach) refuse to participate.

Late-harvest wines

Alsatian wines are mostly sold by single grape variety, with a few exceptions such as the blends Gentil and Edelzwicker. As well as refreshingly dry wines, there are two sweet categories: Vendange Tardive wines, made from grapes picked later and sometimes affected by noble rot, and Sélections de Grains Nobles, from botrytis-affected grapes picked berry by berry, giving rich flavours with complex, sweet fruit and fresh balancing acidity.

Grape varieties

Four aromatic varieties, Riesling, Gewurztraminer, Pinot Gris and Muscat d'Alsace, are allowed for grand cru and late-harvest wines. Riesling is the most widely planted, giving wonderfully fresh wines often revealing apple notes in youth, changing to nuances of petrol with bottle age. Gewurztraminer boasts aromas of lychee and mango offset by spicy touches such as cumin. Pinot Gris is generally fairly rich, with hints of undergrowth and smoke. Muscat enjoys full-on grapey aromas.

Pinot Blanc is less aromatic, making soft, supple wines that are excellent with a wide variety of foods: it has the reputation of a chameleon, as it adapts well to almost any flavour. Sylvaner is lightly aromatic, delivering light, refreshing wines with pleasing acidity. The only red grape, Pinot Noir, accounts for about 10 per cent of production. Light in colour, often like a deep rosé, the wine features delicious cherry fruit. Sparkling wine, Crémant d'Alsace, is made by the méthode traditionelle largely from Pinot Blanc, and Crémant Rosé from Pinot Noir.

ALSACE

REGIONS
░ Bas-Rhin
▒ Haut-Rhin

ABOVE *The general orientation of Alsatian vineyards is facing south-east, but there are many side valleys and amphitheatres giving favoured south or south-western exposure to the sun – which is where some of the best grapes are grown.*

NORTH-EAST FRANCE

Jura and Savoie

The Jura was the birthplace of the wine cooperative movement in 1906 and was the first area to be awarded an appellation in 1936. Yet nowadays it is seldom heard of on the world wine stage, and few of its wines are exported. Today less than 10 per cent of the vineyards planted in the 19th century survive. The wines of Savoie are, shamefully, even less known internationally.

Of the Jura grape varieties, Poulsard produces rosés and partners Trousseau and Pinot Noir to make lightish reds; Savagnin's white wines have nutty flavours, and it is often blended with Chardonnay, which is also used alone. Attractive sparkling wines are marketed as Crémant du Jura. But the glories of the region are *vin jaune* ('yellow wine') and *vin de paille* ('straw wine'). Macvin is a blend of grape juice and spirit drunk as an aperitif in the Jura.

Jura specialities

The unusual, sherry-like vin jaune, made from late-picked Savagnin grapes, is a speciality of Château-Chalon. The wine is kept in cask for over six years and never topped up as it evaporates. A film forms on the surface, much like the flor of sherry. Usually drunk as an aperitif, it is well structured and extremely nutty. Its distinctive, squat 62-cl bottle (see opposite) is called a *clavelin*.

BELOW *Château-Chalon is not a château at all, but a village and an appellation controlée collection of vineyards. Old vintages of its unique sherry-style wine are highly sought after and, consequently, command high prices.*

For vin de paille, the grapes – Chardonnay, Savagnin and Poulsard – are dried before fermentation to intensify the sugars. The traditional method of drying them on straw mats gave its name to this style of production. The wines are aged for two to three years and are rich, sweet and alcoholic – up to 17 per cent – with aromas of dried exotic fruits.

Savoie

These wines are mostly consumed locally, in the region's ski resorts or along the southern shores of Lac Léman. Many indigenous grape varieties are used. Jacquère produces light, fresh white wines, especially in the crus of Apremont and Abymes. Neighbouring Chignin produces good floral wines from Roussanne (known locally as Bergeron). Altesse (locally Roussette de Savoie) makes delicious, light, fruity whites, especially in the cru of Frangy. Chasselas produces good, well-flavoured wines towards Lac Léman, while the spicy Mondeuse grape gives reds from light and fruity to rich

and flavoursome, notably in the Combe de Savoie – particularly the cru of Arbin.

The basic appellation of Vin de Savoie covers most wines, but there are also three separate appellations: Roussette de Savoie for Altesse wines, Crépy for the Chasselas grape, and Seyssel, which makes wines from Altesse and Molette, some of which are sparkling.

> **Louis Pasteur**
> The pioneering scientist Louis Pasteur, whose work on fermentation, bacterial disease and wine conservation was the basis of scientific winemaking, had his laboratory at Arbois in the Jura.

Vin Jaune Château-Chalon Philippe Butin, Jura. Dry, mineral and nutty with overtones of sherry.

Arbois Vin de Paille Domaine Rolet, Côtes de Jura. Sweet, fresh and delicious with a clean, zesty acidity; long lived.

Roussette de Savoie Edmond Jacquin et Fils, Savoie. Medium bodied with floral and apricot aromas and a fresh finish.

JURA AND SAVOIE

REGIONS

Jura

Savoie

SELECTED APPELLATIONS

Jura

1. Arbois
2. Côtes du Jura
3. Château-Chalon
4. L'Étoile

Savoie

5. Crépy
6. Frangy
7. Seysell
8. Apremont
9. Chignin
10. Abymes
11. Arbin

Burgundy

Burgundy is a huge region, stretching almost from Paris to Lyon and from the Loire to the Saône. Its rich gastronomy is famous, including boeuf bourguignon, coq au vin and incomparable cheeses. To complement its food, Burgundy produces some of the greatest red and white wines in the world. The best come from the narrow strip of land known as the Côte d'Or where Pinot Noir and Chardonnay grapes are grown to perfection.

The Burgundian quality classification is like a pyramid. At the bottom are generic wines, such as Bourgogne Rouge or Bourgogne Passetoutgrains. Next are the village appellations, and above these the premiers crus (first growths), from the better vineyards. Both can be blends from several vineyards or sourced purely from a single vineyard (when the vineyard name may be added after the village name). At the top of the pyramid are 30 grands crus (great growths), individual vineyards that give the finest wines, known only by the name of the vineyard.

BURGUNDY BUYING TIPS

The dispersal of church estates after the Revolution and the effects of Napoleonic inheritance law have left most Burgundian vineyards split into small parcels owned by different *vignerons*, or vine growers. Some of these estates, or *domaines*, market their own wines, but most sell to négociants, thus two bottles of apparently identical wine may be totally unalike, having been grown by different vignerons and vinified and brought up in barrel and bottle in different ways. What matters most on a Burgundian wine label is the name of the grower or shipper – if in doubt, buy your Burgundy from a specialist merchant.

BELOW *La Tâche vineyard, belonging to the Domaine de la Romanée-Conti, with Vosne-Romanée beyond. From here come some of the most sublime Pinot Noirs in the world.*

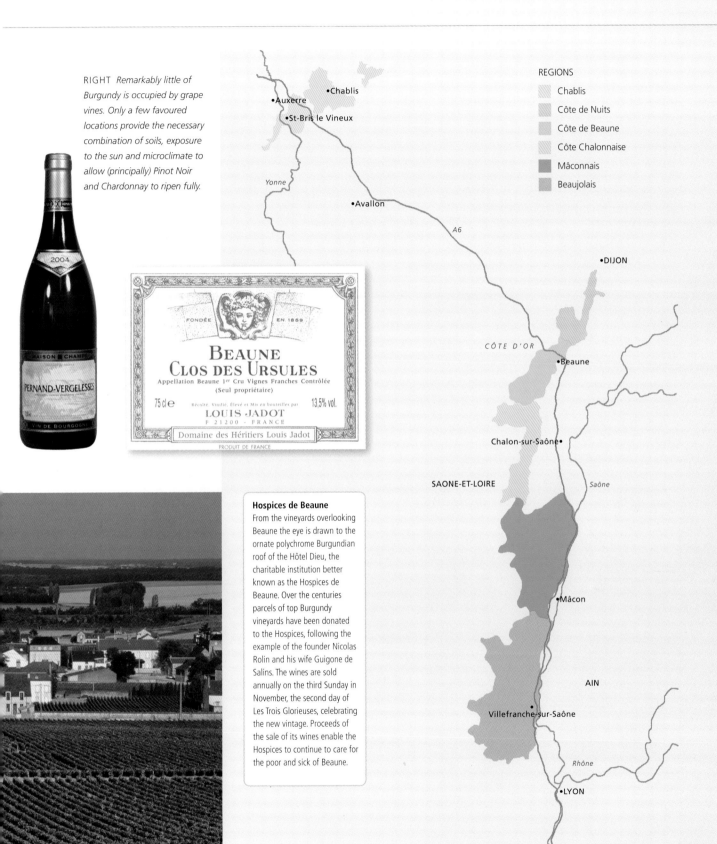

RIGHT *Remarkably little of Burgundy is occupied by grape vines. Only a few favoured locations provide the necessary combination of soils, exposure to the sun and microclimate to allow (principally) Pinot Noir and Chardonnay to ripen fully.*

FONDÉE EN 1859

**BEAUNE
CLOS DES URSULES**
Appellation Beaune 1ᵉʳ Cru Vignes Franches Contrôlée
(Seul propriétaire)

75 cl ℮   Récolté, Vinifié, Élevé et Mis en bouteilles par   13,5% vol.

LOUIS JADOT
F 21200 - FRANCE

Domaine des Héritiers Louis Jadot

PRODUIT DE FRANCE

PERNAND-VERGELESSES

VIN DE BOURGOGNE

2004

REGIONS

Chablis
Côte de Nuits
Côte de Beaune
Côte Chalonnaise
Mâconnais
Beaujolais

•Chablis
•Auxerre
•St-Bris le Vineux

Yonne

•Avallon

A6

•DIJON

CÔTE D'OR

•Beaune

Chalon-sur-Saône•

SAONE-ET-LOIRE

Saône

•Mâcon

AIN

Villefranche-sur-Saône•

Rhône

•LYON

Hospices de Beaune
From the vineyards overlooking Beaune the eye is drawn to the ornate polychrome Burgundian roof of the Hôtel Dieu, the charitable institution better known as the Hospices de Beaune. Over the centuries parcels of top Burgundy vineyards have been donated to the Hospices, following the example of the founder Nicolas Rolin and his wife Guigone de Salins. The wines are sold annually on the third Sunday in November, the second day of Les Trois Glorieuses, celebrating the new vintage. Proceeds of the sale of its wines enable the Hospices to continue to care for the poor and sick of Beaune.

BURGUNDY

Chablis

Burgundy begins in the north with what may be the world's most famous white wine: Chablis. At its best Chablis is exciting and crisp, with sometimes piercing acidity and stony minerality. In style it is perhaps more like the Eastern Loire stars, Sancerre and Pouilly-Fumé, than the rich whites of the southern Côte d'Or, but like all great white Burgundies it is made from the Chardonnay grape.

Chardonnay is a tolerant grape, ripening well in a variety of climates, but it is put to the test here. The vineyards of this northerly region are prone to frost in the spring, and crops can be devastated almost before the vine has begun its work. Hail is another dreaded enemy.

Grands crus

At the core of Chablis are the vineyards of the seven grands crus, their south-west exposure perfectly capturing the sun's ripening rays. Less than 100 ha/250 acres is divided between Bougros, Les Preuses, Vaudésir, Grenouilles, Valmur, Les Clos and Blanchots, and their limited size makes the wines hard to find. The limestone soil is at its most intense here and delivers wines with the greatest power and minerality. La Moutonne is not officially a grand cru but is often considered to be at that level, the wine originating in a 2-ha/5-acre parcel of Preuses and Vaudésir.

Premiers crus

The forty premiers crus are scattered around the appellation on both sides of the Serein River: Fourchaume, Vaillons, Montmains, Côte de Léchet, Montée de Tonnerre, Mont de Milieu and Beauroy are the most commonly encountered. Numerous owners with individual winemaking methods, together with varying vineyard exposures and soils, lead to a wealth of different styles. Well-made premiers crus possess notable intensity of fruit and minerality and can age gracefully from good vintages.

LEFT *Surrounded by Grenouilles, Valmur and Blanchots, Les Clos is the most extensive of the grands crus of Chablis. Generally speaking, it also makes the biggest, longest-lived grand cru wines.*

'*Chablis produces stupendous wines and contentious people.*'

SERENA SUTCLIFFE
THE WINES OF BURGUNDY

Village Chablis and Petit Chablis

These vary enormously in quality, with the better producers making wines that justify their price tags. Wines from the *cave coopérative*, La Chablisienne, are a good benchmark. Debate runs high as to whether soils lacking the Kimmeridgean limestone that distinguishes true Chablis should be included in the appellation, particularly in the case of Petit Chablis (the lowest appellation). Some growers do produce decent wines, and the arguments should be left within the region.

Surrounding areas

A small amount of Sauvignon is produced locally at St-Bris-le-Vineux under the recent (2001) appellation St-Bris. As a bracing white wine it is not dissimilar to its cousins from the eastern Loire. Pinot Noir (sometimes in combination with César or Tressot) is grown for red wines under the Bourgogne Irancy, Côte d'Auxerre, Chitry and Épineuil appellations. Coming from so far north, these reds are decidedly vintage-dependent, but can show charming, light Pinot Noir characteristics in a warm season.

Chablis 'La Sereine' Cave La Chablisienne. Typical village Chablis, consistent and good value.

Chablis Domaine Jean-Marc Brocard. Lots of minerality and good levels of acidity beneath well-defined fruit. The Boissonneuse cuvée is well worth the extra cost.

Chablis 1er Cru 'Montée de Tonnerre' Domaine Louis Michel. Delicious, with good structure behind the fine purity and clean, zesty acidity.

Chablis 1er Cru 'La Forest' Domaine Vincent Dauvissat. Almost at grand cru level, this is full flavoured and generous yet never lacking in acidity or mineral content.

Chablis Grand Cru 'Les Clos' Domaine François Raveneau. Full, intense and extremely expressive after time in bottle, with sublime minerality and perfectly integrated acidity.

Oak or no oak

Most growers feel that the steely, mineral quality of good Chablis is best achieved by fermenting the wine in tanks. However, some producers use oak barrels for aging their biggest wines, giving them some of the buttery fatness of, say, a Meursault.

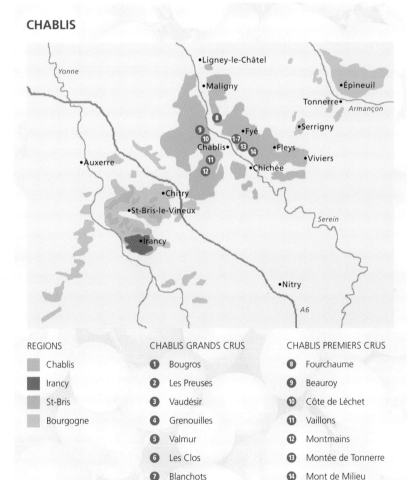

CHABLIS

REGIONS	CHABLIS GRANDS CRUS	CHABLIS PREMIERS CRUS
Chablis	❶ Bougros	❽ Fourchaume
Irancy	❷ Les Preuses	❾ Beauroy
St-Bris	❸ Vaudésir	❿ Côte de Léchet
Bourgogne	❹ Grenouilles	⓫ Vaillons
	❺ Valmur	⓬ Montmains
	❻ Les Clos	⓭ Montée de Tonnerre
	❼ Blanchots	⓮ Mont de Milieu

ABOVE *There are so many small, individual vineyards entitled to be sold as premiers crus that, for ease of marketing, most are sold under the name of one of the more familiar premiers crus listed here.*

BELOW *Chardonnay grapes are harvested for vinification by the local cooperative, La Chablisienne. It is one of the best-run and most reliable cooperatives in France.*

BURGUNDY

Côte de Nuits: Marsannay to Chambolle-Musigny

Driving through the Côte d'Or is akin to a journey through one of the world's greatest wine lists, with village after village offering names to make the mouth water and lighten the wallet. This is where Pinot Noir grows to perfection, demonstrating that terroir is more than just a word invented in a marketing department – the soil and microclimate really do have a huge effect on the wine.

Equally important are the hands that make the wine. Each village has its own wizard, who weaves magic with the grapes, turning them into some of the finest bottles of wine imaginable. While Cabernet Sauvignon is about power and structure, Pinot Noir is about aromas and elegance.

Gevrey-Chambertin

Although the wines of Marsannay and Fixin are honest and often well made, it is with Gevrey-Chambertin that the great wines start. Chambertin and Chambertin-Clos de Bèze head the collection of nine grands crus – solid, profound wines, rich in fruit, that bedazzle the drinker. Chapelle-Chambertin is the only questionable inclusion in the grands crus, with its lighter, earlier-maturing wines. Such premier crus as Clos St-Jacques, especially the wines from Sylvie Esmonin's estate, are challengers for upgrading. Les Cazetiers is another exemplary premier cru. For straightforward village Gevrey-Chambertin, try Les Evocelles from Domaine Lucien Boillot.

Morey-St-Denis

Clos St-Denis and Clos de la Roche are the standard-bearers for Morey-St-Denis, along with Mommessin's Clos de Tart: all offer restrained power and finesse to varying degrees, while Clos des Lambrays never seems to have quite the same definition. Even the generous premiers crus and village wines can be silky when in the hands of a master like Jacques Seysses at Domaine Dujac.

CÔTE DE NUITS (NORTH)

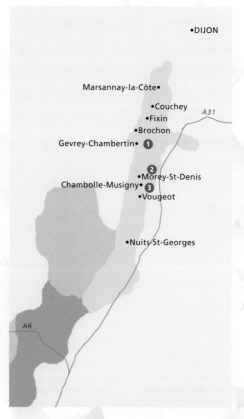

REGIONS

Côte de Nuits

Hautes Côte de Nuits

GRANDS CRUS (North to south)

1 Gevrey-Chambertin

Mazis-Chambertin

Ruchottes-Chambertin

Chambertin-Clos de Bèze

Chapelle-Chambertin

Griotte-Chambertin

Chambertin

Charmes-Chambertin

Latricières-Chambertin

Mazoyères-Chambertin

2 Morey-St-Denis

Clos de la Roche

Clos St-Denis

Clos de Tart

Clos des Lambrays

Bonnes Mares

3 Chambolle-Musigny

Bonnes Mares

Musigny

ABOVE *The narrow strip of vineyards constituting the northern part of the Côte de Nuits occupies a gentle hill with perfect soil, exposure to the sun and altitude to produce great red wine. Outside that strip it is hardly worth bothering!*

Chambolle-Musigny

The grand cru of Bonnes Mares straddles both Morey-St-Denis and Chambolle-Musigny and is another wonderful site for Pinot Noir, giving wines that are full and tannic with sensual fruit above. Christophe Roumier makes stunning wines here, and even his village Chambolle-Musigny gives pleasure year in, year out. The great Musigny vineyard makes more elegant wines with greater perfume – the Comte Georges de Vogüé estate proves this point superbly – and the premiers crus Les Amoureuses, Les Charmes and Les Cras can be stunning, too.

'I forget the name of the place, I forget the name of the girl, but the wine was Chambertin.'

HILLAIRE BELLOC

BELOW *A wall divides the vineyard of Lavaux St-Jacques (left) from Clos St-Jacques. Both are premier crus in Gevrey-Chambertin.*

Ψ Ψ Ψ Ψ Ψ **Chambertin Domaine Armand Rousseau.** Superbly structured and powerful, with strong tannins and hints of liquorice.

Ψ Ψ Ψ Ψ **Clos St-Denis Domaine Dujac.** Wonderful silky fruit with deep colour and a big, expansive finish.

Ψ Ψ Ψ **Gevrey-Chambertin 'Les Evocelles' Domaine Lucien Boillot.** Deeply fruited and chunky in youth with gamier notes in age.

Ψ Ψ Ψ **Gevrey-Chambertin 'Clos de la Justice' Vallet Frères.** Supple and elegant with plenty of red berry fruit.

Ψ Ψ Ψ **Morey-St-Denis 'Cuvée des Alouettes' Domaine Ponsot.** Chewy cherry fruit with some minerality and a firm finish.

Ψ Ψ Ψ **Chambolle-Musigny Domaine Georges Roumier.** Wonderfully elegant fruit aromas with depth and refinement on the palate.

Route des Grands Crus
This 60-km/38-mile tourist route runs through the heart of the Côte d'Or vineyards from Dijon in the north to Santenay in the south. What is immediately apparent as the route unfolds is the rapidly changing nature of the soil structures, almost like being in the heart of an artist's palette. Differences in the soils are principally responsible for the subtle (or occasionally wide) differences in flavour and scent of wines grown in different parts of the same village.

BURGUNDY

Côte de Nuits:
Vougeot to Nuits-St-Georges

As in the northern part of the Côte, the overwhelming majority of wines are red, headed by the world's most expensive red wine, Romanée-Conti. A little white is made in Nuits-St-Georges, and very good it is, but the reds command the greatest attention, being seductively sensual when made by great producers. Again, the producer's name is key, particularly considering the cost of each bottle.

BELOW *Although the wall surrounding the Clos de Vougeot reflects the vineyard's monastic origins, today the vineyard is split between many separate owners.*

Clos-Vougeot Domaine Jean-Jacques Confuron. Rich in spicy black fruit with solid, chewy structure and firm, ripe tannins.

Romanée-St-Vivant Domaine Leroy. Incredibly concentrated black fruit with spice notes and a full, intense palate.

Échezeaux Domaine Jean Grivot. Sweet red and black fruits, often with violet notes, with a firm, dark finish.

Vosne-Romanée 1er Cru 'Les Suchots' Domaine de l'Arlot. Seductive sweet fruit with floral notes, a firm mouthfeel and strong finish.

Nuits-St-Georges 'Les Fleurières' Domaine Jean-Jacques Confuron. Brimming with blackcurrant fruit, with notes of glycerine on the palate and a ripe, expansive finish.

RIGHT *The stone cross at Vosne-Romanée, viewed from Romanée-Conti with Romanée St-Vivant beyond the wall.*

Vougeot

The sleepy village of Vougeot possesses the largest of the grand cru vineyards, Clos de Vougeot, which has over seventy separate growers. There is, therefore, great variation in production quality, but at its best Vougeot is superb, giving generous wines with pure, concentrated fruit and soft, velvety tannins. Jean-Jacques Confuron makes a fine example from vines located in the best portion of the vineyard, immediately in front of the château.

Vosne-Romanée

Domaine de la Romanée-Conti is the jewel in the crown of Vosne-Romanée, making fabulous wines – rich in fruit, gloriously mouthfilling and hideously expensive – from its holdings of Romanée-Conti and La Tâche. Two other grands crus, Richebourg and Romanée-St-Vivant, offer a slightly more affordable chance to discover how sensual Pinot Noir can be, with domaines like Anne Gros and Jean Grivot making marvellous wines. Of the premiers crus, Les Suchots and Les Beaux Monts are sublime in the safe hands of domaines such as Leroy and de l'Arlot. The Grands-Échezeaux and Échezeaux grands crus are marginally better value at the exalted level of the Domaine de la Romanée-Conti, and from other good growers such as Gros.

Nuits-St-Georges

The commune of Nuits-St-Georges is the largest of the Côte. There are no grands crus, and the village and premier cru wines display differing styles according to the soil in individual vineyards. Generally, those to the north of the village give more fragrant and seductive wines, while those from vineyards towards Prémeaux are more structured and solid.

Much depends on the style of the domaine. Again, Confuron and Domaine de l'Arlot are worthy of note, along with the estate wines of the négociant house, Faiveley. Good Côte de Nuits-Villages are made in Comblanchien and Corgoloin. They can be quite elegant and fruity, as can those of the Hautes Côtes de Nuits, although these are generally lighter, with less finesse.

CÔTE DE NUITS (SOUTH)

•DIJON

REGIONS

Côte de Nuits

Hautes Côtes de Nuits

Marsannay-la-Côte•

A31

GRANDS CRUS (North to south)

❶ Vougeot

Clos de Vougeot

❷ Flagey-Échezeaux

Grands-Échezeaux

Échezeaux

Chambolle-Musigny•

❶❷•Vougeot

❸•Vosne-Romanée

❸ Vosne-Romanée

Richebourg

Romanée-St-Vivant

•Nuits-St-Georges

Romanée-Conti

La Romanée

•Prémeaux-Prissey

La Grande Rue

Comblanchien•

•Magny-lès-Villiers

La Tâche

•Corgoloin

A6

ABOVE *After the magnificence of Vosne and the sturdiness of Nuits-St-Georges, the Côte de Nuits somewhat fizzles out heading south, Comblanchien being more renowned for its quarries than for its wine.*

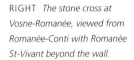

RÉCOLTÉ, ÉLEVÉ ET MIS EN BOUTEILLE AU DOMAINE

ÉCHEZEAUX

GRAND CRU

APPELLATION ÉCHEZEAUX CONTRÔLÉE

13.5 % vol. **2001** 750 ml

DOMAINE JEAN GRIVOT

VOSNE-ROMANÉE · 21700 · CÔTE-D'OR · FRANCE

PRODUCE OF FRANCE

BURGUNDY

Côte de Beaune: Ladoix-Serrigny to Beaune

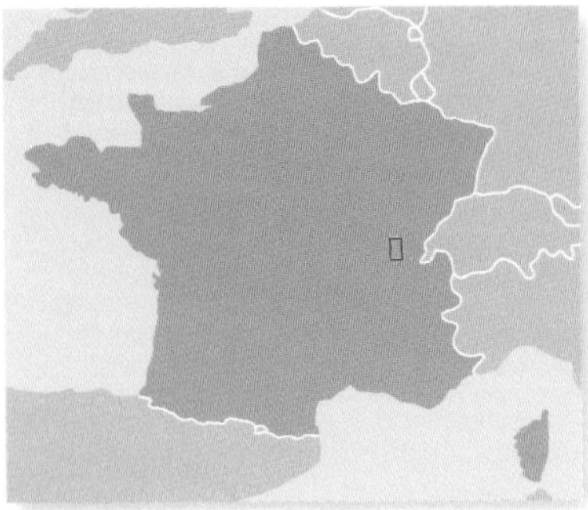

As the Côte de Beaune succeeds the Côte de Nuits the vineyards become broader, the escarpment shallower and a slight change of angle gives some vineyards more exposure to the sun. Serious reds are still made in quantity, but the geology and microclimates ensure that in favoured spots Chardonnay grows to perfection, making what many would regard as the greatest white wine in the world.

Ladoix-Serrigny's enjoyable wines were formerly sold as Côtes de Beaune-Villages but are now under their own appellation. They are good value and easy drinking, but are under the shadow of their neighbour.

Côte de Beaune-Villages
The restricted Côte de Beaune appellation is little seen and should not be confused with Côte de Beaune-Villages, which comes from many communes.

BELOW *Chardonnay grapes being harvested into traditional wicker baskets in Louis Latour's vineyards on the hill of Corton.*

RIGHT *The charming village of Aloxe-Corton, with its commune vineyards in the foreground and its grands crus on the hill of Corton behind.*

Aloxe-Corton

The commune of Aloxe-Corton is home to Corton, Burgundy's largest grand cru and the only red grand cru of the Côte de Beaune, though it also includes a little white wine. Confusingly, each of the grand cru vineyards appends its own name to that of Corton: the greatest of these are Bressandes, Renardes and Clos du Roi, all giving their individual touches to the wines. Chandon de Briailles makes delicious wines, including a little excellent Corton Blanc, but

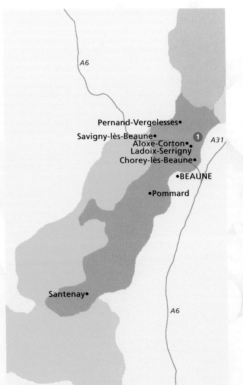

CÔTE DE BEAUNE (NORTH)

REGIONS

- Côte de Beaune
- Hautes Côtes de Beaune

GRANDS CRUS

1 Corton

including (from 28 vineyards)

En Charlemagne

Le Corton

Les Bressandes

Les Maréchaudes

Les Renardes

Le Clos du Roi

LEFT *In general the wines of the Côte de Beaune mature earlier than those of the Côte de Nuits, although Corton and Corton-Charlemagne can develop superbly over many years. The slopes of the hill of Corton are much steeper than elsewhere in the Côte d'Or.*

Map labels: A6, Pernand-Vergelesses, Savigny-lès-Beaune, Aloxe-Corton, Ladoix-Serrigny, Chorey-lès-Beaune, A31, BEAUNE, Pommard, Santenay, A6

Corton-Bressandes Grand Cru Domaine Tollot-Beaut. Delicious cherry fruit, polished structure and a big finish.

🍷🍷🍷 **Corton-Charlemagne Grand Cru Domaine Bonneau du Martray.** Well focused with intense minerality beneath fine fruit.

🍷 **Pernand-Vergelesses Maison Champy.** Fruity with a stony finish. Great value.

🍷🍷🍷 **Beaune 1er Cru Grèves 'Vigne de l'Enfant Jésus' Bouchard Père et Fils.** Open fruity style with elegance and refined, silky texture.

those of Tollot-Beaut are tremendous, and they also produce a small quantity of fantastic Corton-Charlemagne. This magical appellation is only for white wines. These are quite tight in youth, requiring a few years in bottle before showing their paces, but in wines such as those of Bonneau du Martray the combination of minerality and explosive fruit is superb. The red premiers crus and village wines of Aloxe-Corton can be rustic in youth but repay cellaring.

Around the hill of Corton, Pernand-Vergelesses produces good, affordable reds in good vintages, and whites that are quite mineral with steely acidity: Maison Champy in Beaune make some of the best whites, along with Chandon de Briailles. Savigny-lès-Beaune grows good whites but the red premiers crus of Les Vergelesses and Les Marconnets are the best of the village. Simon Bize and Jean-Marc Pavelot both make charming wines, but Tollot-Beaut again excels with the Champ-Chevrey monopole. Chorey-lès-Beaune has no premiers crus, but its light, fruity village wines can be delicious, and the old-vines cuvée at the Château de Chorey displays structure as well as good fruit.

Beaune

Many of the region's négociant houses are found in the capital of Burgundy wines – the walled mediaeval town of Beaune, with its famous Hôtel Dieu. Beaune's vineyards, over two-thirds of which are premier cru, are capable of making outstanding red wines with good depth of fruit. The more northerly have greater elegance, whereas those bordering Pommard can be more structured and earthy. Many of Beaune's négociants own vineyards here, and most have tasting rooms where you can try their wines: Bouchard Père et Fils, Louis Jadot and Champy all offer good quality, and Joseph Drouhin makes a striking white premier cru from the Clos des Mouches vineyard.

BURGUNDY

Côte de Beaune:
Pommard to Santenay

The Côte d'Or's most famous white wine villages lie towards the southern end of the Côte de Beaune. Meursault is the first of a trio of villages that produce some of the greatest white wines in the world; its neighbours, Puligny and Chassagne, share the fabulous Montrachet grand cru vineyard and have each attached its name to theirs. But to the south of Beaune there are also fine reds to savour.

Pommard makes some of the most structured wines, such as the excellent Comte Armand examples. They need cellaring to produce the wonderful, gamey flavours that make Burgundy so glorious. Clos des Epeneaux is a justified favourite. Volnays display greater elegance, with violet notes above berry fruit. Michel Lafarge and Domaine de la Pousse d'Or are noted producers. Monthélie can be similar, if more rustic, while St-Romain and Auxey-Duresses are simpler. All offer good value, with white Auxey-Duresses and St-Romain being delicious in the right hands, such as Michel Prunier.

BELOW *Vines grow right into the heart of the village of Chassagne-Montrachet, as here in the tiny premier cru Ez Cretz vineyard.*

Meursault

There is no grand cru in Meursault but the premiers crus Genevrières, Charmes and Perrières make fabulous wines, famous for their nutty, buttery flavours, creamy texture and brilliant minerality. Domaine des Comtes Lafon makes some of the best – even the village wine, Clos de la Barre, is eye-opening. Another fine producer is Guy Roulot, in whose wines the terroir of each vineyard is always well defined.

Puligny-Montrachet and Chassagne-Montrachet

The best wines of Montrachet, arguably the finest dry white wine vineyard in the world, have a wonderful concentration of sweet fruit, with a depth that gives a huge, unctuous aftertaste, lasting an age. Domaine Ramonet makes great wines here, capable of ageing, as has Domaine des Comtes Lafon since employing biodynamics.

Four further grand cru vineyards share the Montrachet suffix: Bâtard-Montrachet, Bienvenues-Bâtard-Montrachet, Chevalier-Montrachet and the slightly lighter Criots-Bâtard-Montrachet. Some of the best wines come from Domaine Leflaive, exhibiting a wonderful purity. Another fine Puligny producer is Etienne Sauzet, whose premiers crus Les Combettes and Champ-Canet are in rich masculine style. Chassagne also produces fine, fruity reds, especially from Clos St-Jean.

Behind Montrachet, St-Aubin makes good value reds and whites, the premiers crus En Remilly and Les Murgers des Dents de Chien being among the best. Santenay is the final main village of the Côte, making chewy, earthy reds. For both Santenay and St-Aubin look for wines from Marc Colin.

Volnay 1er Cru 'Caillerets Clos des 60 Ouvrées' Domaine de la Pousse d'Or. Old-vine cuvée with plenty of spicy cherry and violet aromas and flavours.

Meursault 'Les Tessons Clos de Mon Plaisir' Domaine Roulot. Rounded and nutty after a few years in bottle, with wonderful minerality.

Puligny-Montrachet 1er Cru 'Champ Canet' Domaine Etienne Sauzet. Big fruit aromas and flavours with well-integrated oak and a full, refined finish.

Montrachet Grand Cru Domaine Ramonet. Sublime fruit, rich and powerful, needing a few years to show at its best.

Chassagne-Montrachet 1er Cru 'Les Caillerets' Domaine Jean-Noël Gagnard. Spicy fruit and minerals dominate, with good structure and power.

St-Aubin 1er Cru 'En Remilly' Domaine Marc Colin. Well fruited with good structure. Best drunk young.

CÔTE DE BEAUNE (SOUTH)

REGIONS
Côte de Beaune
Hautes Côtes de Beaune

GRANDS CRUS (North to south)
1 **Puligny-Montrachet**
Chevalier-Montrachet
Bienvenues-Bâtard-Montrachet
Le Montrachet (shared)
Bâtard-Montrachet (shared)
2 **Chassagne-Montrachet**
Criots-Bâtard-Montrachet
Le Montrachet (shared)
Bâtard-Montrachet (shared)

LEFT *Maranges, at the southern end of the Côte de Beaune, is a useful source of unpretentious reds at sensible prices.*

BEAUNE · Pommard · Volnay · Monthélie · St-Romain · Auxey-Duresses · Meursault · St-Aubin · Puligny-Montrachet · Chassagne-Montrachet · Santenay · Maranges

BURGUNDY

Côte Chalonnaise

The pretty, rolling hills of the Côte Chalonnaise are home to five ever-improving appellations. Their wines may not have the class or fame of the Côte d'Or, but this is a source of delicious Burgundies at affordable prices. Rully, Mercurey, Givry and Montagny provide red and white wines from Pinot Noir and Chardonnay. The only white grape allowed for Bouzeron, the newest appellation, is Aligoté.

LEFT *In a vineyard above Rully Pinot Noir grapes are harvested, producing a good value red with scents of strawberry and cherry.*

🍷 **Bouzeron Domaine Chanzy.** Crisp, fresh and fruity.

🍷🍷 **Mercurey 1er Cru 'Les Combins' Domaine Emile Juillot.** Full-flavoured Pinot with an earthy finish.

🍷🍷 **Montagny 1er Cru 'Cuvée Spéciale' Cave des Vignerons de Buxy.** Fresh and floral with citric notes. Good depth and excellent value.

Rully's whites seem more successful than the reds, with clean, fresh fruit aromas and flavours, best enjoyed young. Mercurey whites are fine with good minerality, while the more abundant reds are chunky with ample depth of flavour. Emile Juillot makes good wines and Faiveley's La Framboisière is admirable. Givry is mainly a producer of red wine with notes of pepper over the fruit. Montagny is exclusively white: many of its easy-drinking wines come from the excellent Cave des Vignerons de Buxy.

Bourgogne Aligoté

Aligoté is famous as a base for Kir, in which the sweetness of crème de cassis neutralizes its bright acidity, but the crisp, fruity wines of Bouzeron need no additions: they are most refreshing, with just the right level of acidity. Aubert de Villaine of Romanée-Conti fame was instrumental in establishing the appellation and makes excellent wines, as does Domaine Chanzy.

CÔTE CHALONNAISE

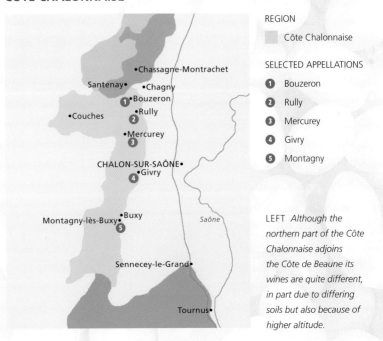

REGION

▨ Côte Chalonnaise

SELECTED APPELLATIONS

1 Bouzeron
2 Rully
3 Mercurey
4 Givry
5 Montagny

LEFT *Although the northern part of the Côte Chalonnaise adjoins the Côte de Beaune its wines are quite different, in part due to differing soils but also because of higher altitude.*

BURGUNDY

Mâconnais

The Mâconnais is a useful source of affordable white Burgundy. Fine-quality, easy-drinking wines, displaying open fruit and minerality, are produced in the rolling hills of this charming countryside. They are sold either as Mâcon-Villages or, often, with the name of a village added to that of Mâcon. Even the tiny village of Chardonnay – possibly the birthplace of the grape – may add its name, confusing many a drinker.

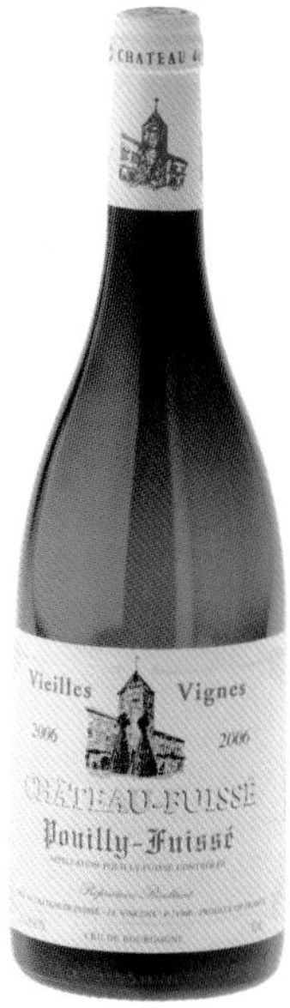

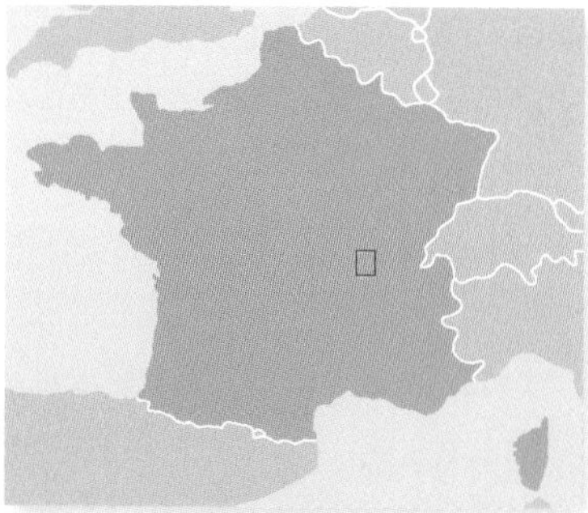

Pouilly-Fuissé Vieilles Vignes Château-Fuissé. Richly fruited, barrel-fermented, complex wine rewarding cellaring.

St-Véran Domaine de la Croix Senaillet. Fresh and lively, notes of hawthorn blossom and citric flavours, underpinned by minerality.

Viré-Clessé Cave de Viré. Open, floral aromas with good length on the palate; hint of wet stones in the finish.

Pouilly-Fuissé

The heart of the area, however, lies around the rocky outcrops of Solutré and Vergisson. Pouilly and Fuissé yield wines that can be lighter, tank-fermented, or fuller, barrel-fermented examples. The best have rich fruit, and at top domaines such as Château de Fuissé they can rival the great wines of the Côte de Beaune. Pouilly-Loché and Pouilly-Vinzelles, satellite appellations, also make good, if less focused, wines.

Viré-Clessé offers good-value, crisp, fresh wines with the minerality so typical of the area. St-Véran is another useful appellation for affordable white Burgundy: it can be richly flavoured or light and citric, depending on its origin.

MÂCONNAIS

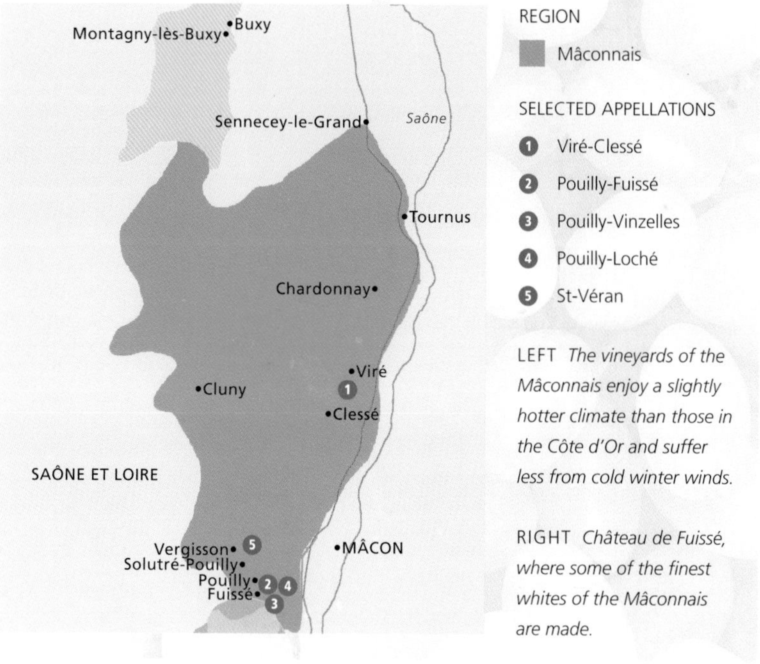

LEFT *The vineyards of the Mâconnais enjoy a slightly hotter climate than those in the Côte d'Or and suffer less from cold winter winds.*

RIGHT *Château de Fuissé, where some of the finest whites of the Mâconnais are made.*

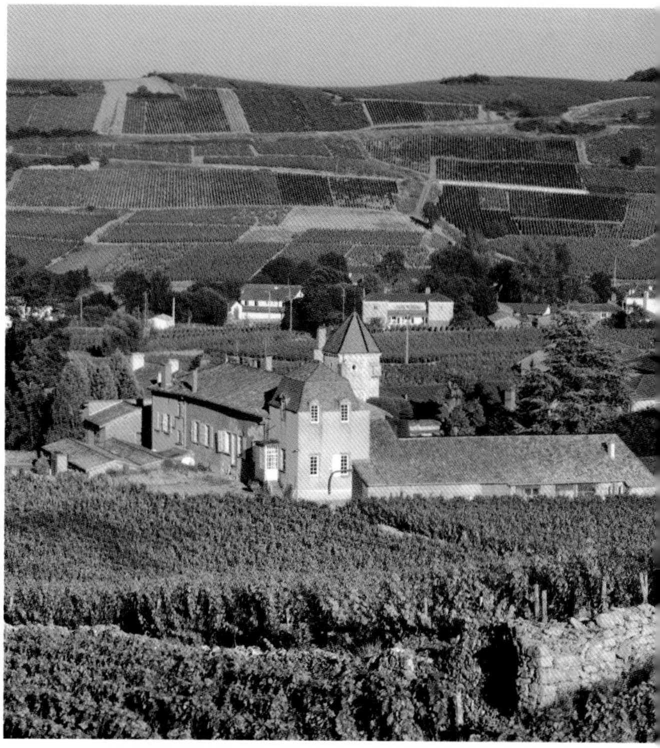

BURGUNDY

Beaujolais

The Beaujolais is rural France. Its hills are dotted with pretty villages of red-roofed houses, bedecked with flowers in summer. Life has a gentle pace and the wines have a gentle feel. Here the Gamay grape grows to perfection, making lip-smackingly fruity wines that give instant delight. Beaujolais generally represents great value; it is not to be sipped and savoured but quaffed with hearty, rustic food.

A good deal of ordinary, basic Beaujolais is still produced in the south of the region, much of it sold as Beaujolais Nouveau, the first wine of the new vintage. It can be delightfully fruity, and may reward keeping for a few months, but too much of it is sharp and acidic. The best wines come from the north.

The crus

Here the soils are more granitic, which Gamay prefers. They are sold either as Beaujolais Villages or, in the case of ten special wines, by the name of a cru. This is normally the name of the producing village, except in the case of Moulin-à-Vent, from the commune of Romanèche-Thorins, which is

LEFT *Beaujolais country is especially attractive in autumn. The vines in the foreground are in Chiroubles, with Morgon and Régnié beyond.*

Beaujolais-Villages Georges Duboeuf. Consistently good, well-fruited Beaujolais.

Morgon Marcel Lapierre. Traditionally vinified, with rich notes of black cherries and good substance.

Fleurie 'Clos de la Roilette' Alain Coudert. Well fruited with hints of spice and a solid finish.

Chénas Domaine du P'tit Paradis. Delicious chewy red fruit with good structure for ageing.

Moulin-à-Vent des Hospices Collin-Bourisset. Solid and chunky with notes of cigar box. Built to last.

BEAUJOLAIS NOUVEAU

The race to get the first bottles of the new vintage on the tables of Europe on the third Thursday of November, which became a marketing phenomenon in the 1970s and 80s, did much to bring the region to the notice of the consumer and put the Beaujolais back on the wine map. Once the great rush is over, the young wine ends up in *pots lyonnais* – the carafes of the Lyon bistros – as affordable, gulping wine for locals and tourists alike.

Light and fruity

Most Beaujolais is made by *macération carbonique* – whole-grape fermentation. Bunches of unbroken grapes are sealed into a vat in which the juice begins fermenting naturally and rapidly, inside the grape. This process maximizes the fresh fruitiness and aroma so characteristic of Gamay.

named after a disused windmill (now a tasting cellar). Manganese in the soil here gives the wines body and structure and allows them to age gracefully, resembling the wines of the Côte d'Or after a few years in bottle.

Evocatively named Fleurie bursts with red fruit and floral notes of violets and roses. Sales are high, and finding good examples is not easy, but growers such as Alain Coudert make sensational wines with some structure. On clear days, there is a spectacular view to Mont Blanc from the Chapelle de la Madone, which dominates Fleurie's hillside vineyards.

Brouilly is the lightest of the crus; more structure can be found in Côte de Brouilly. Chénas wines also have structure, along with those of Morgon, whose Côte de Py wines are robust with distinctive cherry fruit.

The youngest cru, Régnié, makes light, fragrant wines, best suited to young drinking, as is Chiroubles, which has a little more substance and wonderful floral aromas. St-Amour wines are quite elegant, yet seem to put on weight with ageing, while Juliénas is always well structured with its range of red and black fruit flavours and aromas. A small quantity of white Beaujolais is also produced.

RIGHT *Harvesting Gamay grapes below the Chapelle de la Madone, which overlooks the village of Fleurie and can be seen from all ten of the Beaujolais crus.*

BEAUJOLAIS

SAÔNE ET LOIRE

MÂCON•

①
② •Juliénas
③ •Chénas
④
Fleurie• ⑤ •Romanèche-Thorins
Chiroubles• ⑥
•Beaujeu
⑦•Morgon
⑧
⑨
⑩   •Belleville

Villefranche-sur-Saône•

AIN

Saône

•St-Vérand

Chazay-d'Azergues•

LYON•

REGIONS

■ Beaujolais
■ Cru Beaujolais
■ Beaujolais Villages

BEAUJOLAIS CRUS

① St-Amour
② Juliénas
③ Chénas
④ Moulin-à-Vent
⑤ Fleurie
⑥ Chiroubles
⑦ Morgon
⑧ Régnié
⑨ Côte de Brouilly
⑩ Brouilly

LEFT *Being further south, Beaujolais enjoys an earlier harvest than the rest of Burgundy. However, its finest wines, the crus, come from the north of the region.*

RHÔNE VALLEY

Northern Rhône

Syrah is the king of grape varieties in the Northern Rhône, making majestic red wines dominated by spicy red and black fruits with notes of violets and strong tannins, which give them the backbone to age for many years. Sometimes Marsanne, Roussanne and Viognier are used to temper its power and impart elegance to the wines, which can be formidably bold in youth.

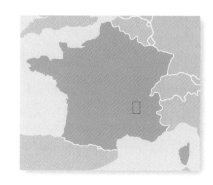

Côte Rôtie

Vine growing in Côte Rôtie goes back to Roman times. Baking in the summer sunshine, the granitic soils of the steeply terraced vineyards are ideal for Syrah. A little white Viognier may be added for extra freshness and elegance. The négociant house of Guigal excels here, with dazzling single-vineyard wines, such as La Landonne and La Turque.

Hermitage

The great hillside vineyards of Hermitage tower above the town of Tain l'Hermitage, making richly flavoured, long-lived wines. Topping the hill is a small chapel owned by the négociant firm of Jaboulet, who have adopted its identity for their signature brand, Hermitage La Chapelle. It is a great icon for Hermitage wines, but estates such as Domaine

NORTHERN RHÔNE

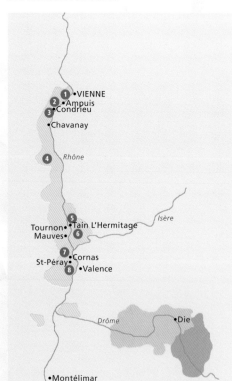

REGIONS

- Côtes du Rhône
- Clairette de Die
- Châtillon-en-Diois

CÔTES DU RHÔNE CRUS

1. Côte Rôtie
2. Château Grillet
3. Condrieu
4. St-Joseph
5. Hermitage
6. Crozes-Hermitage
7. Cornas
8. St-Péray

LEFT The finest wines of the northern Rhône come from the steep hillsides overlooking the river. Expanding appellations to take in vines on lower ground merely weakens the appellation.

Côte Rôtie Cuvée Classique Domaine René Rostaing. Consistent, with great fruit and hints of bacon fat.

Hermitage Domaine Jean-Louis Chave. Magnificent: powerful, peppery fruit with rich tannins. Built to last.

Crozes-Hermitage Domaine des Entrefaux. Good value, with deep, spicy fruit and chocolate notes.

Cornas Domaine Auguste Clape. Meaty and virile with ripe fruit and bold tannins.

Côtes du Rhone Côtes Levant Domaine Remejean. Classic Rhône blend of Grenache and Syrah offering plenty of spicy fruit backed by soft ripe tannins.

Ermitage 'L'Ermite' M. Chapoutier. Incredible wine with sensational peach and floral aromas and big minerality.

Condrieu Domaine Pierre Gaillard. Intense aromas of peach and apricot blossom, with well-integrated oak.

Jean-Louis Chave often eclipse Jaboulet. The flatter lands of neighbouring Crozes-Hermitage do not enjoy the same protection from the biting Mistral winds, making similar wines to Hermitage but less intense.

St-Joseph

Vineyards in Tournon and Mauves make some of the best wines of St-Joseph, an appellation now stretching almost to Côte Rôtie. These offer good value compared to Hermitage and mature earlier. A slightly more rustic style is made in Cornas but wines such as those from the old Alain Voge estate are nonetheless wonderful.

White wines

Excellent white wines are also made, with the longest lived coming from Marsanne and Roussanne in Hermitage. Rich and honeyed in youth, they develop mineral character as they age. White Crozes-Hermitage is for younger drinking. St-Joseph uses mainly Marsanne for its whites, with small amounts of Roussanne to add complexity, as does the lesser-known St-Péray, which has attractive whites especially from

vineyards near the Château de Crussol, and also sparkling wine.

In vogue today are the whites from Condrieu, where Viognier is enjoying a renaissance. At their best in their first few years, they have intense aromas of peach and apricot blossom – Yves Cuilleron and Pierre Gaillard make some of the finest. Unfortunately, expansion within the appellation has led to some disappointing wines. Rare late-harvest wines are quite astounding. Minuscule Château Grillet makes tiny amounts of expensive wines to age.

The Diois

Distinctive sparkling wines are made in the Diois, to the east of the Rhône, the most interesting being Clairette de Die Tradition – gently sparkling and attractively off-dry. The partially fermented juice from Clairette and Muscat Blanc à Petits Grains is bottled and allowed to finish fermenting there, giving a light sparkle to the wines. Still dry white is sometimes made from Aligoté in Châtillon-en-Diois.

ABOVE *The famous hill of Hermitage produces fabulously generous, long-lived red wines. It also produces superb, equally long-lived (and equally expensive) whites.*

RHÔNE VALLEY

Southern Rhône

As Syrah is to the northern Rhône Valley, Grenache is to the south. It must constitute at least 40 per cent of red wines sold as Côtes du Rhône, with Syrah and Mourvèdre its usual partners. Almost all Côtes du Rhône is red, and some of it is good, particularly when made by one of the great Châteauneuf estates. Côtes du Rhône-Villages such as Rasteau, Vinsobres and Beaumes-de-Venise can be even better.

Châteauneuf-du-Pape

The appellation of Châteauneuf-du-Pape, where the Popes had their summer palace in the 14th century, is renowned for its richly flavoured, long-lived reds. Thirteen grape varieties are allowed here: some of them are white, but Grenache reigns supreme. Stones cover the vineyards, retaining daytime heat and acting as radiators to continue the ripening process in the evening. The wines are full of sweet, ripe fruit, with fine-grained tannins for backbone. With a wide palette of varieties to choose from and varied

BELOW *The big stones, so characteristic of Châteauneuf vineyards, can be seen in this view of the remains of the Papal castle from the Clos des Papes vineyard.*

soils and exposures, each estate produces its own style. Some of the best are made at Château de Beaucastel and Domaine du Vieux Télégraphe. Characterful white wines are normally fresh and lively when dominated by Grenache Blanc and Bourboulenc and sometimes richer with Roussanne.

Meaty reds

Grenache can be up to 80 per cent of the blend in robust Gigondas, with Syrah and Mourvèdre adding spicy and leathery notes and some complexity. Domaine Santa Duc and Château de St Cosme are making excellent wines – the latter's Valbelle cuvée is particularly fine.

Lirac is a Châteauneuf lookalike, offering good value for its honest, chewy reds and whites, with excellent rosés too. Côtes du Ventoux reds have structure and brighter fruit flavours, while fresh and fruity white wines dominate in the Côtes du Lubéron. Standards are also rising in the Côtes du

Vivarais, Coteaux du Tricastin and Costières de Nimes, where dedicated growers and winemakers are producing very attractive, warm, fruit-driven reds.

Dessert wines

As well as strong reds, Beaumes-de-Venise makes fresh, sweetly fruited fortified wines from Muscat Blancs à Petits Grains. It is a delightful aperitif or light dessert wine. Fortified red wine Rasteau partners chocolate or red fruits well.

Tavel rosé
Some of the region's best rosé is produced in Tavel, where Grenache tops a long list of permitted grape varieties. It is known for its light pink colour, taking on an onion-skin appearance with age. Enjoy it young and fruity.

BELOW *Increasingly vineyard proprietors in the southern Rhône are making and estate-bottling their own wines, with the result that standards are constantly rising. There are excellent négociant wines from companies such as Perrin and St Cosme.*

Châteauneuf-du-Pape Château de Beaucastel. A high proportion of Mourvèdre gives notes of leather and undergrowth. Needs age.

Châteauneuf-du-Pape Domaine de la Vieille Julienne. Rich, full-fruited and meaty. Great in youth and age.

Gigondas Château de St Cosme. Rich in black fruits, with strong tannins and balanced acidity.

Lirac 'Cuvée Confidentielle' Château St-Roch. Chewy, ripe fruit with good structure. Can be drunk young, but best after two to five years.

Côtes du Rhône-Villages 'Khayyam' Mas de Libian. Deeply coloured and gloriously fruited. Attractively priced.

Tavel Rosé Château d'Aqueria. Fresh, vibrant rosé with good style. Ideal with food.

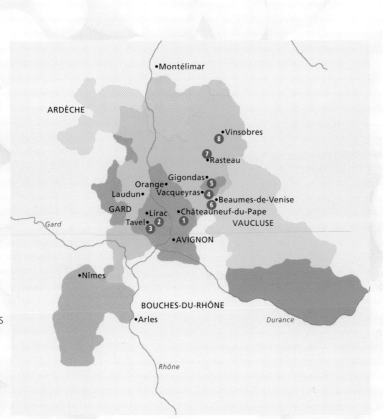

SOUTHERN RHÔNE

REGIONS
- Côtes du Vivarais
- Coteaux du Tricastin
- Côtes du Rhône
- Côtes du Rhône-Villages
- Côtes du Ventoux
- Côtes du Lubéron
- Costières de Nîmes

CÔTES DU RHÔNE CRUS
1. Châteauneuf-du-Pape
2. Lirac
3. Tavel
4. Vacqueyras
5. Gigondas

CÔTES DU RHÔNE VILLAGES CRUS
6. Beaumes-de-Venise
7. Rasteau
8. Vinsobres

SOUTHERN FRANCE

Provence

Provence is renowned for its wonderful climate and the quality of its light, which has attracted artists such as Van Gogh, Matisse and Picasso. It is also noted for its rosé. Around 80 per cent of Provençal wines are rosé, and the place is awash with the stuff, some good, a lot undistinguished, and much of it consumed by tourists and locals in the cafés and restaurants of the Riviera.

Côtes de Provence is a large appellation, producing about half of all French rosé, chiefly from Grenache, Syrah, Cinsault and Carignan. Bandol offers fine-quality rosé and some of the best reds. Mourvèdre gives full-bodied, leathery wines with a wonderful rusticity suited to rich winter foods, while Coteaux Varois makes a fresher style.

Cabernet Sauvignon is grown around Aix-en-Provence and also at Les Baux-de-Provence. Domaine de Trévallon makes impressive wines here, but as more than the statutory 20 per cent of Cabernet is used they have to be labelled as *vin de pays* ('country wine'). Other good reds are found in Palette, also noted for its whites.

Cassis produces interesting whites made from up to eight different grapes, with Marsanne and Clairette predominant, and good Vermentino is found in Bellet. Most of this is drunk locally. Unfortunately these wines are produced in very limited quantities in an expensive part of France. Consequently they are never cheap.

Bandol Cuvée Classique Domaine Tempier. Full bodied with leather and undergrowth notes.

Cassis Clos Ste-Magdeleine. Clean peach fruit with herbal notes and a citric and mineral background.

Bandol Rosé 'Mas de la Rouvière' Domaines Bunan. Cinsault-dominated with delightful pink colour and hints of red fruits and peaches.

BELOW *The Clos Ste-Magdeleine vineyard overlooks the Mediterranean above the old fishing port of Cassis, once a haunt of Dufy and Matisse.*

PROVENCE

- Avignon
- *Rhône*
- *Durance*
- ALPES-MARITIME
- Arles
- Salon-de-Provence
- Nice
- BOUCHES-DU-RHÔNE
- Aix-en-Provence
- Draguignan
- Cannes
- Brignolle
- MARSEILLE
- VAR
- St-Tropez
- Cassis
- *MEDITERRANEAN SEA*
- Bandol
- Toulon

REGIONS

- Les Baux-de-Provence
- Coteaux d'Aix-en-Provence
- Palette
- Côtes de Provence
- Cassis
- Bandol
- Coteaux Varois
- Bellet

ABOVE *Given the extent of Provençal vineyards and the region's popularity, it is perhaps surprising that so few areas have developed anything more than a local reputation.*

SOUTHERN FRANCE

Corsica

This hot, dry mountainous island, birthplace of Napoleon Bonaparte, has a wealth of microclimates and soils scattered around the valleys and hillsides of the coastal areas. Few of the better wines are seen in export markets. Much of the wine is produced as Île de Beauté vins de pays, mainly from the Chardonnay, Cabernet Sauvignon and Merlot grown on the eastern side.

Aromatic Vermentino
Both Patrimonio and Ajaccio make good whites with delicious melon-style Vermentino fruit, as does Cap Corse, where excellent sweet Muscats also originate.

CORSICA

MEDITERRANEAN SEA

Cap Corse

① ②

Patrimonio • • Bastia
③

•Calvi
⑨

•Corte

④

⑧

•Ajaccio

⑤

•Propriano
⑦   ⑥   •Porto Vecchio

SELECTED APPELLATIONS
① Corse-Coteaux du Cap Corse
② Muscat du Cap Corse
③ Patrimonio
④ (Vin de) Corse
⑤ Corse-Porto-Vecchio
⑥ Corse-Figari
⑦ Corse-Sartène
⑧ Ajaccio
⑨ Corse-Calvi

ABOVE Corsica's climate is little influenced by the Mediterranean Sea and is hotter and drier than in mainland France.

RIGHT *The rugged landscape and searing heat of Corsica ensure that its wines have abundant personality. This is the organic vineyard of Antoine Arena in Patrimonio.*

Corse-Porto-Vecchio Domaine de Torraccia. Round and earthy with decent body and soft tannins.

Corse-Sartène Rosé Domaine Saparale. Light, fresh rosé with delightful aromas of red summer fruits.

Muscat du Cap Corse Vin Doux Naturel Domaine Pieretti. Sweet and aromatic Muscat aromas and flavours, with perfect refreshing acidity.

Patrimonio is a principal appellation. Local Nielluccio, the equivalent of Tuscany's Sangiovese, flourishes in limestone soils and makes big, flavoursome reds with strong tannins, bright acidity and a rustic edge. The granitic soils and higher altitudes of Ajaccio, planted mainly with Sciacarello, make lighter reds with firm tannins and notes of pepper, as well as some fragrant rosés.

Calvi's reds have a wild, herbal style, while Sartène makes a more open style, often adding a proportion of Barbarossa. Figari wines can have more finesse but are produced in tiny quantities. In Porto Vecchio, Grenache often supplements Nielluccio and Sciacarello to make elegant, softer wines.

SOUTHERN FRANCE

Languedoc-Roussillon

Some of France's most delicious and inexpensive wine comes from the swathe of vineyards between the Rhône Delta and Spain. This region was a major contributor to Europe's notorious wine lake, but noble Rhône varieties have replaced high-cropping varieties to produce wines packed with the sensuous herbal aromas of the *garrigue* – the wild, open countryside of the Mediterranean.

Much of the production is of varietal vins de pays, seen in every supermarket and wine shop throughout Europe. Their keen prices and good quality make them ideal for everyday drinking. But there is far more to the region.

Languedoc

The Languedoc appellation covers a vast tract of land with a wide range of soils and climatic conditions. Most wines are blended from several grape varieties, giving them complexity

LANGUEDOC-ROUSSILLON

REGIONS

Coteaux du Languedoc

Faugères

St-Chinian

Minervois

Cabardès

Côtes de la Malepère

Limoux

Corbières

Fitou

Côtes du Roussillon

Côtes du Roussillon-Villages

Banyuls and Collioure

SELECTED APPELLATIONS

1. Pic St-Loup
2. Clairette du Languedoc
3. Picpoul de Pinet
4. La Clape
5. Muscat de Lunel
6. Muscat de Frontignan
7. Muscat de Mireval
8. Muscat de St Jean-de-Minervois
9. Muscat de Rivesaltes
10. Maury

ABOVE *Once, most of these wines left the region anonymously in bulk road tankers. Now many are estate bottled. Some, such as the Mas de Daumas Gassac, are world-renowned, and wines from Collioure fetch big prices in export markets.*

Limoux fizz
Sparkling wines from Limoux – Blanquette (mainly Mauzac) and Crémant (Chardonnay and Chenin) – are worth noting. There is also a sweet version made from Mauzac with a delightful flavour of apples, the perfect partner for tarte tatin.

RIGHT In the 1980s Mas de Daumas Gassac set new and high standards for the Midi, being described by Gault and Millau as 'a Languedoc Château Lafite'. Its garrigue vineyard is farmed organically.

and varied characters. Syrah, Grenache, Mourvèdre, Carignan and Cinsault give intensity with notes of the garrigue (such as wild thyme) in reds and finely fruited rosés. Whites have a multitude of origins, from the great Rhône varieties through Vermentino to Macabeu (Spain's Macabeo). Consequently there is no general style.

Increasingly well-made reds are emerging from Cabardès and Côtes de la Malapère in the west. Solid reds emanate from the Languedoc crus of St-Chinian and Faugères, aided by their schistous soils which give wines with good definition and bright, spicy fruit. Picpoul de Pinet is a fresh, light white.

Minervois

Red wine, much of which is simple and fruity, dominates Minervois. The central region of Minervois-La Livinière makes higher quality wines. Here Syrah, Grenache and Mourvèdre need to account for 60 per cent of the blend, giving the wines more structure and finesse. Cooperatives and private producers continue to raise standards.

Corbières

The large, dry region of Corbières produces appetizing wines, dominated by Carignan. It is full bodied with big spicy notes – Corbières-Boutenac is particularly meaty. Fitou is similar, yet rarely as fine. Good, fruity rosés are made throughout the region.

Côtes du Rousillon

The same main grape varieties are grown in Côtes du Rousillon, but Syrah and Mourvèdre are increasingly encountered, especially in Côtes du Roussillon-Villages, where the use of Carignan is outlawed. *Vins doux naturels* (sweet wines) from Rivesaltes, Banyuls and Maury, based on Grenache, are the outstanding wines of the area. Some Muscat is also made.

SOUTHERN FRANCE

South-west France

From Bordeaux to the foothills of the Pyrenees, the south-west of France produces a rich variety of wines that have been out of the limelight for many years but have recently risen in popularity. Despite this, they still offer good value. Some unusual grape varieties survive here, such as Fer Servadou, Ondenc, Len de l'El, Gros and Petit Manseng, Arrufiac and Petit Courbu, bringing individuality to the wines.

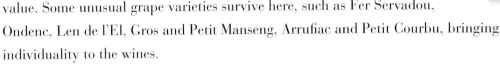

Blockbuster reds

The wines of Gaillac readily demonstrate the region's variety, with strongly flavoured reds, fresh, fragrant dry whites and sweet whites, plus light, fruity sparkling wines and soft rosés. Around Fronton gentle, easy-drinking reds are made. On the other hand, Cahors was traditionally noted for its 'black wines' – rich, intense reds, full of tannins, taking years to soften. Modern winemaking results in softer wines, but they retain the spicy, rich fruit the Malbec grape delivers. For truly blockbuster reds, Madiran takes some beating: the tannic Tannat grape makes intense wines that, even when softened by barrel ageing, still require years of cellaring.

Buzet makes good Bordeaux lookalikes, chiefly in the local cooperative, the largest producer. Another good cooperative produces Côtes du Marmandais in a similar style. Red Marcillac is rustic and sturdy. France's only Basque wine is Irouléguy, produced in red, white and rosé varieties, the red robust and characterful.

BELOW *Vineyards near Monbazillac. Wines qualifying for the Monbazillac appellation are sweet – and very good – but red and dry wines are also produced under different appellations.*

SOUTH-WEST FRANCE

REGIONS

- Bergerac
- Côtes de Duras
- Côtes du Marmandais
- Buzet
- Cahors
- Marcillac
- Côtes du Frontonnais
- Gaillac
- Madiran/Pacherenc du Vic Bilh
- Jurançon
- Béarn
- Irouléguy

SELECTED APPELLATIONS

1. Monbazillac
2. Montravel
3. Pécharmant
4. Saussignac

LEFT *There is no dominant style to the wines of south-west France. Wines of all kinds are made and many are still produced traditionally from indigenous grapes. It is to be hoped that these characterful wines do not fall foul of internationalization.*

Gaillac Château Lastours. Crisp, clean, dry white with notes of apple.

Cahors 'Cuvée Maurin' Domaine la Bérangeraie. Rich in black berry fruit with hints of pepper and fine-grained tannins.

Madiran Château Montus. Rich, intense red with full aromas of stewed fruits and spice, with excellent ageing potential.

Jurançon Moelleux 'Cuvée Thibault' Domaine Bellegarde. Delicious peachy, nutty palate with notes of orange and hints of botrytis.

Bergerac Sec 'Moulin des Dames' Château Tour des Gendres. Richly flavoured white with floral aromas and great intensity on the palate.

Monbazillac Domaine de l'Ancienne Cure. Dried fruit aromas with a luscious, honeyed palate.

In Bordeaux's shadow

Côtes de Duras borders Bordeaux's Entre-Deux-Mers and makes decent whites, reds and rosés, along with a little sweeter white. But the best wines of this northern area are from Bergerac. Wines that were once also-rans by Bordeaux standards now show genuine quality in a variety of styles. Grape varieties are the same as in Bordeaux and the whites are generally dry, fresh and lively, or richer and more complex when barrel fermented. Reds are full-flavoured, and some of the best are sold under the Côtes de Bergerac or Pécharmant appellations.

Monbazillac is the best known of a cluster of sweet white wine appellations, where *Botrytis cinerea* often affects the crop, giving wines with exotic fruit aromas. Saussignac, with its small production, is worth searching out, as is neighbouring Montravel for its dry whites and reds, plus sweet wines under appellations Côtes de Montravel and Haut-Montravel.

●●● Regions 26–38

●●● Italy

Italy is one of the most prolific wine-producing countries in the world. Grapes were cultivated there when the Greeks established colonies in the eighth and seventh centuries BC, but it is really only in the last thirty years that its full potential has been recognized. At last growers have realized that, even in the baking heat of the far south, it is possible to produce quality wines utilizing the latest winemaking techniques.

Italian winemakers throughout the country now acknowledge the importance of low yields, of terroir, of scrupulous winery practices and of the country's own grape varieties. Standards are rising fast (see box on page 76 for details of Italy's classification system), as are prices for the best wines.

While Italy's red wines have long been its finest, its whites are improving rapidly – not only the well-known Soaves and Orvietos but also a new wave of exciting wines such as Greco di Tufo and Fiano di Avellino. One thing has not changed, however: for Italians, the primary purpose of wine is to accompany and complement food, and what fabulous food it is!

NORTH-WEST ITALY

Liguria, Valle d'Aosta and Lombardy

In terms of wine, north-west Italy is most famous for the great wines of Piedmont (see page 74), yet for the traveller there are other delicious finds to be made in this diverse corner. From the Alpine scenery of the Valle d'Aosta, boasting some of the highest vineyards in Europe, via the broad plains of the Po Valley to the precipitous cliffs of the Ligurian Riviera, many unusual wines await pleasurable discovery.

Liguria

Winemaking along the Ligurian Riviera is limited by its formidable terrain, with terraced vineyards clinging precariously to the coastal cliffs overlooking the Mediterranean. Planted with Vermentino and the local varieties Bosco and Albarola, they make the delicious white wine of the Cinque Terre, ideal to quaff with local seafood and fish dishes. Commercial winemaking is mainly centred in the Riviera Ligure di Ponente DOC, using Pigato and Vermentino for whites. Reds are made from Ormeasco and Rossese: the latter, with its own appellation of Rossese di Dolceacqua, is a light fruity wine for easy drinking.

Valle d'Aosta

In the Valle d'Aosta a wealth of grape varieties is permitted: Nebbiolo, Pinot Noir, Chardonnay and Moscato (Muscat) are

BELOW LEFT *A complete spectrum of wines is made in north-west Italy: red, white, pink, still, sparkling, dry and sweet.*

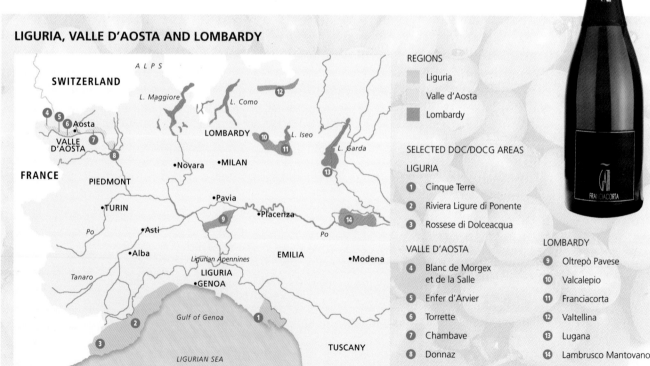

LIGURIA, VALLE D'AOSTA AND LOMBARDY

REGIONS
- Liguria
- Valle d'Aosta
- Lombardy

SELECTED DOC/DOCG AREAS

LIGURIA
1. Cinque Terre
2. Riviera Ligure di Ponente
3. Rossese di Dolceacqua

VALLE D'AOSTA
4. Blanc de Morgex et de la Salle
5. Enfer d'Arvier
6. Torrette
7. Chambave
8. Donnaz

LOMBARDY
9. Oltrepò Pavese
10. Valcalepio
11. Franciacorta
12. Valtellina
13. Lugana
14. Lambrusco Mantovano

RIGHT *Vines cling precariously to the cliffs overlooking the Mediterranean above the village of Manarola in the Cinque Terre.*

 Pigato 'Le Russeghine' Bruna, Riviera Ligure di Ponente. Fresh and floral, with great balance and a good finish.

Chardonnay Château Feuillet, Valle d'Aosta. Small production but great value, with intense fruit, a full palate and fresh acidity.

Valtellina Sfursat Nino Negri, Lombardia. Complex aromas and spicy plum fruit. Made from grapes dried for three months before vinification.

Franciacorta Satèn Brut Enrico Gatti, Lombardia. Wonderful aromas, silky mouthfeel and lingering finish. Delicious.

Franciacorta sparkling wines
To develop complexity, the non-vintage wines – which can range from very dry to medium dry – spend at least 18 months maturing in bottle before disgorgement. The silky Satèn wines are bottled at a slightly lower pressure and must age for two years.

planted alongside indigenous vines. It is well worth seeking out the reds of Donnaz, Enfer d'Arvier and Torrette, and the crisp white Blanc de Morgex et de la Salle. Little of the sturdy Malvoisie escapes the Valle d'Aosta, where it is much prized by the locals. Interesting Moscato *passito* (dried grape wine) is also made in the DOC of Chambave.

Lombardy

In what is one of the most populated regions of Italy other industries tend to overshadow winemaking. The Oltrepò Pavese produces many indifferent wines, as to a lesser extent does Valcalepio. Decent whites from Trebbiano are made in the Lugana DOC, while good Nebbiolo-based reds originate in Valtellina, sometimes made from dried grapes. Lambrusco is produced on the plains of Emilia, with one of its five DOCs stretching into Lombardy.

The true gems of Lombardy are the sparklers of Franciacorta. These world-class wines are based mainly on Chardonnay and Pinot Noir, although Pinot Bianco is also allowed. All three varieties thrive in the infertile soils of this beautiful landscape, giving wines that, when produced by the traditional method, as used in Champagne, are the best sparkling wines of Italy. Rosé and vintage wines are also produced, along with still wines under the Terre di Franciacorta DOC: clean, fresh whites and flavoursome reds made from Cabernet Sauvignon, Barbera and Nebbiolo.

NORTH-WEST ITALY

Piedmont

For most wine enthusiasts, Piedmont is summed up in two magnificent red wines – Barolo and Barbaresco – and a famous, if notorious, sweet sparkler, Asti Spumante. In fact the region produces a great many wines in a multitude of guises. Most originate in the gentle hills surrounding the chic town of Alba, the world's white truffle capital, but there are significant outposts in the north, such as Ghemme and Gattinara.

Regal wines

Barolo and Barbaresco, both produced from the Nebbiolo grape, are near neighbours. In youth, they exhibit delightful perfumes reminiscent of violets and roses, backed by bright acidity and angular tannins. After some time they become majestic, complex offerings, with notes of tar and tobacco behind their rich, meaty, well-fruited flavours.

The vineyards of both appellations cover the charming Langhe hills like a patchwork quilt, with Nebbiolo vines interspersed with plantings of Barbera and Dolcetto in less favoured sites. Nebbiolo (from *nebbia*, meaning fog) is the latest of the varieties, often not achieving perfect ripeness until late October, when morning mists hanging in the valleys block out precious sunlight until well after daybreak. Driving through the hills it is easy to appreciate the varied exposures and altitudes of the vineyards, and it is becoming increasingly fashionable for labels to state the vineyard of origin, although some growers still blend wines from several locations. With such a variety of aspects and winemakers it is difficult to generalize, but most agree that the wines of

Old oak or new

There are two schools of thought on winemaking here. Traditionalists, such as Mauro Mascarello, age their wines in large old casks called *botti*, while modernists, like Enrico Scavino, prefer to use *barriques* (barrels) of new French oak. There is no right or wrong way. Both methods can produce incredible wines, capable of ageing wonderfully in bottle to give pleasure over many years.

'The king of wines and the wine of kings.'

HOW THE PEOPLE OF
PIEDMONT DESCRIBE
BAROLO

LEFT *Nebbiolo vines surround the village of Barolo, the rolling hills providing a wealth of subtly differing microclimates.*

PIEDMONT

REGION
◻ Piedmont

SELECTED DOC/DOCG AREAS

①	Alba	⑪	Gattinara
②	Asti	⑫	Gavi or Cortese di Gavi
③	Barbaresco	⑬	Ghemme
④	Barolo	⑭	Langhe
⑤	Brachetto d'Acqui	⑮	Monferrato
⑥	Carema	⑯	Roero
⑦	Colli Tortonesi		
⑧	Dolcetto di Dogliani		
⑨	Dolcetta di Ovada		
⑩	Erbaluce di Caluso		

LEFT *The climate of Piedmont is governed by the mountains, Alps and Apennines, which surround it on three sides. Mountains account for 43 per cent of its area, while gentler hills cover 26 per cent – the great wines are made in the hills.*

the communes of La Morra and Barolo are the most aromatic and earliest maturing, while those of Castiglione Faletto, Serralunga and Monforte have greater structure and concentration, requiring longer cellaring.

Barbaresco's hills are slightly steeper than those of Barolo, and the wines tend to have greater elegance. In the delightful hilltop village of Barbaresco the renowned Angelo Gaja, one of the world's greatest growers, produces incomparable examples of both Barolo and Barbaresco. But he has also pioneered the planting of international varieties such as Cabernet Sauvignon, Merlot and Chardonnay, often renouncing the use of the two great appellations in favour of the Langhe DOC. His single-vineyard Sorì Tildìn and Sorì San Lorenzo are rare and expensive but quite superb. The cooperative cellar of the Produttori del Barbaresco remains a safe bet for high-quality, affordable wines.

Nebbiolo is grown throughout Piedmont, notably under the appellation Nebbiolo d'Alba, and onwards to Roero and Carema, thence to Ghemme and Gattinara, where its local name is Spanna.

Easy-drinking reds

While Nebbiolo is the grape for the flagship wines, Barbera and Dolcetto are far more widely planted. Barbera is the softer of the two, giving wines of good red fruit character, ranging from light and easy drinking in the Asti and Monferrato appellations to full and rich examples such as Bricco San Biagio from Ciabot Berton in La Morra, part of the Alba appellation. Interesting Barberas are also produced in the Colli Tortonesi.

Dolcetto, despite a name that implies sweetness, is actually bone dry, with bright acidity and flavours of sour cherries. Dolcetto d'Alba and Dolcetto d'Asti are the most common, but good examples also come from Dogliani, Ovada and around Monferrato. One rarity worth searching out is the gently sparkling Brachetto d'Acqui, a light, fresh red with low alcohol and delicious red and black fruit flavours – a perfect accompaniment to strawberries.

ITALIAN WINE CLASSIFICATION

The classification **Denominazione di Origine Controllata (DOC)** was introduced in the 1960s in an attempt to regulate Italian wines by controlling where they can be made, yields, grape varieties and production methods. To recognize the superior qualities of certain wines, such as Barolo and Chianti, **DOCG (Denominazione di Origine Controllata e Garantita)** was introduced in the 1980s. Ordinary wines were classified **VDT (Vini da Tavola)**. However, many exceptionally good wines were sold under the VDT classification, very often because they used grape varieties not permitted under DOC regulations. These are now covered by the designation **IGT (Indicazione Geografica Tipica)**.

White wines

In the Langhe and Roero hills, Arneis makes satisfying dry whites. Those from Roero are lighter, with bright fresh fruit, floral aromas and an underlying minerality suited to the local food. Towards Alessándria, the Cortese grape makes dry whites under the Gavi appellation. Those from the commune of Gavi are called Gavi di Gavi, though this does not imply better quality. They are simple with bright floral aromas, a mineral backbone and citrus notes on the palate, similar to those from the nearby Colli Tortonesi.

Moscato is the most widely planted white variety, producing delicious, sweet sparkling and semi-sparkling wines with pronounced grapey flavours. These light, fresh wines retain some natural sugar and are light in alcohol. Another excellent dessert wine, much fuller and far rarer, is Erbaluce di Caluso, made by the *passito* method – drying the Erbaluce grapes to intensify the sugars. It is sweet, with gentle aromas and a full, velvety palate.

FAR RIGHT *Barbaresco vineyards near Neive and one of Barbaresco's most famous and expensive wines, Gaja's Sorì Tildìn (labelled Langhe), which carries rich aromas of raspberries and vanilla and a full, yet strict palate in youth, with big tannins and hints of cocoa in the end.*

NORTH-EAST ITALY

Trentino-Alto Adige

Italy's northernmost wine region, the Alto Adige or Südtirol, has developed substantially since the 1980s, when light reds from the local Schiava grape began to be superseded by aromatic white varieties and the classic Bordeaux reds. Today, some of Italy's best white wines are made here. At the same time winemaking has come a long way in the terraced, valley-side vineyards of the Trentino region to the south.

Alto Adige

It was not until 1919 that this Alpine region bordering the Austrian Tyrol finally became part of Italy, and it embraces both Austrian and Italian cultures: most of its inhabitants still prefer to speak German. These days its white wines show clearly defined fruit flavours and aromas, with Pinot Grigio, Chardonnay and Pinot Bianco leading the way. The Isarco and Venosta valleys provide first-rate Riesling, while a little high-class Sauvignon Blanc is made under the Terlano DOC. Gewürztraminer is thought to have originated locally – its name derives from the village of Tramin – and shows class and refinement here.

Well-structured reds from Cabernet Sauvignon, Merlot and Lagrein are popular, although Schiava remains the most planted and grows best in the Santa Maddalena DOC. Lagrein likes the gravel soils of Gries, close to the centre of Bolzano, where its spicy fruit and smoky, meaty aromas show best. Pinot Nero also fares well, and a little red dessert wine is made from Moscato Rosa. From the right producer it enchants, with aromas of roses and cloves over sweet, ripe fruit.

Pinot Grigio 'Castel Ringberg' Elena Walch, Alto Adige. Delicious spicy pear fruit with good minerality and acidity.

Gewürztraminer 'Kolbenhof' J. Hofstätter, Alto Adige. Intensely aromatic and extremely concentrated on the palate. Delicious!

Lagrein Cantina Bolzano, Alto Adige. Full bodied with big spicy fruit and soft, yet evident, tannins.

Pinot Grigio 'Storie di Vite' Cantina La Vis, Trentino. Fresh pear-dominated aromas and flavours with good balancing acidity.

Teroldego Rotaliano 'Granato' Foradori, Trentino. Full blackberry fruit with notes of tar and smoke. Long on the palate.

TRENTINO-ALTO ADIGE

Map showing: SWITZERLAND, ALPS, ALTO ADIGE, AUSTRIA, Brunico, Merano, Terlano, Bolzano, Caldaro, DOLOMITES, TRENTINO, Trento, Valle dei Laghi, Rovereto, LOMBARDY, L. Garde, Verona, Adige, Po, VENETO, Vicenza, Treviso, VENICE, Padova, Gulf of Venice, FRIULLI-VENEZIA-GIULIA, ADRIATIC SEA

REGIONS
Alto Adige
Trentino

SELECTED DOC/DOCG AREAS
ALTO ADIGE
1. Valle Venosta
2. Valle Isarco
3. Terlano
4. Santa Maddalena

TRENTINO
5. Teroldego Rotaliano

LEFT *The cool, Alpine climate of Trentino-Alto Adige adds a clarity and freshness to the natural fruitiness of its wines.*

Trentino

Here cooperatives dominate wine production. The principal varieties grown are Chardonnay (the most widely planted), for the thriving sparkling wine industry, and Pinot Grigio, Merlot, Cabernet Sauvignon and other international varieties to satisfy the mass market for light, easy-drinking wines, red and white. But it is worth seeking out the better versions, such as the Pinot Grigio from Cantina La Vis in the Cembra Valley or Pojer and Sandri's Pinot Nero. Interesting Müller-Thurgau is made in the higher vineyards, such as that from the Istituto Agrario di San Michele all'Adige.

A few indigenous varieties make intriguing wines, such as the Teroldego grown in the gravelly soils of the Campo Rotaliano, where it gives deep, well-flavoured reds capable of ageing. Foradori make an excellent example under the Vigneti delle Dolomiti IGT. Marzemino (mentioned in Mozart's *Don Giovanni*) makes fresh, easy-drinking reds in the Vallagarina. Although the Nosiola grape makes indifferent dry whites, when dried to intensify the sugar it produces excellent Vin Santo in the Valle dei Laghi.

ELENA WALCH
CASTEL RINGBERG
Pinot Grigio
ALTO ADIGE

2008

ABOVE *The bittersweet, light red wines of Caldaro (Kalterersee) are produced from Schiava grapes grown in idyllic surroundings.*

NORTH-EAST ITALY

Veneto

The Veneto is a powerhouse of production, not just for north-east Italy but for the whole country. The best-known wines of the region, Soave and Valpolicella, come in various guises. Both have been much maligned over the years, as high-volume production for the mass market resulted in lightweight, flavourless wines. Times have changed: good examples can regularly be found that show true class and style.

Soave

Soave, one of Italy's most popular whites, is made principally from Garganega, which offers gentle fruit and floral nuances. Barrels are often used for Soave Classico, giving the wine greater substance. Recioto, made from dried grapes, has a delicious sweet edge and is fuller and richer on the palate. Sparkling Soave is also made.

Valpolicella

Corvina, Rondinella and Molinara grapes make the light, cherry fruit Valpolicella, with a refreshingly bitter undertone. If they are partially dried, a much stronger and richer version – Amarone – is produced, of which the best examples can be real blockbusters, packed with rich, dark, dried-fruit flavours with a bittersweet finish and abundant alcohol. If the grapes are dried still further and not all the sugar is used during fermentation, a sweet Recioto is produced, resembling liquid raspberries. Masi and Tommaso Bussola make excellent examples. A Ripasso Valpolicella is also made, by fermenting the new vintage Valpolicella over the lees of Amarone to increase its depth and character. Bardolino is similar to traditional Valpolicella, and from the same area comes a fresh and tasty rosé called Chiaretto.

Wide variety of wines

Still wines from several varieties are made under the Gambellara, Colli Euganei, Colli Berici and Breganze DOCs. Cabernet Sauvignon and Merlot dominate the reds, Pinot Bianco the whites. Just north of Venice, Lison-Pramaggiore

and Piave turn out many light, quaffable wines from a range of grapes, particularly Merlot. Cabernet Franc and Cabernet Sauvignon feature strongly, too, and richer, more serious blends have been appearing from this trio of Bordeaux varieties. Good dry whites from the Verduzzo grape, together with crisp Sauvignon Blanc and fresh, lively Chardonnay, feature alongside Pinot Grigio, the fashion for which has caused increased plantings recently. Light Bianco di Custoza is a good aperitif.

Sparkling wines

Prosecco from the Conegliano and Valdobbiadene DOCGs is increasingly popular. It ranges in style from fresh, crisp and dry (Brut) to softer, fruitier and sweeter, confusingly labelled Extra Dry. Both offer fair value, as do the other sparkling wines now appearing from Chardonnay and Pinot Bianco.

ABOVE *A Soave Classico vineyard overlooking historic Soave Castle.*

LEFT *Valpolicella Classico vines growing in the hills above Fumane, north-west of Verona.*

RIGHT *While the Veneto might be considered a single geographical unit, in vinous terms its variety is enormous, with red, pink and white wines of all kinds.*

Aromatic grappa
The Veneto is long associated with the production of grappa, a brandy distilled from what is left (skin, stems and pips) after the juice has been pressed from the grapes to make wine. Usually colourless, fine grappas reveal the characteristics of their grape varieties in their fresh, lively aromas. Much prized, barrel-aged grappas take on a yellow or brown hue.

VENETO

ALPS
SWITZERLAND
ALTO ADIGE DOLOMITES
AUSTRIA
Adige
•Bolzano
FRIULLI-VENEZIA-GIULIA
•Trento
•Belluno
•Udine
LOMBARDY
TRENTINO
•Pordenone
VENETO
•Conegliano
⑪•Bassano del Grappe
Treviso• ⑨
⑩
TRIESTE•
L. Garde
③
⑥•Vicenza
Verona• ④⑤
VENICE•
Soave ⑦
Gulf of Venice
① ②
•Padova
⑧
ADRIATIC SEA
Po

REGION
Veneto

SELECTED DOC/DOCG AREAS
① Bianco di Custoza
② Bardolino
③ Valpolicella
④ Soave and Recioto di Soave
⑤ Gambellara
⑥ Breganze
⑦ Colli Berici
⑧ Colli Euganei
⑨ Piave
⑩ Lison-Pramaggiore
⑪ Prosecco di Conegliano-Valdobbiadene

Soave Classico 'Contrada Salvarenza' Gini. Stylish barrel-fermented Soave with fruity and floral flavours over a mineral background and creamy finish.

Recioto di Soave 'Le Colombare' Leonildo Pieropan. Honey and apricot aromas combine with exotic flavours on the palate. Gentle and sweet.

Amarone della Valpolicella Classico Tommaso Bussola. Enormous wine with aromas and flavours of dried fruits. A soft, sweetish core is followed by a big, dark finish.

Cabernet 'Podere Le Tavole' Fattoria Monte Fasolo, Colli Euganei. Full flavoured and dominated by black fruit and cherries with good backbone.

Prosecco di Valdobbiadene Astoria Extra Dry. Fresh with delicious pear fruit and a clean finish.

NORTH-EAST ITALY
Friuli-Venezia Giulia

Long reputed for high quality, fruity white wines from a host of local and international varieties, Friuli-Venezia Giulia is today dominated by the fashionable Pinot Grigio. It is the most planted variety in the extensive Grave DOC and in the two fine white areas Collio Goriziano (or simply Collio) and Colli Orientali. Mario Schiopetto and Josko Gravner have been the motivators behind the search for uncompromised quality.

Pinot Grigio's popularity notwithstanding, Merlot gives the best wines in the Grave DOC, and is extensively planted. Cabernets Franc and Sauvignon join in Bordeaux-style blends and on their own. Pinot Nero yields fruity, light reds and local Refosco dal Peduncolo Rosso makes chewy, full-flavoured wines. Barrel ageing is becoming more prevalent for reds as growers strive for greater structure.

Fruity whites

Most white wines are made and aged in stainless steel to preserve their bright fruit aromas, though a few growers employ oak barrels and add a little barrique-aged wine to the blend to increase complexity. Sauvignon Blanc and Friulano

(previously Tocai Friulano) are widely grown for their aromatic intensity, alongside Riesling, Pinot Bianco and Chardonnay, with fine examples from Isonzo's Vie di Romans.

The low-cropping Picolit makes concentrated yet fresh dessert wines, and the DOCG Ramondolo provides intense wines, rich in dried apricot and honey flavours, from the Verduzzo grape.

FRIULI-VENEZIA GIULIA

ALPS
AUSTRIA
Adige
DOLOMITES
FRIULLI-VENEZIA-GIULIA
TRENTINO
•Trento
Udine
Pordenone•
Gorizia•
VENETO
TRIESTE•
•Treviso
•Vicenza
•VENICE
•Padova
Gulf of Venice
Po
ADRIATIC SEA

REGION

Friuli-Venezia Giulia

ABOVE *Friuli-Venezia Giulia benefits from a fortuitous mixture of Alpine and Adriatic influences.*

SELECTED DOC/DOCG AREAS

1 Friuli Grave
2 Collio Goriziano
3 Colli Orientali del Friuli
4 Ramondolo
5 Carso

🍷🍷 **Merlot Friuli Grave Vistorta.** Generously flavoured, with ripe red and black berry fruit.

🍷🍷 **Pinot Grigio Castello di Spessa, Collio.** Spicy pear flavours with a clip of acidity.

🍷🍷 **Friulano Oscar Sturm, Collio.** Light, floral aromas, a fresh palate and notes of almond.

ABOVE LEFT *The Ribolla vineyard of the late Mario Schiopetto, who brought German technology and French know-how to Friulian winemaking.*

CENTRAL ITALY
Emilia-Romagna

Bologna may be the capital of Emilia-Romagna, but the city of Modena packs a serious punch, too. It is the home of Maserati automobiles (with Ferraris coming from just down the road in Maranello); the great Italian tenor Luciano Pavarotti was born there; and Modena is surrounded by the vineyards of Lambrusco: millions of bottles of this cheap, sweet, lightly sparkling wine are exported every year.

Emilia

Mass-market Lambrusco bears little resemblance to the dry, strawberry-scented, *frizzante* (semi-sparkling) wines enjoyed by the locals with the region's hearty foods. Four DOCs (plus another in Lombardy) and different clones of the Lambrusco grape ensure a variety of styles, with that from Sorbara reckoned the best.

The foothills of the Apennines provide many varietal wines designated Colli Piacentini, Colli di Parma and Colli Bolognesi, with an interesting range of still, sparkling and passito styles.

Romagna

High-volume, ordinary wine is made in Romagna, but decent wines – still and sparkling – from Albana, Sangiovese (especially Superiore), Cabernet Sauvignon, Pinot Nero and Chardonnay can be found. Perhaps the best is sweet passito such as Antonio Gallegati's 'Regina di Cuori'. Local reds such as Bosco Eliceo Fortana are enjoyable but rarely exported.

EMILIA-ROMAGNA

MILAN · VENETO · VENICE · ADRIATIC SEA · Piacenza · Po · Parma · Ferrara · ① · ③ · Reggio Emilia · Modena · ② · LIGURIA · EMILIA-ROMAGNA · BOLOGNA · GENOA · ④ · Ravenna · Imola · ⑥ · ⑦ · ⑤ · Rimini · SAN MARINO · TUSCANY · TYRRHENIAN SEA · FLORENCE

REGION	SELECTED DOC/DOCG AREAS	
☐ Emilia-Romagna	① Colli Piacentini	④ Colli Bolognesi
	② Colli di Parma	⑤ Trebbiano di Romagna
	③ Lambrusco	⑥ Albana di Romagna
		⑦ Sangiovese di Romagna

🍷 **Lambrusco di Sorbara Cleto Chiarli.** Dry and fresh, with delicious fruit and eye-catching pink froth.

🍷🍷 **Sangiovese di Romagna Superiore Riserva Bissoni.** Soft and full-flavoured with complex aromas and flavours, often with notes of truffle.

ABOVE RIGHT *The fertile plain of the Po River dominates much of Emilia-Romagna, which is more famous for its Parmesan cheese and Parma ham than its wines.*

FAR RIGHT *The vineyards of medieval Castell'Arquato produce white Monterosso and Ortrugo and red Bonarda and Gutturnio.*

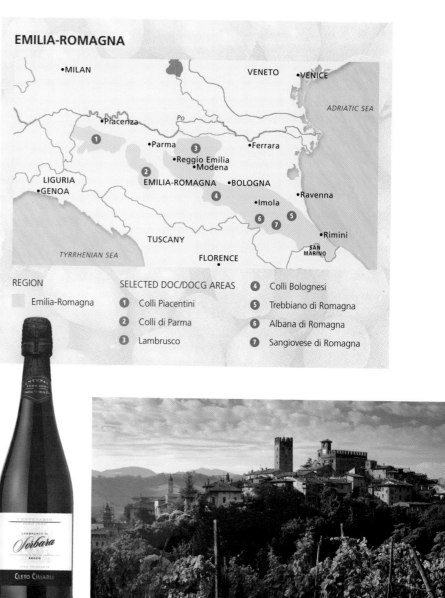

CENTRAL ITALY

Tuscany Central Hills

Tuscany is one of the great tourist destinations of Europe. Florence, Siena and other towns offer the traveller magnificent art treasures, architecture, cultural events and extraordinary history. Its sleepy hills are home to Italy's best-known red wine, Chianti, which went through a bad patch when its quality declined in the 1960s and 70s, but has reinvented itself since the 1980s: today fine examples can be found.

The Chianti formula

Sangiovese is the main variety used in Chianti production, though it was not until 1996 that the DOCG regulations allowed it to be made from that grape alone. In the mid-19th century Baron Bettino Ricasoli, a powerful figure in Tuscan winemaking and politics, dictated that Chianti should be based on Sangiovese with the addition of Canaiolo, with the white Malvasia grape used to soften the hard edges of younger wines. The prolific white variety Trebbiano was added to the blend in the 20th century. Since 1984, the inclusion of white varieties has been severely limited and yields have also been controlled, ensuring better quality of fruit and intensifying the style of the wines. Small additions of Cabernet Sauvignon and Merlot are allowed, to admit the so-called 'Super Tuscans' (see page 89) to DOCG status.

Different styles

The heart of Chianti is the Classico zone, in part the original region classified in 1716 by Grand Duke Cosimo III. Six further zones also take the Chianti prefix – Rufina, Colli

BELOW LEFT *The hilly country of central Tuscany provides a host of different microclimates bringing subtle nuances to each vineyard, emphasized by today's terroir-driven winemaking.*

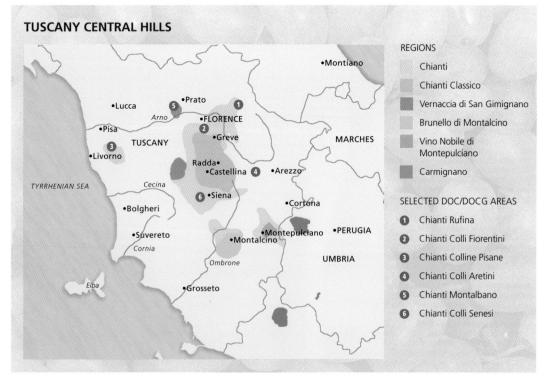

TUSCANY CENTRAL HILLS

•Montiano

•Lucca •Prato ①
⑤
Arno •FLORENCE
•Pisa ②
•Greve
③ TUSCANY MARCHES
•Livorno
Radda•
•Castellina ④ •Arezzo
TYRRHENIAN SEA *Cecina*
⑥ •Siena
•Bolgheri •Cortona
•Suvereto •Montepulciano •PERUGIA
Cornia •Montalcino
UMBRIA
Ombrone
Elba
•Grosseto

REGIONS

Chianti

Chianti Classico

Vernaccia di San Gimignano

Brunello di Montalcino

Vino Nobile di Montepulciano

Carmignano

SELECTED DOC/DOCG AREAS

① Chianti Rufina

② Chianti Colli Fiorentini

③ Chianti Colline Pisane

④ Chianti Colli Aretini

⑤ Chianti Montalbano

⑥ Chianti Colli Senesi

Fiorentini, Colline Pisane, Colli Aretini, Montalbano and Colli Senesi. Soil structures and altitudes vary in each, and these factors, together with the growers' individual winemaking philosophies, give rise to many differing styles: the wines range from light and fruity to deep, complex and structured, capable of ageing.

In the Chianti Classico zone, lower vineyards tend towards a sandy soil structure, giving chewy, full-flavoured wines. Those at higher elevations grow on limestone, which imparts elegance to the wine. New oak is now often used in place of the traditional botti for ageing. Chianti Rufina and Chianti Colli Senesi also produce good wines from higher altitude vineyards. The finest examples of each area are classified as Riserva, benefiting from extended ageing before release.

Vineyards around the beautiful walled town of San Gimignano produce delicious white wines from the local Vernaccia grape. Several styles are made, ranging from light and fruity to richer, barrel-fermented wines.

Chianti Classico 'Castello di Brolio' Barone Ricasoli. Bright, spicy cherry fruit with notes of Virginia tobacco and strong tannins in youth.

Chianti Classico 'Pèppoli' Antinori. Abundant sweet red fruit with overtones of vanilla.

Chianti Rufina 'Cedro' Fattoria Lavacchio. Organic Chianti with elegant bitter cherry fruit and good structure.

Chianti Colli Senesi San Giorgio a Lapi. Intense aromas and flavours of berries and red fruits, with chunky tannins behind.

Namesakes
Vino Nobile di Montepulciano (see page 86) is not to be confused with Montepulciano d'Abruzzo (see page 93). The former, made mainly with Prugnolo Gentile, is named after the Tuscan town that sits amid the producing vineyards, while the latter, from Abruzzo in eastern Italy, is made using the Montepulciano grape.

BELOW *The magnificently sited Castello di Volpaia estate at Radda produces excellent Chianti Classico, Coltassala, Balifico, Bianco di Volpaia and Vin Santo wines, as well as honey, vinegar and olive oil.*

Sangiovese variations

Another great Tuscan red is Brunello di Montalcino. Brunello, the local name for Sangiovese, is the sole grape variety allowed. The quality is high and, with a much smaller area under vine, Brunello is rarer than Chianti and attracts justifiably higher prices. Today's wines have good extraction of colour and flavour, and their tannins and acidity require softening before the wines become approachable. Opinion is divided on whether oak barrels or traditional botti should be used during the four years' ageing required by the DOCG (five for Riserva wines), of which two years must be in wood. A lesser version, Rosso di Montalcino, is more affordable while still providing much pleasure.

Vino Nobile di Montepulciano is another addition to the roll call of Tuscan greats. Unlike Brunello di Montalcino, it must be made from a blend of varieties, with not more than 80 per cent Prugnolo Gentile (a clone of Sangiovese used for Brunello): grapes such as Mammolo and Canaiolo Nero are added. Another regulation prohibits the use of oak barrels and insists that the wine is aged in botti. This gives it a more traditional style, leaving the tannins slightly more angular while preserving the bright fruit aromas and flavours. The lighter Rosso di Montepulciano offers good value.

RIGHT *Sangiovese vines crowd round the little church of Santa Restituta near Montalcino.*

Carmignano

The small Carmignano region, north-west of Florence, is the last of the great red wine areas of central Tuscany. Its claim to fame is that Cabernet Sauvignon was cultivated there long before the present fashion for Super Tuscans, planted as long ago as the 16th century, after Catherine de' Medici became Queen of France. As with the other red wines of central Tuscany, Sangiovese plays the major part, but in the area's cooler climate it struggles to achieve the levels of ripeness of the more southerly regions. Cabernet Sauvignon and occasionally Merlot are added in small quantities to the Sangiovese for greater fullness. Wines for younger drinking are sold as Barco Reale di Carmignano.

WINE FIT FOR THE SAINTS

Vin Santo (literally 'holy wine') is a traditional feature of many Tuscan wineries. Made mainly from Trebbiano and Malvasia grapes that have been dried for several months before pressing to increase the sugar to liquid ratio, the must is fermented in *caratelli* (small barrels). The wines then age in cask from two to six years, during which they gently oxidize, giving a deep golden hue and a distinctive nutty, toffee flavour, which is delicious with *cantucci* biscuits or pastries. A rare red version is made in the Carmignano region.

CENTRAL ITALY

Tuscany Coast

The modern wines of Bolgheri near the Tuscan coast were born of one man's love of Cabernet Sauvignon. In the 1940s, Marquis Mario Incisa della Rochetta planted the variety, then largely unrecognized in Italy, on his Tenuta San Guido estate. He released it commercially in 1968 as Sassicaia, which was soon recognized internationally as a wine to rival the great Cabernet Sauvignon-based wines of Bordeaux.

TUSCANY COAST

REGIONS
- Lucca
- Pisa
- Bolgheri
- Maremma

SELECTED DOC/DOCG AREAS
1. Colline Lucchesi
2. Montecarlo
3. Montescudaio
4. Bolgheri
5. Bolgheri Sassicaia
6. Val di Cornia

Sassicaia Tenuta San Guido. Sweet black fruit with nuances of eucalyptus in an overcoat of toasty oak. Built to last.

Ornellaia Tenuta dell'Ornellaia. Pure fruit with complex notes behind. Full yet elegant.

Val di Cornia 'Coldipietrerosse' Bulichella. Dry, full-flavoured Cabernet blend with ripe red and black fruits.

Colline Lucchesi Rosso Tenuta di Valgiano. Elegant aromas of spicy fruit, structured palate with fine-grained tannins and a long, gentle finish.

Montecarlo Bianco Fattoria del Buonamico. Decent value and easy drinking, with peach and apricot aromas and flavours.

ABOVE RIGHT *The influence of the Mediterranean on Tuscany's coastal wine regions allows such international grapes as Cabernet Sauvignon, Merlot and Syrah to perform superbly, giving rise to wines well worthy of the Super Tuscan designation.*

LEFT *Vines and olives at the Guardiavigna vineyard at Castiglione d'Orcia, part of the Podere Forte estate recently restored by Pasquale Forte, a leader in the electronics industry.*

Other estates, such as the Tenuta dell'Ornellaia, were created in the early 1980s. By the mid-1990s Cabernet Sauvignon and Merlot had been officially recognized as being so suited to the region that they were permitted under DOC laws, the wine having previously been sold as *vino da tavola*.

The temperate climate near the coast is perfect for the gentle ripening of Cabernet Sauvignon, Merlot and Syrah grapes. Ideal sugar levels are achieved, with good pigmentation and acidity. As well as the strong, well-bred reds, dry rosés are made largely from Sangiovese, and pleasant whites from Vermentino and Trebbiano.

Super Tuscans

Bolgheri Sassicaia now enjoys its own DOC. From its formative years it inspired many of Tuscany's winemakers to reject the DOC laws and incorporate grapes such as Cabernet Sauvignon in their blends. The resulting wines stood apart and were much sought after. The term 'Super Tuscan' was soon applied to them and they commanded higher prices than most Chiantis, which were often austere. Although the

law now permits these reds to be called Chianti, many still use the VDT and IGT categories.

Val di Cornia is another local DOC on the rise. Cabernet Sauvignon, Ciliegiolo and Sangiovese contribute to the reds but Merlot attracts most interest. Petra's 'Quercegobbe', made from 100 per cent Merlot, is a shining example of what can be produced, with the minerality of the soil underpinning ripe fruit.

Bordeaux interlopers have also established themselves in Montescudaio. Its limestone soils are well suited to Cabernet Sauvignon and Merlot, which have improved the quality of the local wines previously dominated by Sangiovese.

Lucca, birthplace of one of Italy's greatest opera composers, Giacomo Puccini, gives its name to the Colline Lucchesi, where medium-bodied Sangiovese-based reds are made; Tenuta di Valgiano produces a great example, adding Syrah and Merlot to Sangiovese. Attractive whites are made in the Montecarlo DOC, with the predominant Trebbiano Toscano as a base. Pinots Grigio and Bianco also feature, together with Roussanne, Semillon and Sauvignon Blanc.

CENTRAL ITALY

Umbria and Le Marche

With no coastline to help subdue extreme summer temperatures, Umbria relies on the higher altitudes of its Apennine vineyards for wine production. Orvieto, Torgiano and Montefalco are the big names. The hills of Le Marche gently unfold towards the extensive Adriatic coastline. The cooler northern zone specializes in Verdicchio production, while the reds of Rosso Conero and Rosso Piceno benefit from the more Mediterranean climate of the southern stretches.

Umbria

Orvieto is one of Italy's best-loved whites, made mainly from Procanico (a clone of Trebbiano) and Grechetto. Today most of the production is of good quality, refreshing, dry wine, but a few of its traditional – and delicious – *abboccato* wines with a sweet edge are still made.

Grechetto is also a major player in the white wines of Torgiano, but these are overshadowed by the Sangiovese-based reds, with fine examples produced by Lungarotti.

Since the 1990s Sagrantino di Montefalco has impressed with its powerfully built, deeply coloured, tannic wine, structured for ageing. Sangiovese is the principal grape of the lighter Montefalco Rosso. The hills overlooking Lake Trasimeno produce increasingly interesting reds and whites.

Splendid IGT wines are made from international varieties, a trend started by the Tuscan Antinori family on their Castello della Sala estate: their 'Bramito del Cervo' Chardonnay is among the finest.

Orvieto Classico Secco Barberani. Fresh and fruity with a soft palate and clean acidity.

Sagrantino di Montefalco Colpetrone. Rich in black fruit with a big tannin structure in youth. This repays ageing but is also fun to drink young with hearty food.

Verdicchio dei Castelli di Jesi Classico Superiore Fontevecchia. Deliciously nutty and full flavoured with well-balanced acidity.

Rosso Conero 'San Lorenzo' Umani Ronchi. Decent value with plentiful aromas and good depth of fruit.

Offida Rosso 'Zeii' San Giovanni. Well-made blend of Montepulciano, Cabernet Sauvignon and Merlot. Full flavoured with red and black fruits, hints of pepper and fine tannins.

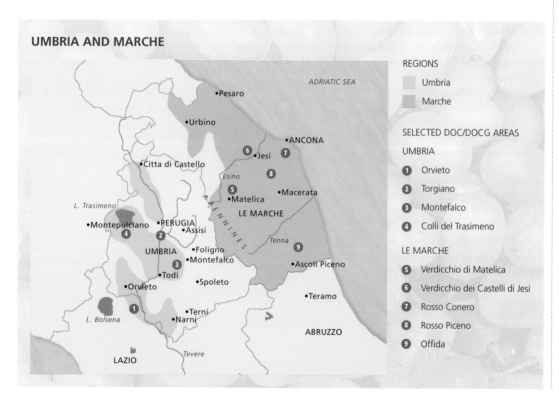

UMBRIA AND MARCHE

ADRIATIC SEA

- •Pesaro
- •Urbino
- •ANCONA
- ⑥ •Jesi ⑦
- •Citta di Castello
- *Esino*
- ⑧
- ⑤
- •Matelica •Macerata
- *L. Trasimeno*
- LE MARCHE
- •Montepulciano •PERUGIA
- ④ ② •Assisi
- UMBRIA •Foligno *Tenna* ⑨
- ③ •Montefalco
- •Todi •Ascoli Piceno
- •Orvieto •Spoleto
- *L. Bolsena* •Teramo
- ① •Terni
- •Narni
- ABRUZZO
- LAZIO
- *Tevere*

REGIONS

Umbria

Marche

SELECTED DOC/DOCG AREAS

UMBRIA

① Orvieto

② Torgiano

③ Montefalco

④ Colli del Trasimeno

LE MARCHE

⑤ Verdicchio di Matelica

⑥ Verdicchio dei Castelli di Jesi

⑦ Rosso Conero

⑧ Rosso Piceno

⑨ Offida

LEFT *The wines of Umbria and Le Marche may be near neighbours, but they are separated by the massive hills of the Apennines, and bear few similarities to one another.*

International varieties
The world's thirst for basic varieties is being satisfied under the IGT Marche classification. Whites such as Pinot Grigio and Chardonnay are made, but the most successful are the reds from Syrah, Cabernet Sauvignon and Merlot.

Le Marche

Verdicchio dei Castelli di Jesi is one of the region's gems: a full-flavoured, nutty, dry white, and an excellent partner to the local fish dishes. The Classico zone makes the best. Verdicchio is also grown in the DOC of Matelica and plays a major part in Esino Bianco.

Rosso Conero tops the reds, with excellent examples from Garofoli, Moroder and Fazi-Battaglia, amongst others, particularly single-vineyard bottlings. It is rich in flavour with bold fruit and notes of tobacco, mainly produced from the Montepulciano grape, although Sangiovese can be added. This is more usual in the larger Rosso Piceno DOC, whose wines tend to be a little tighter. One of the most recent DOCs is Offida, producing whites from Pecorino or Passerina grapes as well as reds from Montepulciano blended with Cabernet Sauvignon. Vernaccia Nera is the basis of Terreni di San Severino – wines with spicy fruit and good structure.

BELOW *A storm brews over a Verdicchio dei Castelli di Jesi Classico vineyard at Montecarotto in Le Marche.*

CENTRAL ITALY

Lazio and Abruzzo

Given Rome's 2,500-year history, its importance at the centre of the Roman Empire and the Roman Catholic Church, and its modern significance as the capital of Italy, it is surprising that until recently Lazio has never enjoyed local wines of real quality. Similarly, the vineyards of neighbouring Abruzzo are only now beginning to realize their full potential. But well-priced, easy-drinking wines are at last widely available.

LEFT *A typical Roman pine brings a touch of welcome cool shade to a corner of an otherwise baking Frascati vineyard.*

Est! Est!! Est!!!
The story goes that a 12th-century German bishop, visiting Rome, sent his servant on ahead to search for lodgings. The servant marked those he thought suitable with the inscription 'Est!' ('It is'). When he arrived at Montefiascone, on the southern shore of Lake Bolsena, he was so smitten by the local wine that he wrote 'Est! Est!! Est!!!' on the inn door.

RIGHT *Vineyards become sparser travelling from north to south through Italy, as the average temperature rises and water supplies become scarcer.*

Frascati Superiore 'Antico Cenacolo' Cantina Cerquetta. Well flavoured, fruity and balanced with distinctive notes of almonds.

'I Quattro Mori' Castel de Paolis, Lazio. Syrah-dominated with Bordeaux varieties. A wealth of berry fruit aromas with a spicy fruit palate and finely grained tannins.

Cesanese del Piglio 'Corte dei Papi', Lazio. Fresh, ripe fruit with moderate depth and dark, slightly bitter finish.

Montepulciano d'Abruzzo Fattoria la Valentina. Open style, full of bright, ripe and spicy fruit.

Montepulciano d'Abruzzo Cerasuolo 'Taverna Nova'. Bright strawberry aromas, clean, juicy palate and fresh clean finish.

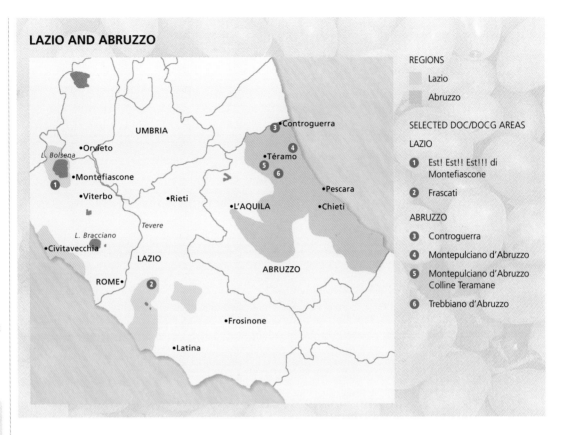

LAZIO AND ABRUZZO

REGIONS
Lazio
Abruzzo

SELECTED DOC/DOCG AREAS

LAZIO
1 Est! Est!! Est!!! di Montefiascone
2 Frascati

ABRUZZO
3 Controguerra
4 Montepulciano d'Abruzzo
5 Montepulciano d'Abruzzo Colline Teramane
6 Trebbiano d'Abruzzo

Lazio

Malvasia and Trebbiano grapes give light, fresh whites for young drinking. The volcanic soils and high altitudes of the Alban hills outside Rome produce large quantities of Frascati, only the best examples of which display notes of lemon and a telltale clip of bitter almonds in the finish. Recently, additions of Viognier and Sauvignon Blanc have given more flavour and depth to some blends. From north of Rome, Est! Est!! Est!!! di Montefiascone is better known for its ridiculous name than for the quality of its wine. Sparkling wines are also produced, but the sweeter Cannellino wines, made from late-picked grapes in Frascati, are more impressive.

Lazio makes little red wine of note, but powerful and tannic Cesanese del Piglio, made predominantly from Cesanese di Affile grapes, shows just what is possible. Cabernet Sauvignon, Merlot and Syrah are also grown to good effect, such as in the wines of Castel de Paolis; however, as the DOC does not permit their use, these wines are currently sold under the IGT denomination.

Abruzzo

Abruzzo is almost entirely hills, providing suitably cool spots for vineyards in an otherwise hot climate. Cabernet Sauvignon and Merlot are successful in the wines of Controguerra in Abruzzo, but the Montepulciano variety reigns here, and it can produce excellent reds. The softer versions are well suited to young drinking but the more extracted, richer wines, aged in barrel, can improve in bottle for years and are now seen more widely. Superior to plain Montepulciano d'Abruzzo, Montepulciano d'Abruzzo Colline Teramane wines are stylish, with good body and greater nuances of spice. The same grapes also make one of Italy's best rosés, Cerasuolo d'Abruzzo, with distinctive berry aromas and good depth of fruit.

White Trebbiano d'Abruzzo is made from either the Trebbiano Toscano grape, producing rather thin wines, or the Trebbiano d'Abruzzo, with more intense flavours and greater complexity. Pecorino and Chardonnay are now to be found and are making good IGT wines.

SOUTHERN ITALY

Puglia and the South

Southern Italy was once something of a vinous no-go area, producing ordinary wines (at best) mostly sold in bulk. But reduction of yields, investment in vineyards and wineries, and modern winemaking techniques have brought great change for the better. Winemakers are today crafting exciting wines that sit comfortably on the world stage. What is more, they are utilizing local grapes rather than international varieties.

Puglia

In volume terms Puglia is the south's largest producer. It makes good whites and rosés but is principally red wine country. Negroamaro and Malvasia Nera give bittersweet fruit and earthy tannins to the red wines of Salice Salentino Rosso. Squinzano and Copertino are similar, and some are now barrel-aged and worth cellaring for a few years. Primitivo di Manduria is a bold, spicy and complex wine when well made and can offer good value. The vineyards of Castel del Monte make decent cherry- and berry-dominated wines. Puglia's best whites, from Locorotondo, have soft, delicate fruit flavours with a dry finish.

PUGLIA AND THE SOUTH

REGIONS

Puglia

Basilicata

Campania

Calabria

SELECTED DOC/DOCG AREAS

PUGLIA

1 Salice Salentino

2 Squinzano

3 Copertino

4 Primitivo di Manduria

5 Locorotondo

6 Castel del Monte

BASILICATA

7 Aglianico del Vulture

CAMPANIA

8 Taurasi DOCG

9 Greco di Tufo DOCG

10 Fiano di Avellino DOCG

11 Lacryma Christi

12 Vesuvio

13 Falerno del Massico

CALABRIA

14 Cirò

15 Greco di Bianco

LEFT *In this particularly hot part of Italy irrigation must be wisely used, although some good wines are also made by dry cultivation.*

Basilicata and Campania

One of the best red grape varieties grown throughout the south is Aglianico, showing genuine class in the best wines. On the volcanic slopes of Mount Vulture it makes excellent, full-bodied, spicy wine with notes of smoke over dark fruit flavours, generally repaying a few years' cellaring.

Another notable Aglianico is Taurasi, which can be wonderfully complex, with bright black fruit and floral aromas in youth backed by hints of tar. Excellent producers include Mastroberardino and Feudi di San Gregorio. Aglianico is a major component in Falerno del Massico (descended from ancient Rome's favourite Falernum), though this can be almost pure Primitivo. Additionally, a richly flavoured white wine is produced. One of Italy's starriest wines, Montevetrano, uses Aglianico to a small extent, but Cabernet Sauvignon and Merlot predominate in this rare, concentrated blockbuster.

There are two DOCG Campanian white wines, Fiano di Avellino and Greco di Tufo. Fiano tends to be light in body with delightful floral aromas, while Greco, grown on volcanic tuff, has an underlying minerality supporting clean fruit flavours. Around Mount Vesuvius just about every style of wine is made under the Vesuvio and Lacryma Christi DOCs. Lacryma Christi enjoyed rather undeserved fame for many years, aided by its presumptuous name, but yield reductions have recently led to better quality.

Calabria

In Calabria, Cirò offers the best wines. Cirò reds have floral and spicy aromas with a chunky, tannic backbone. There are fruity rosés, too. Throughout the region the simple whites are best enjoyed with the local food, apart from the sweeter wines of Greco di Bianco, made in the passito style – richly coloured with high alcohol and bright, citrus aromas.

Salice Salentino Rosso Riserva Leone de Castris, Puglia. Full flavoured with smoky aromas over black fruits.

Aglianico del Vulture 'La Firma' Cantine del Notaio, Basilicata. Big fruit and structure with plenty of ripe tannins.

Montevetrano, Campania. Intense spicy black fruit with seamless tannins and incredible balance. Sensational!

Greco di Tufo dei Feudi di San Gregorio, Campania. Full aromas of peach with a structured and mineral palate.

Cirò Rosso Classico Librandi, Calabria. Dried berry fruit with spice. Well flavoured. Good value.

RIGHT *The conical roofs of Apulian stone houses (*trulli*) bring a distinctive touch to a vineyard at Cisternino.*

Leone de Castris

VITIVINICOLTORI DAL 1665

SALICE SALENTINO

denominazione di origine controllata

2005

RISERVA

ITALY'S ISLANDS

Sicily

Sicily, the largest of the Mediterranean islands, had an important wine culture in antiquity. In more recent centuries it languished as quality declined, but it is now developing impressively. The island has a wide variety of terrains, from coastal to mountain, with a diversity of soil structures. Attentive vine growing and winemaking enables a complete spectrum of wines to be made.

LEFT *A vineyard at Curcuraci, north of Messina, overlooking the Straits of Messina.*

🍷🍷🍷 **Passito di Pantelleria 'Ben Ryé' Donnafugata.** Intense, fruity aromas, dried fruit palate and a luscious finish.

🍷🍷 **Nero d'Avola 'Tenute Dorrasita' Cantine Foraci.** Abundant spicy red and black fruits, with great balance on the palate.

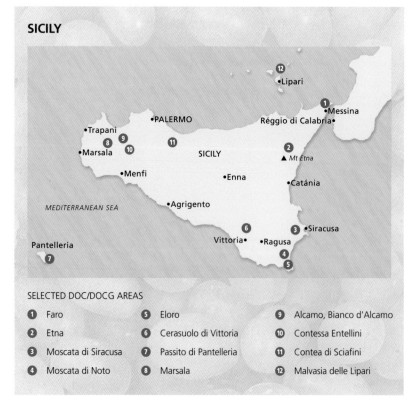

SICILY

MEDITERRANEAN SEA

Pantelleria

SELECTED DOC/DOCG AREAS

① Faro	⑤ Eloro	⑨ Alcamo, Bianco d'Alcamo
② Etna	⑥ Cerasuolo di Vittoria	⑩ Contessa Entellini
③ Moscata di Siracusa	⑦ Passito di Pantelleria	⑪ Contea di Sciafini
④ Moscata di Noto	⑧ Marsala	⑫ Malvasia delle Lipari

Today, indigenous Nero d'Avola and Grillo grapes are grown alongside the internationals, Cabernet Sauvignon and Chardonnay. The pale colour of cherry-flavoured Cerasuolo di Vittoria belies its potency, and Bianco d'Alcamo is the most interesting of the whites: it has a dry yet elegantly fruity style, perfect for seafood. Mount Etna's slopes produce fair red and white wines, but IGT wines often attract the greatest attention, such as the delicious Nero d'Avola and Grillo wines from the organically farmed vineyards of Cantine Foraci, or Do Zenner's old-vine Nero d'Avola.

Sweet wines

That most popular of Italian desserts, zabaglione, has ensured worldwide renown for Marsala. It is a quality fortified wine in its own right, produced in many forms from off-dry to sweet, and in varying colours and lengths of ageing: the Riserva and Vergine versions are worth discovering. The island of Pantelleria makes excellent moscato wines by natural and passito methods.

ITALY'S ISLANDS

Sardinia

While Sicily has been developing its wine production, Sardinia has been grubbing up its vines. Vineyard acreage has dwindled considerably since the early 1980s. Those vineyards that have survived have tended towards the higher quality end of production. Consequently the Sardinian wines to be found in export markets today are usually worthy of consideration. And the island boasts one particularly unusual speciality: the centuries-old Vernaccia di Oristano, a sherry-like aperitif.

Good examples of the DOCG white, Vermentino di Gallura, are ripe with considerable concentration and floral aromas. Other Vermentinos lack the concentration of Gallura but are elegant and fruity nonetheless. Dry, semi-sweet and sweet Malvasia from Cagliari is popular as an aperitif and dessert wine, while Malvasia di Bosa is perhaps most revered locally.

For red wines, the varieties of Cannonau (a relation of Grenache) and Carignano (Carignan) are the leading lights. Carignano del Sulcis wines are made from wonderful old vines that survived the grubbing up, and the quality is such that new plantings have been undertaken. Cannonau gives reds that have impressive depths of colour and aroma with plenty of spicy fruit. Both varieties also produce sweet dessert wines. One of the best is Sella e Mosca's Anghelu Ruju, made in the passito style from Cannonau grapes. This is a full-flavoured, rich wine with a port-like character.

ABOVE RIGHT *Some of Sardinia's best white wines come from Gallura in the north of the island. This Vermentino vineyard is at Berchidda, 30 km/18 miles south-west of Olbia.*

RIGHT *In addition to the DOCG and DOC areas specified on the map there are DOCs for Cannonau and Vermentino covering the whole island.*

Vermentino di Gallura 'Piras' Cantina Sociale Gallura. Intense fruit and floral aromas lead to a full, fresh palate with ample fruit.

Carignano del Sulcis 'Grotta Rossa' Cantina Sociale di Santadi. Intense colour with good fruit aromas and flavours and a dry finish.

SARDINIA

MEDITERRANEAN SEA

TYRRHENIAN SEA

- •Olbia
- •Sassari
- •Alghero
- •Bosa
- •Nuoro
- •Oristano
- Gulf of Oristano
- •CAGLIARI
- Gulf of Cagliari

SELECTED DOC/DOCG AREAS

1. Vernaccia di Oristano
2. Vermentino di Gallura
3. Carignano del Sulcis

GROTTA ROSSA®

CARIGNANO DEL SULCIS
DENOMINAZIONE DI ORIGINE CONTROLLATA

●●● Regions 39–55

NORTH-EAST SPAIN
39 Rioja
40 Navarra
41 Aragón
42 Catalunya
43 Priorat

NORTH-WEST SPAIN
44 Ribera del Duero
45 Rueda
46 Toro and Cigales
47 Galicia

CENTRAL SPAIN
48 Madrid to Alicante

SOUTHERN SPAIN
49 Andalucía
50 Jerez

NORTHERN PORTUGAL
51 Vinho Verde
52 Douro Valley
53 Barraida and Dão

SOUTHERN PORTUGAL
54 Estremadura and Ribatejo
55 Alentejo, Setúbal Peninsula
    and Algarve

●●● Spain and Portugal

For centuries two of the world's finest fortified wines, sherry and port, proudly carried the Iberian Peninsula's vinous flag. They remain great today, but quality table wines, particularly red wines, have taken their place in public perception. Rioja led the way, first by rescuing French merchants when phylloxera struck in the 19th century, and then by becoming the world's best value red wine in the 1970s.

Good Rioja is now more realistically priced. With intelligent winemaking, however, previously unremarkable regions of both countries are now producing pleasant, inexpensive wines, offering arguably the best value to be found in Europe.

But it is at the top end that the greatest excitement is found, albeit at serious prices. In Portugal the port houses have discovered that exceedingly good red wines can be made from traditional port grapes. And in Spain, areas such as Ribera del Duero and Toro have joined Rioja in pushing the quality even higher. Great things are happening.

NORTH-EAST SPAIN

Rioja

Rioja is one of Spain's great wines and certainly its most available worldwide. Today's Rioja owes much to the bad fortune of others, for when phylloxera struck the vineyards of Bordeaux it attracted the French merchants in search of stock to fulfil their clients' needs, thus developing an export market. Towns such as Haro and Logroño became hosts to some of the big names of the trade.

Climatic effects

As a region, Rioja is divided into three zones. Rioja Alta has the largest area under vine and, although sheltered by the Sierra Cantabrian mountains from the immediate effects of the Atlantic Ocean, it is nevertheless influenced by it. The cool climate and limestone- or ferrous-based clay soils are ideal for the production of high quality grapes with the right levels of acidity necessary for ageing. Rioja Alavesa also comes under Atlantic influence, while the flatter, hotter and drier Rioja Baja has a more Mediterranean climate. It produces wines with more body and tannin but lacking the elegance of its neighbours.

BELOW *A verdant vineyard near Mendavia contrasting with the characteristically barren landscape of the Rioja Baja.*

Grape varieties

Tempranillo is the principal grape variety, growing to perfection in Rioja Alta. Its hallmark berry fruit aromas and flavours give wines that are quite delicious in youth but are also, in the right hands, capable of ageing for decades. Garnacha (Grenache), Graciano and Mazuelo are added to some blends, each imparting different nuances to the wines. Cabernet Sauvignon, Merlot and Syrah are now cultivated, but are generally alluded to as 'other varieties'. Viura, Malvasia and Garnacha Blanca make the region's small output of white wines, with recent changes in legislation permitting Sauvignon Blanc, Chardonnay and Verdejo along with half a dozen lesser-known grapes, for both white and red. As yet, they are rarely seen. While single-vineyard wines are produced and marketed, the majority are blended to accord with 'house style'.

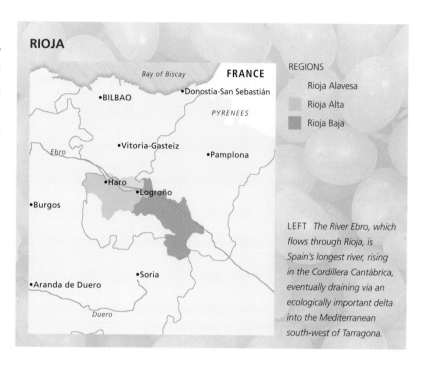

RIOJA

REGIONS
Rioja Alavesa
Rioja Alta
Rioja Baja

LEFT *The River Ebro, which flows through Rioja, is Spain's longest river, rising in the Cordillera Cantábrica, eventually draining via an ecologically important delta into the Mediterranean south-west of Tarragona.*

Denominación de Origen Calificada (DOCa):
Top wine classification, for Rioja only. The Catalan equivalent, for Priorat only, is Denominació d'Origen Qualificada (DOQa).

Denominación de Origen Pago (DO Pago):
For single estates of high quality.

Denominación de Origen (DO): High quality wines from designated regions. In Catalan, Denominació d'Origen (DO).

Vino de Calidad con Indicación Geográfica (VCIG): For good wines not quite of DO quality.

Vino de la Tierra (VdlT): Country wine (similar to French Vin de Pays).

Vino de Mesa (VdM): Table wine. The Catalan equivalent is Vi de Taula (VdT).

Classification

The everyday red wines of Rioja are referred to as either Tinto Joven ('young red') or Sin Crianza ('without oak'), and are excellent for quaffing without ceremony. Some winemakers use carbonic maceration for their production, especially in Rioja Alavesa. Other wines see just a short time in cask and will be labelled Rioja Tinto (although this can also apply to Tinto Joven and Sin Crianza). More serious examples are aged for longer in barrels, often of American oak, giving a distinct vanilla aroma to the wines.

The length of ageing decides the wines' classification. Crianza must spend two years at the winery, with at least 12 months in barrel. More serious are the Reservas, which are at least three years old when they are released, with the same minimum requirement of 12 months in cask. The top classification is Gran Reserva, for which the wines will have been aged for a minimum of two years in barrel and three years in bottle before being allowed near a corkscrew. These are generally made only in the finest vintages, although some of the more commercial bodegas seem to make them nearly every year.

These classifications have been in place for many years, and some of today's bodegas are turning away from the idea that length of time in barrel should determine the quality, in favour of shorter periods of maturation to attain fruitier wines with fresher aromas and flavours. Far more of the tighter-grained French oak is now to be seen in cellars. The so-called Super Reservas undergo their malolactic fermentation in a new oak cask before being aged in a second new oak cask. This has a price implication as barrels are expensive and, while the resulting wines bear little resemblance to their traditional brothers, they can be quite astounding, as is the case with Sierra Cantabria's 'Amancio'.

Another recent feature is the rise of single-vineyard wines. Traditionally, wines were blended from different parcels of vineyard and even from different regions, thereby producing a house style that had only vintage variation. The single-vineyard wines are more terroir-driven, with the winemakers seeking to allow the expression of origin to dominate, rather than the style of the bodega.

White and rosé wines

White Riojas used to be rather dull – and at times oxidized – but modern winemaking has given them a new lease of life. Now many are fresh, clean and fruity, making for pleasurable easy drinking. More serious examples are also made by barrel fermentation and can develop in bottle for some years. Fine, fruity rosés are now becoming fashionable. They are best drunk young, while the bright strawberry aromas and soft berry flavours remain youthful.

Rioja Tinto Bodegas Sierra Cantabria. Great value Rioja with good berry fruit and vanilla notes.

Rioja Crianza Marqués de Cáceres. Consistent and easy drinking, with red fruit flavours and soft tannins.

Imperial Gran Reserva Compañía Vinicola del Norte de España (CVNE). Good defined aromas of berry fruit with notes of coffee, dried fruit flavours on the palate, and hints of toast.

Viña Ardanza Reserva La Rioja Alta SA. An excellent old-style Reserva with complexity, body and style.

'San Vicente' Señorío de San Vicente. Single-vineyard wine, with intensity of flavour combined with great finesse and subtlety.

'Torre Muga' Bodegas Muga. Modern style with good depth and power, generally requiring some bottle age.

'La Nieta' Viñedos de Páganos. Single-vineyard wine with intense aromas of ripe berry fruit with intense concentration on the palate.

'Organza' Bodegas Sierra Cantabria. Barrel-fermented white with rich and expansive tropical fruit underpinned by good minerality.

RIGHT *The stark rocks of the Sierra Cantabria provide a dramatic background to this vineyard in the Rioja Alta and protect it from devastating Atlantic gales.*

NORTH-EAST SPAIN

Navarra

From relatively humble beginnings, Navarra is today producing an array of attractive wines. The delicious rosés made from Garnacha were first to catch the attention of wine lovers. Experimentation at the government research station, which advises and trains winemakers and vine growers, has led to a good understanding of the different varieties that flourish in the region's various climatic areas, and some wines of distinction are now produced.

Chivite Colección 125 Blanco Bodegas Julián Chivite. Barrel-fermented Chardonnay with great class, intensity of flavour and complexity that leaves a lasting and creamy finish.

Rosado de Lágrima Bodegas Ochoa. Fine, fruity rosé displaying soft, berry aromas and a clean, refreshing acidity.

Crianza 'Señorío de Sarría' Bodega Sarría. Well-made blend of Tempranillo and Cabernet with plenty of ripe, black fruit and toasty oak.

Red wine is the major production here, and the northern areas nearer the Atlantic Ocean are well suited to varieties such as Cabernet Sauvignon and Merlot. The hotter and drier areas of Ribera Alta and Ribera Baja are more Mediterranean-influenced, producing excellent Garnacha and Tempranillo.

There is growing use of oak ageing, with a system of Crianza, Reserva and Gran Reserva similar to Rioja's (though using more French oak). Oak is also used for the fermentation of Chardonnay, giving wines that – provided they are not over-oaked – are full flavoured and chewy. The reds can be quite complex, varying from the more traditional blends of Tempranillo and Garnacha to those including the great Bordeaux varieties, which have an elegant touch. A little late-harvest Muscat is also made. Those from Bodegas Chivite are well worth seeking out.

BELOW The Bodega del Señorío de Sarria produces some of the best value, reliable wines in the whole of Spain.

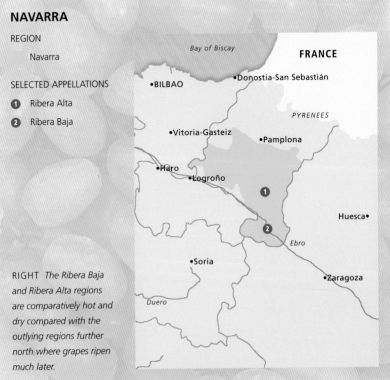

NAVARRA

REGION
    Navarra

SELECTED APPELLATIONS
① Ribera Alta
② Ribera Baja

Bay of Biscay

FRANCE

•Donostia-San Sebastián

•BILBAO

PYRENEES

•Vitoria-Gasteiz

•Pamplona

•Haro

•Logroño

①

Huesca•

②

Ebro

•Soria

•Zaragoza

Duero

RIGHT The Ribera Baja and Ribera Alta regions are comparatively hot and dry compared with the outlying regions further north where grapes ripen much later.

NORTH-EAST SPAIN

Aragón

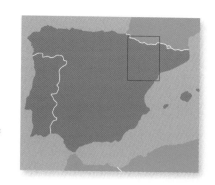

Although Aragón wines are little seen abroad (with the exception of Cariñena), they will certainly be seen shortly if their quality continues to rise and prices remain so attractive. One of the region's most exciting areas is Somontano, in the foothills of the Pyrenees. Largely unheard of until the latter part of the 20th century, Somontano is now making quite a stir for the quality of both its red and white wines.

Somontano's local red variety, Moristel, is still grown to good effect, but Cabernet Sauvignon, Merlot and Tempranillo have adapted well to the mild climate. Good Chardonnay is made by Viñas del Vero, and for delicious Gewürztraminer try the Enate from Alto Aragón.

Campo de Borja, Calatayud and Cariñena mainly produce reds. Garnacha fares best when blended with Tempranillo, although interesting varietal wines are made from older vines. Cabernet Sauvignon, Merlot and Syrah are also plentiful. These good-value reds are bold, with attractive aromas and abundant flavour. They are generally produced for young drinking, but wood ageing can be successful, as in Care from Bodegas Añadas. Such wines are now being exported vigorously. Campo de Borja produces attractive fruity rosés as well as sweeter Mistela, a form of fortified dessert wine.

Enate Chardonnay 234 Viñedos y Crianzas del Alto Aragón, Somontano. Exotic, white fruit aromas with a fresh yet soft palate and good finish.

Marboré Bodega Pirineos, Somontano. A complex blend that produces big structure and abundant fruit with firm tannins, taking time to soften.

Baltasar Gracián Garnacha Viñas Viejas Bodegas San Alejandro, Calatayud. Full bodied with plenty of chewy fruit and well-integrated oak.

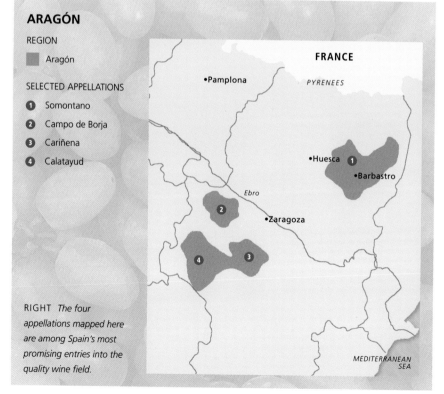

ARAGÓN

REGION

◾ Aragón

SELECTED APPELLATIONS

① Somontano
② Campo de Borja
③ Cariñena
④ Calatayud

RIGHT *The four appellations mapped here are among Spain's most promising entries into the quality wine field.*

FRANCE

•Pamplona

PYRENEES

Ebro

•Huesca ①
•Barbastro

②

•Zaragoza

④ ③

MEDITERRANEAN SEA

BELOW *The Moorish hill village of Alquézar backed by the Sierra y Cañones de Guara, at the northern edge of the Somontano DO.*

NORTH-EAST SPAIN

Catalunya

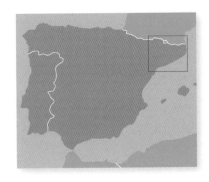

Catalunya has a long history of winemaking, and was one of the first Spanish regions to plant international varieties. Its fame in the latter half of the 20th century was built on white wines, ideal for consumption with Mediterranean dishes such as paella. Increasing tourism demanded the development of red and sparkling wines, and both are now available in quantity and quality.

Miguel Torres was a pioneer in the initial evolution of the region's red wine, and the company remains one of the finest large-scale producers. Their empire now extends to both North and South America.

Penedès

In Penedès, historically the most famous area, all three colours of wine are now produced. For red wines, the traditional varieties of Rioja are used alongside the major

BELOW *The 11th-century Castillo de Milmanda, in the Conca de Barberá DO, is owned by Miguel Torres. As well as Cabernet Sauvignon and Pinot Noir, Chardonnay is cultivated here, producing the company's leading white wine.*

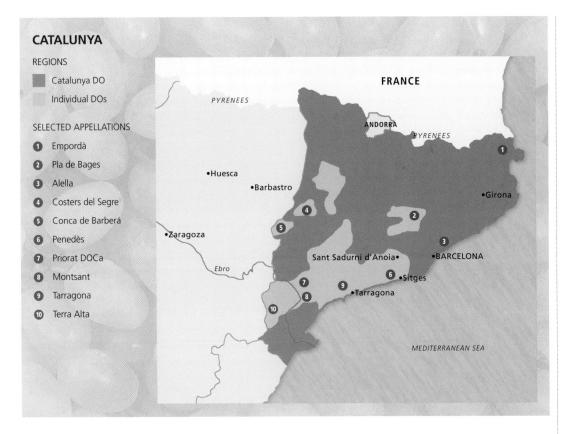

CATALUNYA

REGIONS

▮ Catalunya DO

▮ Individual DOs

SELECTED APPELLATIONS

1. Empordà
2. Pla de Bages
3. Alella
4. Costers del Segre
5. Conca de Barberá
6. Penedès
7. Priorat DOCa
8. Montsant
9. Tarragona
10. Terra Alta

Map labels: FRANCE, PYRENEES, ANDORRA, PYRENEES, •Huesca, •Barbastro, •Girona, •Zaragoza, Ebro, Sant Sadurní d'Anoia•, •BARCELONA, •Sitges, •Tarragona, MEDITERRANEAN SEA

LEFT *The climate in Catalunya's vineyards ranges from Mediterranean coastal heat to the cool of the mountains, providing the region with a wide range of wines.*

🍷 **Catalunya 'Viña Esmeralda' Torres.** Aromatic white with a soft, fruity palate.

🍷 **Costers del Segre 'Viña 27 Chardonnay' Raimat.** Fruit-driven with clean, balancing acidity.

🍷🍷🍷 **Costers del Segre Cérvoles, Seleccio en Vinya, Celler de Cantonella.** Flavoursome red with spice and herbal notes over black fruit.

🍷🍷 **Montsant 'Castell de Falset' Agricola Falset-Marca.** Spicy black fruit with tobacco and mineral notes.

🍷🍷🍷 **Montsant 'Flor de Primavera' Celler de Capçanes.** Classy Kosher blend with complex aromas over ripe, black and red fruit.

🍷🍷 **Penedès Reserva 'Gran Coronas' Torres.** Cabernet Sauvignon-dominated blend with berry fruit and sweeter vanilla notes.

ones of Bordeaux with higher altitudes proving suitable for Pinot Noir. As well as the fruity, easy-drinking Joven wines, others are aged in barrel using the same laws as Rioja.

Originally it was white wines that brought renown, when the local grape varieties, Parellada, Macabeo and Xarel-lo, were used to produce Cava (see page 108). They have now been joined by Chardonnay and the aromatic varieties Gewürztraminer and Riesling. The area was the first in Spain to use temperature-controlled fermentation in stainless steel, protecting the bright aromas of the more delicate white varieties.

Good value wines

Montsant is showing prowess, making wines similar to those of Priorat (see page 109), which it almost surrounds, but without the finesse. Montsant was previously part of the Taragona DO, but the individuality of the wines led to the creation of its own DO in 2001. Bold, concentrated and chewy wines offer good value. They are made from Garnacha and Mazuelo with recently planted Cabernet Sauvignon, Syrah and Tempranillo. Chardonnay and Garnacha Blanca give pleasant dry whites.

Another area still offering good value is Costers del Segre, where imported and local varieties make varied styles of wine. The Codorníu-owned Raimat estate was important in the development of the DO and is responsible for much of today's production.

Nestling up against the French border, Empordà has attracted new blood and is producing good reds and dessert wines. Its most notable offering, Garnatxa d'Empordà, is made from sun-dried Garnacha grapes, resembling the vins doux naturels of neighbouring Rousillon in France. It can be long-lived and is excellent with chocolate desserts.

A handful of other regions, such as Alella, Terra Alta and Pla de Bages, are yet to cause waves on the international wine scene, but the catch-all DO Catalunya permits the blending of wines from many parts of the region and is used for an increasing number of good value wines.

Cava

Cava is the pre-eminent sparkling wine of Spain. White or pink, sweet or dry, it has become popular in both home and export markets and is frequently served as an affordable alternative to Champagne.

Although Cava can be produced in several of Spain's vineyard regions, most is produced in Catalunya and more particularly in Penedès, where the town of Sant Sadurní d'Anoia has become the production capital. Cava was first made in the late 1800s by Josep Raventós of the Codorníu company, which remains one of the major producers.

Production is similar to that of Champagne, with the bubbles being formed by secondary fermentation in bottle, but the wines do not have to be aged long and the grape varieties used differ. Traditionally these were mainly Macabeo, Parellada and Xarel-lo, but more recently Chardonnay has been added together with Pinot Noir. The grapes are picked while their acidity remains high, giving the wines a freshness to balance their sparkle and appealing clean fruit flavours.

Styles vary according to the amount of sugar added. The driest are Extra Brut and Brut, and the scale of sweetness rises through Extra Seco and Seco, with Semi-seco and Dulce being sweet. No celebration would be the same in Spain without a glass or two of this delicious fizz.

 Freixenet Cordon Negro Brut. The leading export brand, with a consistent, fresh, fruity style.

Codorníu 'Jaume Codorníu' Brut. Fine and elegant, with delightful floral aromas and a gentle touch of yeast.

Castillo Perelada Brut Rosado. Light berry aromas with a fresh and fruity palate and clean finish.

The name of the wine
The Champenois objected to the use of 'Champaña' in the wine's original name, so 'Cava' was adopted in 1970, relating to the underground cellars where it is matured.

LEFT *Bottles of Cava are stored, necks down, in the cellars of the house of Freixenet. Sediments formed during fermentation in bottle settle in the necks, from which they are removed by freezing.*

NORTH-EAST SPAIN

Priorat

This tiny Catalunyan region has shot to stardom since the late 1980s. It now makes some of Spain's most sought-after red wines. Recognition came swiftly, and so rapid was its rise to fame that Priorat became only the second region after Rioja to be granted DOCa status. A small group of winemakers pioneered the modern wines, and today there are over 600 growers.

'Finca Dofí' Alvaro Palacios. Glorious blackberry fruit with notes of chocolate and mineral, with big tannins in youth: repays cellaring for some years.

Clos Mogador. Excellent concentration of sweet black fruit with good minerality in both aromas and palate. Another candidate for cellaring.

'Clos de l'Obac' Costers del Siurana. Intensely flavoured with impressive fruit, minerals, toast and spice. Generally takes 10 years from the vintage to show at its best.

Priorat Tinto 'Zeta'. Rich, almost jammy black fruits with spice and an oaky finish.

Vineyards are located on steep slopes, which many growers have terraced, though others frown on the practice. Llicorella soils give the wines their special mineral qualities and restrict the vines to a naturally low yield, giving grapes of great intensity and notable concentration.

Cabernet Sauvignon and Syrah have been successfully planted alongside old-vine Garnacha and Cariñena. The best wines are made from old-vine Garnacha with other varieties adding to the complexity, giving full flavours, great intensity of black fruits and a distinct minerality. They benefit from cellaring for a few years. With such rapid stardom attracting major investment, prices range from expensive to exorbitant.

PRIORAT

PYRENEES

FRANCE

ANDORRA

PYRENEES

• Barbastro

Sant Sadurní d'Anoia • **BARCELONA**

• Sitges

R. Ebro | • Tarragona

MEDITERRANEAN SEA

REGION

Priorat

ABOVE Commercial Priorat is a modern sales success, yet today's vineyards are nowhere near as extensive as they were in the mid-19th century.

LEFT *Ploughing by horse is still the order of the day in the Clos l'Ermita vineyard of Alvaro Palacios in Priorat.*

White Priorat
Dry white wines are also made, mainly from Garnacha Blanca, Macabeo and Pedro Ximenez.

NORTH-WEST SPAIN

Ribera del Duero

Modern winemaking is a recent phenomenon in Ribera del Duero: the DO was created only in 1982. Then the lone star among a handful of bodegas was the legendary Vega Sicilia, which had enjoyed fame for decades and is still regarded as one of the world's finest red wines. Ribera has seen a dramatic increase in the number of bodegas, and is now one of Spain's top appellations.

Growing conditions

Limestone is a key feature of Ribera's various soils, and the local clone of Tempranillo (Tinto Fino or Tinta del Pais) enjoys it. Altitude is another significant factor. It means the daytime heat is tempered by cooler nights in summer and early autumn, but increases the risk of spring frost, which can lead to little or no fruit in some years. Harvests seldom start before early October and can last until the end of the month, when rain is more likely.

Grape varieties

Tempranillo must account for 75 per cent of red wine blends; alongside it, Cabernet Sauvignon, Merlot and Malbec, introduced to the area by Vega Sicilia in the late 19th century, are also grown. Garnacha is used to produce rosé wine, but this is in decline due to the demand for highly priced reds.

Albillo, the region's only white grape, makes a little fruity white wine for young drinking. As it is not allowed DO status, the small production is mainly consumed locally.

'One of the most profound wines ever made in Spain.'

ROBERT PARKER ON
THE 2003 PINGUS

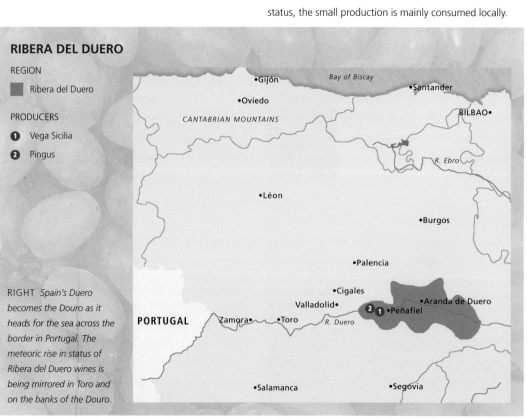

RIBERA DEL DUERO

REGION

Ribera del Duero

PRODUCERS

1 Vega Sicilia

2 Pingus

Bay of Biscay

•Gijón

•Oviedo

•Santander

CANTABRIAN MOUNTAINS

BILBAO•

R. Ebro

•Léon

•Burgos

•Palencia

•Cigales

Valladolid•

•Aranda de Duero

PORTUGAL

Zamora•

•Toro

R. Duero

2 1 •Peñafiel

•Salamanca

•Segovia

RIGHT *Spain's Duero becomes the Douro as it heads for the sea across the border in Portugal. The meteoric rise in status of Ribera del Duero wines is being mirrored in Toro and on the banks of the Douro.*

Ageing in oak
Both open-grained American oak, which imparts vanilla notes, and the tighter-grained French oak are used for ageing by the different bodegas.

RIGHT *The high plain of Old Castile is largely unremarkable countryside, empty and sparsely cultivated. In the Duero Valley, which crosses the plain, the sight of neatly tended rows of vines raises the spirits of wine lovers.*

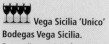 **Vega Sicilia 'Unico' Bodegas Vega Sicilia.** Extraordinary wine of great quality and consistency, released only after 10 years' minimum ageing.

'Pingus' Dominio de Pingus. Possibly Spain's rarest and most sought-after wine. Superb balance and great elegance.

Pago de los Capellanes Reserva. Delicious, ripe red fruit and well-integrated oak with mineral nuances.

Arzuaga Reserva Bodegas Arzuaga Navarro. Stylish berry fruit with a silky, complex palate and an elegant, structured finish.

'Regina Vides' Hermanos Sastre. Full flavoured, chewy and incredibly complex, with an array of ever-changing nuances behind deep black fruit flavours.

Vega Real Roble Bodegas Vega Real. Forest fruits and vanilla dominate this full-bodied yet easy-drinking red.

Rising quality

The legal ageing requirements are the same as in Rioja. 'Roble' wines – young reds that have not been aged long enough to earn Crianza status – are increasingly seen, giving opportunities for good-value drinking while providing younger bodegas with much needed cash flow. These generally have the same depth of fruit but lack the complexity that results from longer periods in cask.

Blends vary between bodegas, but all the wines have power and depth of flavour with good levels of acidity and plenty of spicy fruit. The best examples can age gracefully for up to 20 years, evolving into majestic and complex wines with delicious savoury qualities. There are over 200 bodegas in operation – as many of the vineyards are still in their infancy, quality levels are surely set to rise further as the vines age. The best may be yet to come.

NORTH-WEST SPAIN

Rueda

The high plateau of Rueda is noted for fresh and lively white wines, made mainly from the Verdejo grape. Modern winemaking has transformed the character of the region's wines and they are now appearing on the international market. Viura is also planted and, more recently, Sauvignon Blanc has increased in importance. As tastes in white wine change, traditional Rioja companies have invested here with an eye to the future.

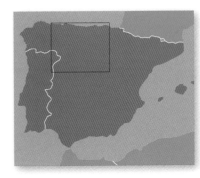

ABOVE *Harvesting Viura grapes in Rueda.*

In Rueda, some irrigation is permitted, to offset the hot, dry summers. Mechanical harvesting, often at night to protect the grapes from oxidation, allows them to be picked at perfect maturity, ensuring a good balance between fruit and acidity. Vinification in temperature-controlled stainless steel vats further protects the fruit aromas, though there is a move by some producers to vinify in barrel, to make more complex, fuller wines.

The white wines generally are fresh and zesty with Verdejo imparting its bright citric notes and Sauvignon Blanc in particular extracting mineral notes from the soils, making them food friendly. Blends are sold as Rueda Blanco.

A little red wine is produced, predominantly from Tempranillo grapes, with some Cabernet Sauvignon, Merlot and Garnacha allowed for blending. Most is sold as soft and fruity Joven. There is also some interesting rosé.

🍷 **Monte Palma Verdejo Bodegas Cerrosol.** Expressive aromas and flavours of tropical and citrus fruits with good refreshing acidity.

🍷🍷 **Ermita Veracruz Verdejo.** Floral and grassy scents, citric notes and a slight bitterness in the finish.

🍷 **Blanco Nieva Pie Franco Viñedos de Nieva.** Green apple and grass nose with clean acidity.

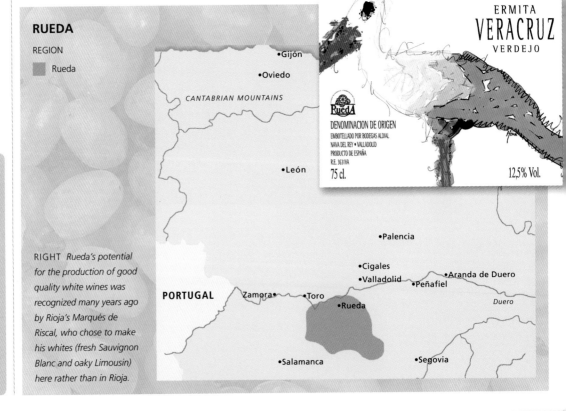

RUEDA

REGION

▢ Rueda

RIGHT *Rueda's potential for the production of good quality white wines was recognized many years ago by Rioja's Marqués de Riscal, who chose to make his whites (fresh Sauvignon Blanc and oaky Limousin) here rather than in Rioja.*

ERMITA
VERACRUZ
VERDEJO

RuedA
DENOMINACION DE ORIGEN
EMBOTELLADO POR BODEGAS ALDIAL
NAVA DEL REY • VALLADOLID
PRODUCTO DE ESPAÑA
R.E. 3631VA
75 cl.   12,5% Vol.

NORTH-WEST SPAIN
Toro and Cigales

Toro has long been known for its strong, deeply coloured wines but, until recently, little of high quality was produced. After it acquired DO status in the late 1980s, percipient winemakers focused their attention on the area, largely because of parcels of ungrafted old vines, some over 130 years old, which have proved capable of making outstanding wines. The future of Cigales is similarly bright, for both inexpensive and upmarket reds.

Tinta de Toro, the local clone of Tempranillo, is the main grape. It has adapted well to the area's climate and sandy soils, but requires careful attention in the vineyard to bring good fruit to the winery. Some Garnacha is also grown.

Much of the wine is sold as Joven, often after carbonic maceration. Traditional fermentation is used for the wines aged in cask, accounting for only 25 per cent of the production. The top wines are excellent, with remarkable colour, masses of unctuous, black, chewy fruit flavours and plenty of ripe tannins.

Cigales has not yet created the same level of interest. However, its delicious, refreshing rosés, which may contain a proportion of white grapes, are a good enough reason to search for its wines.

'Termanthia' Bodegas Numanthia Termes, Toro. A sensational wine, with incredible concentration of ripe fruit backed by mineral notes and fine-grained tannins.

'Pintia' Bodegas y Viñedos Pintia, Toro. Perfectly balanced and well fruited. Good value for the quality.

Calderona Rosado Nuevo Bodegas Frutos Villar. Good strawberry fruit aromas and flavours with a creamy texture.

TORO AND CIGALES

REGIONS

- Toro
- Cigales

Gijón
Oviedo
CANTABRIAN MOUNTAINS
Léon
PORTUGAL
•Palencia
•Cigales
•Valladolid •Aranda de Duero
Zamora• •Toro •Peñafiel
Duero
•Rueda
•Salamanca •Segovia

PINTIA
TORO
Denominación de Origen
COSECHA 2006

ABOVE LEFT *Vines in a gently rolling vineyard at Morales de Toro, just to the east of the ancient town of Toro. The red soils are predominantly clay or sand.*

LEFT *Toro's altitude, some 600–750 m/2,000–2,500 ft above sea level, ensures cool nights, resulting in good colour in the grapes.*

NORTH-WEST SPAIN

Galicia

Compared with the barren landscape of much of Spain, Galicia is positively lush. Its proximity to the Atlantic Ocean brings increased rainfall and a cooler climate, which is ideally suited to white wine production. But where other areas have made a move to international varieties, Galicia has stuck almost exclusively to native grapes. Foremost among them is the fashionable Albariño, which has brought Rías Baixas to prominence.

Rías Baixas

The Rías Baixas region is really a collection of small, distinct areas, mainly clustered around coastal inlets, each of which gives an individual character to its wine through differing aspects and altitudes. Traditionally the vines are trained on pergolas to protect them from humidity.

Albariño's bright aromas range from fruity (apple, pear, peach) to floral, and its refreshing acidity and sound structure make it an excellent partner to the local seafood specialities of Galicia. Some producers ferment the wine in barrel for greater structure and complexity, but it is the clean and lively tank-fermented version that captivates the palates of consumers worldwide.

Moving inland

Albariño is also grown in Ribeiro but blends from Treixadura, Torrontés, Godello and Loureiro are its hallmark. Easy drinking with good aromas, these wines offer good value. Whites from emerging Monterrei are usually blends, too. In Valdeorras, Godello makes well-flavoured, fresh whites with gentler acidity. Temperature-controlled fermentation in stainless steel tanks has greatly improved quality here.

Other elegant Godello whites are made further inland in Bierzo, although it is mainly noted for its reds. The indigenous Mencia grape thrives in the drier climate and sandier soils, making fruity rosés and elegant, structured young reds. Some aged reds are made and, with a dramatic rise in production since the early 1990s, the future looks good.

Ribeira Sacra

Galician red wines are rarities. Some of the best, though seldom seen internationally because of their low production, are again Mencia-based, from the picturesque valleys of Ribeira Sacra. They have bright, fruity aromas and plenty of chewy fruit on the palate. The difficulty of working the steep terraces may have deterred some investors, but the potential is considerable. Here, Albariño has fewer citric notes and greater depth of fruit and, if it remains in fashion, Ribeira Sacra could become a challenger to Rías Baixas.

GALICIA

REGIONS

Rías Baixas

Ribeiro

Ribeira Sacra

Valdeorras

Monterrei

Bierzo

RIGHT *Although good roads link the main cities, patience is needed to explore many of the wine-producing areas, in which tiny roads twist and turn with the tumbling countryside.*

BELOW *Beautifully sited vineyards overlook the Rio Sil in the Ribeira Sacra DO east of Ourense.*

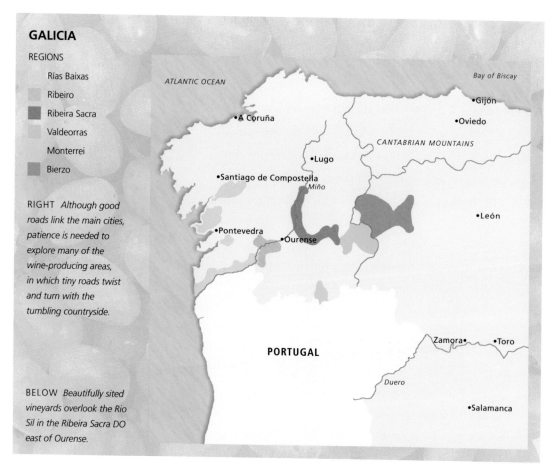

ATLANTIC OCEAN

Bay of Biscay

•Gijón

•A Coruña

•Oviedo

CANTABRIAN MOUNTAINS

•Lugo

•Santiago de Compostella
Miño

•León

•Pontevedra

•Ourense

PORTUGAL

Zamora• •Toro

Duero

•Salamanca

Rías Baixas Albariño Bodegas Fillaboa. Elegant with bright peach aromas and clean, crisp acidity.

Rías Baixas Albariño de Fefiñanes '1583' Bodegas del Palacio de Fefiñanes. Delicately oaked, finely fruited and complex, with great elegance.

Ribeiro Viña do Campo Blanco Bodegas Docampo. A blend of Treixadura and Torrontés with bright perfume and chewy palate.

Valdeorras 'Gaba do Xil' Godello Telmo Rodríguez. Aromas of pineapple, flowers and hints of aniseed, with moderate body and a touch of minerality.

Pétalos del Bierzo Descendientes de J. Palacios. Pure Mencia with full red fruit aromas, good minerality and complexity.

CENTRAL SPAIN

Madrid to Alicante

As in most of the country, the wines of Spain's central vineyards have recently improved, but they had a lot of catching up to do. Most were sold for distillation or disguising as sangria. In this difficult, hot, dry climate it has taken the advent of better vineyard management and modern technology in the wineries to produce wines of drinkable quality and export value, and there are bargains to be found.

La Mancha is Spain's largest DO. Here, healthy vines require little attention so production costs are kept low. The drought-resistant Airen grape produces light, fruity whites with cool fermentation. Tempranillo (locally called Cencibel) makes either young reds or more serious, barrel-aged wines with spicy red fruit flavours. Cabernet Sauvignon and Syrah also feature, with Cabernet Sauvignon Dominio de Valdepusa from Marqués de Griñon's La Mancha estate having been praised by influential wine writer, Robert Parker.

Good Tempranillo-based reds, richly fruited and often oaked, are made in the smaller enclave of Valdepeñas. The reds of Manchuela and Almansa and Valencia's Utiel-Requena show promise from a variety of different vines. Rosés can be refreshing and attractive. Jumilla and Yecla reds also display good flavour. In the Vinos de Madrid and Ribera del Guardiana DOs, international varieties are sometimes blended with Tempranillo or Garnacha to add complexity to these burgeoning reds.

La Mancha Canforrales Clàsico Tempranillo Bodegas Campos Reales. Plenty of ripe berry fruit, good structure and balance. Unoaked.

Yecla Castaño 'Coleccion' Bodegas Castaño. Sweet, ripe fruit, well integrated oak and notes of spice and liquorice.

Valdepeñas 'Córcovo' Reserva Bodegas J.A. Mejía e Hijos. Open, red fruit aromas, vanilla notes and good length.

CENTRAL SPAIN

PORTUGAL

• MADRID ❽
Tajo
• Cuenca
• Castellón
• Cáceres
❾
❶ ❸ ❺ • VALENCIA
• Ciudad Real • Albacete
• Badajoz Guadiana ❷ ❹
❻ ❼
Guadalquivir • Alicante •
Murcia •
• Córdoba • Jaén MEDITERRANEAN SEA
• Montilla Lorca • Cartagena •
• Huelva SEVILLE
• Granada
SIERRA NEVADA

REGIONS	SELECTED DOs	
Madrid	❶ La Mancha	❺ Utiel-Requena
Castilla-La Mancha	❷ Valdepeñas	❻ Jumilla
Valencia	❸ Manchuela	❼ Yecla
Murcia	❹ Almansa	❽ Vinos de Madrid
Extremadura		❾ Ribera del Guardiana

LEFT A huge quantity of wine is made in the various regions mapped here. Some is dreadful, some decent, some very good. It should not cost a lot to track down the good ones.

FAR LEFT In this well-cared-for Valepeñas vineyard vines do not have to compete with weeds for precious water.

SOUTHERN SPAIN

Andalucía

Spain's most southerly region has long been famous for its fortified wines, with sherry (see Jerez, page 118) being the most prominent. Indeed, Montilla-Moriles was considered part of the sherry area until the early 20th century, giving its name to *amontillado* wines ('in the style of Montilla'). Other wines in a similar style are made throughout the province and, although currently out of fashion, they represent excellent value and delicious drinking.

🍷🍷 **Málaga Virgen Pedro Ximénes López Hermanos.** Well rounded with delicious nut and toffee flavours and a good balancing acidity.

🍷🍷🍷 **Málaga Molino Real 'Mountain Wine' Telmo Rodriguez.** Partially dried grapes give intense peach flavours with a clean, zesty finish.

🍷🍷 **Montilla-Moriles 'Gran Barquero' Fino Pérez Barquero.** Beautifully tight and dry with salty notes and clean acidity.

Pedro Ximénez is the star variety in Montilla, its naturally high sugar often producing wines of up to 16 per cent alcohol without the need for fortification. Dry, medium and cream styles are produced and are often cheaper than sherry. Lately, dry table wines have shown promise.

Málaga makes an array of differing wine styles. The sweeter fortified wines from Pedro Ximénez can be exquisite and boast distinct flavours of raisins, caramel and nuts. Excellent dessert wines from Moscatel are emerging, such as the fresh and aromatic Molina Real. The Sierras de Málaga DO is a recent creation to supply the increasing demand for lighter, drier wines. Wine from Condado de Huelva was first exported to the West Indies in 1502.

BELOW LEFT *Andalucía's fierce heat has precluded the making of quality table wines until recently. Most are sold and consumed locally.*

BELOW *It is claimed that Ancient Greeks taught the people of Málaga how to prune vines: these are at Mollina, near Antequera.*

ANDALUCÍA

REGION

Andalucía

SELECTED DOs

1 Condado de Huelva

2 Jerez

3 Málaga, Sierras de Málaga

4 Montilla-Moriles

SOUTHERN SPAIN

Jerez

Lying inland from Cádiz, the town of Jerez de la Frontera is surrounded by vineyards producing one of the least appreciated and best-value fortified wines in the world. 'Sherry' is the long-standing anglicization of its name. Unfortunately a northern European taste for sickly 'cream' sherry led to a corruption of the true style from the 1960s onwards. Happily, good examples are still produced and readily available in the export market.

The wine's fate is determined immediately after fermentation. Light and delicate wines may develop a surface layer of yeast, known as flor, which protects the wine from oxidation while it matures. These wines are dry, destined to become Finos and Amontillados, gently fortified to around 15 per cent. Unfortunately some are artificially sweetened by the blending in of sugary Pedro Ximénez, taking away the wine's refreshing qualities. Fuller wines are matured in contact with the air and given a larger dose of fortification to prevent the formation of flor. These Olorosos are capable of developing superbly over many years. A contributory factor to such development is the solera system.

The solera

Essentially this is a number of tiers of barrels, with the oldest wine at the bottom and the youngest at the top. When wine is drawn off the bottom barrel for bottling, it is replaced by some of the next oldest wine from the layer above, and so on. Some of the oldest wine remains in the bottom barrel, adding complexity to the younger wine with which it mixes. The more tiers of barrels the better the system works – and the more expensive it is to set up and maintain. For that reason a number of the biggest and oldest companies make some of the best aged Olorosos, such as Domecq's Sibarita and González Byass' Matúsalem.

Manzanilla 'La Gitana' Bodegas Hidalgo. Salty, nutty, bone dry, refreshing.

Fino 'Tio Pepe' Gonzalez Byass. Benchmark Fino, rounder than La Gitana, no less invigorating.

Oloroso 'Pata de Gallina' Emilio Lustau. Unblended almacenista sherry. Deep, figgy nose. Initially dry flavour turns to lingering, round, concentrated aftertaste.

Pedro Ximénez 'San Emilio' Emilio Lustau. The Pedro Ximénez grape produces an incredibly sweet wine, normally used in blending. Thick, dense, treacly and irresistibly grapey.

Sherry grapes
Just three white grape varieties are used for sherry production. Palomino Fino is the aristocrat, producing fine-flavoured sherry when grown on chalk soil. Moscatel produces deliciously sweet wines, without the refreshing acidity of Palomino. Pedro Ximénez gives incredibly dense, raisiny nectar, and is mostly used in small quantities in sweeter blends.

JEREZ

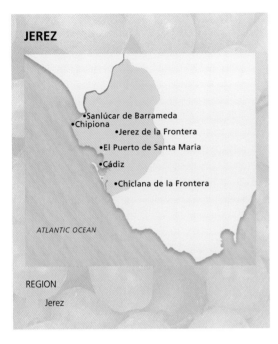

- •Sanlúcar de Barrameda
- •Chipiona
- •Jerez de la Frontera
- •El Puerto de Santa Maria
- •Cádiz
- •Chiclana de la Frontera

ATLANTIC OCEAN

REGION

Jerez

Sherry styles

Fino is the driest sherry, admirably suited to the tastiness of local tapas such as anchovies or olives. Some of it, matured in cellars close to the Atlantic at Sanlúcar de Barrameda, is called Manzanilla and has a particular salty tang, making it wonderfully refreshing and appetizing.

Genuine Amontillado is really a Fino that has been aged a good deal, losing its flor and its sharpness and gaining a deeper, nutty flavour through contact with the air. It should retain its natural dryness and linger in the mouth. Good examples are Tio Diego (Valdespino) and Tio Guillermo (Garvey). The greatest of these wines may be 20 or 30 years old, their intense flavours concentrated by evaporation during long barrel ageing. Palo Cortado is a rarely encountered, fragrant style, roughly between Amontillado and Oloroso. Oloroso is dark, soft, full-bodied and fragrant.

Sherry enthusiasts seek out *almacenista* wines, raised and matured by individual growers, and the very rare single-vintage sherries.

FAR LEFT *Barrels of wine (oldest at the bottom) in the Bodega of Juan Garcia Jarana, an* almacenista, *who makes and raises his own wine. In Jarana's case much of this is marketed by the excellent company Emilio Lustau.*

LEFT *Despite their proximity to the Atlantic Ocean, the vineyards of Jerez are some of the hottest imaginable. In fact the ocean's main influence is debatable: does it really give that distinctive and delicious salty tang to Manzanilla?*

BELOW *Andalucía is sunbaked and dry. When rain falls it is imperative not to waste a drop. A vineyard worker prepares the soil between the vines to retain rainfall in a Jerez vineyard.*

LUSTAU
SOLERA RESERVA
FINE SHERRY WINE

PX
Pedro Ximénez
SAN EMILIO
SHERRY

Golden brown and very sweet, smooth and luscious

SOLERA RESERVA
JEREZ DE LA FRONTERA
PRODUCE OF SPAIN

NORTHERN PORTUGAL

Vinho Verde

Most of the Vinho Verde that is exported is white, but its name, meaning 'green wine', refers not to its colour but to its youthfulness, and a good proportion of the region's production is red: this is consumed locally, its tannic style being considered too rustic for foreign palates. As all the wines are designed for young drinking, a specific vintage is rarely stated on the label.

Although Vinho Verde is not truly sparkling it often has a distinct fizz, derived from the carbon dioxide absorbed during malolactic fermentation. Today, not all the wine undergoes this process, and producers may add carbon dioxide to recreate the style. High acidity gives the wines a definite bite, so for export they are often softened, the higher sugar levels making them more consumer friendly.

Six separate areas, with differing climates, produce Vinho Verde, and the list of permitted grape varieties is extensive. Loureiro and Trajadura are the best of the white varieties in the south, giving fairly light, fresh wines, ideal to accompany the local seafood. Close to the border with Spain's Galicia, however, Alvarinho (Albariño) makes more structured whites, higher in alcohol and with more expressive aromas.

PORTUGUESE CLASSIFICATIONS

Denominação de Origem Controlada (DOC): Quality wine region, equivalent to the French Appellation d'Origine Contrôlée.

Indicação de Proveniência Regulamentada (IPR): Up-and-coming wines.

Vinho Regional (VR): Regional wine. Often indicates that non-indigenous grape varieties are used.

Vinho de Mesa: Table wine.

Vinho Verde Quinta de Azevedo. Fresh, light and fruity with a light sparkle.

Vinho Verde Casal Mendes. Just off-dry with delicate apple fruit, clean acidity and a gentle spritz.

Vinho Verde Alvarinho Aveleda 'Follies'. Floral and peach aromas, medium body with citrus notes.

RIGHT *As in neighbouring Spanish Galicia, the Portuguese Minho has a comparatively damp climate, a contributory factor in the high acids and low sugars of Vinho Verde grapes.*

LEFT *Many winemaking traditions survive in Portugal despite the enormous improvements in quality brought by modern practices. These Vinho Verde vines are trained on pergolas.*

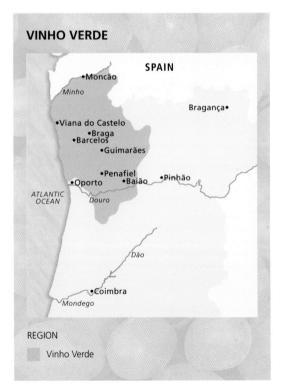

VINHO VERDE

SPAIN

•Monção

Minho

Bragança•

•Viana do Castelo
•Braga
•Barcelos
•Guimarães

•Penafiel
•Oporto •Baião •Pinhão

ATLANTIC OCEAN

Douro

Dão

•Coimbra

Mondego

REGION

Vinho Verde

NORTHERN PORTUGAL
Douro Valley

The poor schist soils and arid climate of the scenic Douro Valley make the vine work hard to find water, and the steep vineyards have been terraced to make viticulture possible. Port (see page 122) has always been so important to the region that table wines were largely ignored. Yet in the 1950s proof of what was possible was revealed by Barca Velha, which remains world class.

RIGHT *The port companies, old and new, have had to invest heavily in their vineyards to maintain the exceptional qualities of their ports and table wines, as evidenced in the exemplary state of this broadly terraced Quinta do Noval vineyard.*

BELOW RIGHT *The Douro Valley is a wine region for the future, with a raft of exceptional wines emerging from what was traditionally fortified wine territory.*

Quinta do Vale 'Dona Maria'. Complex blend of local varieties packed with berry fruit. Concentrated and powerful.

Quinta de la Rosa 'Val da Clara'. Good depth of flavour with plenty of ripe fruit and an elegant finish.

Casa Ferreirinha 'Barca Velha'. Often regarded as the finest of Portuguese wines, it generally requires a decade or so to show at its complex best.

Traditionally, many grape varieties were planted, often mixed within vineyards. Now the vineyards have been replanted with individual varieties, such as Touriga Nacional, Touriga Franca and Tinta Roriz, specifically for the production of table wines. Such is the potential quality of these wines that foreign investment has been attracted into the region. New-wave table wines produced by traditional port companies such as Niepoort are creating great interest.

With such varied altitudes, aspects and grape varieties, no single style stands out, although reds predominate. The wines range from rich and powerful to lighter and more aromatic. But with contemporary labour costs and an established home market, it is certain that the greatest examples will always remain expensive.

DOURO VALLEY

SPAIN

•Moncão
Minho

Bragança•

•Vila Nova de Guia

•Vila Real

Oporto•
Baião• Pinhão•

Vila Nova de Guia
Douro

ATLANTIC OCEAN

Dão
•Guardã

•Coimbra
Mondego

REGION

Douro Valley

Port

Port is unquestionably one of the world's greatest fortified wines. Its role varies enormously from country to country. In one it may be drunk as an aperitif – perhaps white and chilled – while in another it is served as a great after-dinner drink, conferred with ritual etiquette (it should always be passed to the left). It may be barrel-aged or bottle-aged, drunk straight from the bottle or decanted.

> **White port**
> Made from white grapes, white port is similar to red port, but less sweet. Ageing in cask gives it a golden colour. It is usually served chilled as an aperitif.

Treading the grapes

In order to extract the maximum colour and flavour from the grapes in the relatively short period before fortification, the grapes were trodden in stone *lagares*, or troughs, with songs and lively music to accompany the task. This traditional process continues today, but the crushing is more usually done by mechanical means, especially for commercial styles. Once the wines are made, they are transported downriver – traditionally in *barcos rabelos* – to age in the cellars of the lodges in Vila Nova de Gaia.

LEFT *The treading of grapes (seen here at Dow's) is not just a nostalgic gimmick. Because the fermentation of port is unusually short it is important that maximum pigments and tannins are extracted at the beginning. The human foot is perfect for this, with the added benefit of not crushing the pips, which would impart bitter flavours.*

Back in the 1600s Douro wines were fairly rough, but they became popular in Britain when French wine became unavailable during periods of war between the two nations. Brandy was added to protect the wines during their transportation, and the British developed a taste for the fortified wine. They established companies in Oporto to guarantee supply, and soon began buying grapes and making wines themselves. Many of these old companies are still in business, such as Warre (1670), Croft (1678) and Sandeman (1790).

It is unclear exactly when grape brandy was first added to wine during fermentation but the technique is still employed today, arresting the process when around half of the natural sugar remains unconverted. This produces a sweet wine with a relatively high level of alcohol (around 20 per cent), yet remaining remarkably natural and balanced given the artificiality of the process.

Styles of port

Of the three regions of production, the vineyards around the town of Pinhão are reputedly the best. Various wines are produced, each with its own distinctive style. The finest are vintage ports, made in a single year and aged in cask for two years before bottling, unfiltered. These age well in bottle for decades, and throw a sediment or crust during this time, so require decanting before drinking. They are made only in the finest years, and each house declares a vintage independently. If they are unsure of final quality, some houses will declare under a second label, such as Fonseca's Guimaraens brand.

Occasionally the vintage is not a success everywhere, yet certain estates, known as *quintas*, will produce a wine worthy of a vintage. These 'single-quinta wines' are sold under the name of the quinta: Taylor's Quinta de Vargellas is an excellent example.

Vintage wines require long ageing to achieve their full potential. Late-bottled vintages, however, are wines from a single vintage, aged in cask for up to six years then bottled after light filtration, and immediately ready to drink. Wines blended from several vintages, bottled earlier without filtration, are called crusted ports, as they form a sediment in bottle. They need to be decanted before drinking and offer excellent value.

Thanks to the fortification process, ports can age for longer in cask than many other wines, taking on a lighter, browner colour. These are known as tawny ports and have a distinctive dried berry and nutty aroma. They are generally sold by the average age of the blend – 10, 20, 30 or even 40 years. If they come from a single vintage they are termed *colheita* ('crop').

Ruby port is the basic style, having been aged in tank before being blended to the style of the brand, much like Champagne, then filtered and bottled. The best are labelled Reserve or Vintage Character.

Most port houses belong to big parent companies, but independent family companies such as Borges, Churchill, Niepoort, Santa Eufemia and Ventozelo succeed admirably.

Dow Late-bottled Vintage Port. Richly flavoured with good balance between sweetness and acidity.

Niepoort 20 Years Old Tawny. Excellent tawny with complex dried fruit aromas and a fresh, nutty finish.

Fonseca Vintage Port. Capable of ageing well, richly fruited and powerful yet retaining a great sense of balance and freshness.

BELOW LEFT *Traditionally, newly made wines were transported downriver in* barcos rabelos, *distinctive sailing barges. The practice is commemorated annually in the Barcos Rabelos Regatta, held on the Douro on St John's Day (24 June), each sail celebrating the name of a historic port house.*

NORTHERN PORTUGAL

Bairrada and Dão

These two regions lie side by side – Barraida nearer the coast and Dão sheltered by mountains. Each produces predominantly red wines, although Barraida's best-known wine is Mateus Rosé from Sogrape. Under an unsatisfactory cooperative system established in the 1940s both regions all too often made mouth-puckering, lacklustre wines, but forward-thinking producers are now showing just what can be done.

Bairrada

The Baga grape, on which Mateus Rosé is based, is naturally high in acidity and susceptible to rot, which in this humid coastal region can spread rapidly and devastate the harvest. Rain can also be a problem at this time, so many growers who worked through the cooperatives harvested early; their grapes never achieved full ripeness but had green tannins alongside piercing acidity. Now, smaller producers are using techniques such as de-stemming the grapes before fermentation and working with ripe fruit from older vines. Work in the vineyards has improved and international varieties such as Cabernet Sauvignon are now being planted. As a result, excellent wines are coming to the market, rich in fruit and full bodied. Although smoother than their ancestors, the best repay cellaring for a while.

Dão

Many of Dão's wines were flat and lifeless until Portugal joined the EU in the mid-1980s. At that point the stranglehold of the cooperatives was broken, and companies such as Sogrape have been instrumental in the development of wines and the resultant increased quality, with much investment in new technology.

Dão is protected from the worst of the Atlantic weather, making it warmer in summer for the essential ripening period. Its sandy, granitic soils are well suited to a number of varieties, with Touriga Nacional, Tinta Roriz (a clone of Tempranillo) and Jaen being most favoured. Its wines are

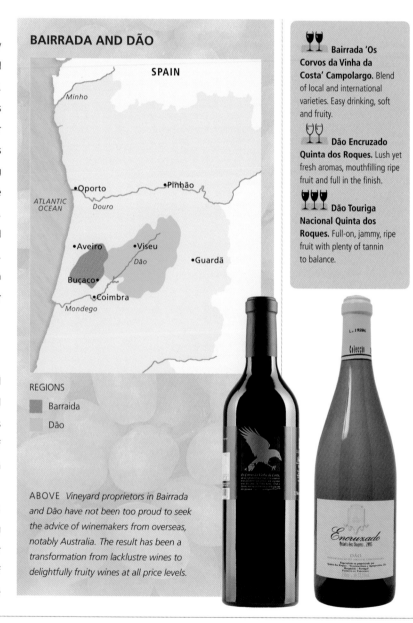

BAIRRADA AND DÃO

SPAIN

Minho

•Oporto   •Pinhão

ATLANTIC
OCEAN   Douro

•Aveiro   •Viseu
Dão
•Guardã

Buçaco•

•Coimbra
Mondego

REGIONS

▇ Barraida

▨ Dão

ABOVE *Vineyard proprietors in Bairrada and Dão have not been too proud to seek the advice of winemakers from overseas, notably Australia. The result has been a transformation from lacklustre wines to delightfully fruity wines at all price levels.*

🍷🍷 **Bairrada 'Os Corvos da Vinha da Costa' Campolargo.** Blend of local and international varieties. Easy drinking, soft and fruity.

🍷🍷 **Dão Encruzado Quinta dos Roques.** Lush yet fresh aromas, mouthfilling ripe fruit and full in the finish.

🍷🍷🍷 **Dão Touriga Nacional Quinta dos Roques.** Full-on, jammy, ripe fruit with plenty of tannin to balance.

mainly richly flavoured, concentrated and deeply coloured, although Jaen can give lighter, fruitier wines. Touriga Nacional is usually present, though sometimes in too small a proportion to be helpful, adding its telltale floral notes and elegance to the blends. The use of oak for maturation is on the increase, as is the number of varietal wines.

Smaller producers are emerging at the top of the pile. Quinta dos Roques, for example, is making a great impression, not only for its sturdy, oaked reds but also for delicious whites (again oaked) from the local Encruzado variety, which generally produces wines of structure and good acidity with slightly tropical notes.

BELOW *The vineyards of Luís Pato are producing some of the most exciting wines in Portugal, mostly reds, some from single vineyards, others from single varieties.*

SOUTHERN PORTUGAL

Estremadura and Ribatejo

Estramadura is the powerhouse in terms of quantity of Portuguese wine production. Ribatejo comes second, largely supplying the local market but, while much is still basic, fair wines are now to be found. As elsewhere in Portugal, production has been dominated by cooperatives, but entry into the EU made funds available for modernization, which is improving the general quality, and good growers are now marketing their own wines.

LEFT *Even in the 21st century many of Portugal's vineyards are interspersed with other crops such as olives. The fragmentary nature of the vineyards is apparent in this scene in the Ribatejo.*

BELOW *Much prized locally, wines from the small regions of Bucelas (dry white) and Colares (dark, tannin-laden red) are rarely encountered far from Lisbon.*

🍷🍷🍷 **Quinta do Monte d'Oiro Reserva, Alenquer.** Fresh red fruits with hints of lavender, always well balanced and with finesse.

🍷🍷 **Tagus Creek Grande Vinho, Ribatejo.** This blend of international and local varieties gives plenty of black fruit and chunky tannins.

🍷🍷 **Quinta de Lagoalva de Cima Syrah. Ribatejo.** Good intensity with spicy and savoury notes on the palate.

D.F.J. Vinhos makes affordable, fruit-driven red wines and lively whites from local and international varieties under its Grand'Arte label. Smaller estates are carving reputations in the Alenquer DOC, such as Quinta do Monte d'Oiro and Quinta de Chocapalha, both of whom are succeeding with native and international varieties, red and white.

In the Ribatejo good reds are made from Cabernet Sauvignon and Syrah. Quinta de Lagoalva de Cima's fine wines include a delicious Syrah and a blend of indigenous varieties, both of which are fairly bold. The estate also breeds bulls and horses, two other specialities of the area.

One of Portugal's superstar winemakers, João Portugal Ramos, is making affordable wines under his Tagus Creek label, named from the river that flows through Ribatejo. Fiuza and Bright make value wines, too, including varietals such as Sauvignon Blanc.

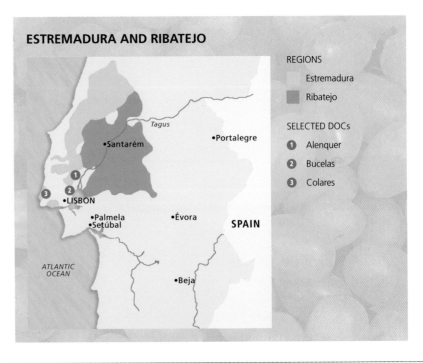

ESTREMADURA AND RIBATEJO

REGIONS

Estremadura

Ribatejo

SELECTED DOCs

① Alenquer

② Bucelas

③ Colares

Tagus

•Portalegre

•Santarém

•LISBON

•Palmela
•Setúbal

•Évora

SPAIN

ATLANTIC OCEAN

•Beja

SOUTHERN PORTUGAL

Alentejo, Setúbal Peninsula and Algarve

The most important of Portugal's southern vineyards are in Alentejo. This hot, arid area was once most famous for its cork production, but the quality of its wine is now recognized internationally. Its vineyards, reliant on irrigation, are mainly planted with indigenous varieties, although Cabernet Sauvignon, Merlot and Syrah are all found. The cooperatives are now making clean, well-fruited reds, and this is an area on the up.

João Portugal Ramos makes impressive blends and single-variety wines, white and red. The reds display notable concentration of ripe fruit, and are good value for such quality. His Tricadeira is well worth seeking out. International investment is important here, too. For instance, Domaines Barons de Rothschild of Bordeaux have joined forces with José Berardo at Quinta do Carmo, making serious wines.

The Setúbal Peninsula boasts a delicious fortified Muscat (Moscatel de Setúbal). José Maria da Fonseca is its top producer, and also makes a wide range of table wines, notably a number of good reds produced in a brand new winery, including a sterling wine from the Castelão variety. In the Algarve, things are still waiting to happen.

BELOW RIGHT *A Moscatel vineyard belonging to Bacalhôa Vinhos. This company is typical of many in Portugal, having interests in several different regions and producing many wines in a wide range of styles, while maintaining satisfactory quality throughout.*

'Trincadeira' João Portugal Ramos, Alentejo. Full-flavoured with ripe fruit and wilder notes. Big, toasty finish.

'Monte Velho' Tinto Herdade do Esporão, Alentejo. Very affordable, easy-drinking red, in a modern and commercial style.

Moscatel de Setúbal 'J.P. Moscatel' Bacalhôa Vinhos de Portugal. Fortified white with delicious dried fruit flavours, notes of orange peel and nuts and a rich yet fresh finish.

ALENTEJO, SETÚBAL PENINSULA AND ALGARVE

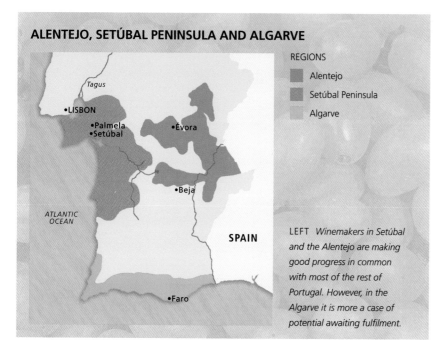

REGIONS
- Alentejo
- Setúbal Peninsula
- Algarve

Tagus · LISBON · Palmela · Setúbal · Évora · Beja · Faro · ATLANTIC OCEAN · SPAIN

LEFT *Winemakers in Setúbal and the Alentejo are making good progress in common with most of the rest of Portugal. However, in the Algarve it is more a case of potential awaiting fulfilment.*

●●● Regions 56–62

●●● Germany

One of life's greatest treats is to sip a glass of chilled Riesling from the Mosel or Rhein (Rhine), incomparable at all levels from aperitif to dessert. Germany is at the northern extremity of European wine growing, and its cool climate is one of the most important factors contributing to the sheer elegance and refinement of these wines, which miraculously balance their irresistible pure fruitiness with a refreshing natural acidity.

These wines have never been of higher quality than they are today. Yet Germany is also at a vinous crossroads, because it is now producing very good food wines, white and red, in a totally different style – the whites drier and more alcoholic, the reds fuller bodied than formerly. They are able not only to satisfy the home market but also to compete on the international stage. There is huge potential in the burgeoning vineyards of the former DDR and also in the plantings of cool-climate red varieties, particularly Pinot Noir, or Spätburgunder as it is known in Germany.

Germany's quality system

German wines are classified differently from those of all other countries, in that quality is measured by the natural sugar content of the harvested grapes, indicating the potential alcohol that can be produced by vinification. A legal minimum of natural alcohol is laid down for each category. In general, the riper the grapes are, the richer and more complex the wines will be.

Deutscher Tafelwein (T)

German table wine, equivalent to basic French *vin de table*, from one of five designated regions. Natural alcohol level: at least 5 per cent.

Landwein (L)

Superior table wine, equivalent to *vin de pays*, from one of 19 designated regions. Natural alcohol level: 0.5 per cent more than *Tafelwein*.

Qualitätswein bestimmer Anbaugebiete (QbA)

'Quality wine from a designated region' entirely from one of 13 designated regions, from approved local grape varieties, displaying local character, reaching a natural potential alcohol level before fermentation and a minimum level of 7 per cent by volume after fermentation. They may be chaptalized (have sugar added) to raise the final level. Most German wines are QbA.

Qualitätswein mit Prädikat (QmP)

'Quality wine with distinction' falls into one of six categories determined by the ripeness of the grapes and when and how they are picked.

Kabinett, made from fully ripened grapes: fine, usually light wines with low alcohol content.

Spätlese ('late harvest') made from even riper grapes: greater intensity of flavour and concentration. Can range from quite dry to fairly sweet.

Auslese, made from selected, very ripe bunches: intense in bouquet and taste, usually, but not always, sweet.

Beerenauslese (BA), made from individually selected, overripe grapes, usually infected by *Botrytis cinerea* (noble rot): notable for their longevity.

Eiswein, also made from overripe grapes, harvested and pressed while frozen: remarkable wines with enormous concentration of fruit, acidity and sweetness.

Trockenbeerenauslese (TBA) made from individually selected berries, overripe (and usually infected by noble rot) and dried up almost to raisins.

Classic and Selection wines were introduced in 2000. They are either *trocken* (dry) or *halbtrocken* (half-dry), though this is not shown on the label. Classic wines originate from specific grape varieties in specified regions that give a consistent style and quality. Selection wines are the same but from specific vineyard sites, where grapes have been hand-harvested from vines producing lower yields.

Prädikat levels are indicators of a wine's weight and body but do not guarantee quality. To ensure quality the Verband Deutscher Prädikatsweingüter (VDP), representing 200 premium growers, embraces a strict code of practice and a tiered system for classifying vineyard sites. A VDP site may be an entire Einzellage ('individual site') or a small parcel from that site. Dry wines from a top site – Erste Lage – are designated Grosses Gewächs (Erstes Gewächs in the Rheingau).

> **Kabinett wines**
> Today, these are the driest of the QmP wines, very likely utterly delicious and thoroughly well made, but without the greatness of an Auslese or TBA. Long ago, however, Kabinett wines were the best wines, for the term Kabinett (or Cabinet) is derived from Cabinet-Keller (Cabinet cellar) in which such wines were reserved for selling at a later date. This term was first used in 1712 in the Cistercian Eberbach Abbey.

BELOW *Noble rot grapes may not look particularly attractive but the wines they produce in Germany's classic regions are some of the finest expressions of concentrated grape flavour of all.*

SOUTH-WEST GERMANY
Ahr and Mittelrhein

Though it is one of Germany's most northerly regions, the Ahr Valley perversely enjoys a reputation for red wine. History and geology have conspired to make this the ideal home for Spätburgunder (Pinot Noir). The steep, slatey valley sides retain the day's heat, acting as radiators to give extra hours for grape ripening. The backbreaking work required to tend these vineyards means that the wines are expensive and rarely exported.

Ahr wines were once light – some still are – but the best modern examples are fuller and drier. Cooperatives dominate production, yet there are quality small growers such as Jean Stodden and Weingut Kreuzberg. Also good, but less expensive, are Peter Lingen's wines.

Tourists flock to the Mittelrhein, with its medieval castles and the Lorelei Rock. Its vineyards, however, have seriously declined in number. They benefit from the light reflected from the Rhein, which also tempers the cool climate. Riesling is the principal variety. In the southern parts the clay and slate soils, in good exposures, give fresh, well-fruited wines with a clean acidity. In some years richer, botrytis-affected wines are made. Little is exported.

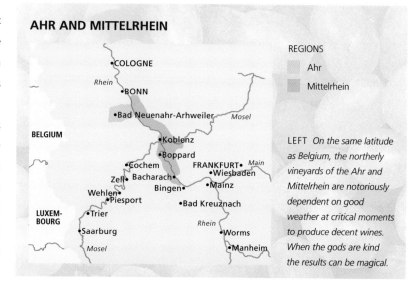

AHR AND MITTELRHEIN

REGIONS
Ahr
Mittelrhein

LEFT *On the same latitude as Belgium, the northerly vineyards of the Ahr and Mittelrhein are notoriously dependent on good weather at critical moments to produce decent wines. When the gods are kind the results can be magical.*

🍷🍷🍷 **Blauschiefer Spätburgunder Meyer-Näkel.** Aromas of bitter cherries with smoky nuances, good concentration and often a touch of bacon fat in the finish.

🍷🍷🍷 **Neuenahrer Schieferlay Trocken Kreuzberg.** Red berry fruit with notes of cask. Soft, yet spicy on the palate, with hints of minerality.

🍷🍷 **Bacharacher Hahn Riesling Kabinett Toni Jost.** Bright, fresh fruit with an underlying slatey minerality and crisp acidity.

RIGHT *Burg Stahleck castle (dating back to 1135) above Bacharach is today a youth hostel. Behind it, the precipitous Posten vineyard produces steely Riesling.*

TONI JOST
HAHNENHOF

2007
Bacharacher Hahn
Riesling Kabinett

Produce of Germany

ALC 9 % VOL   MITTELRHEIN   750 ML
Enthält Sulfite Qualitätswein mit Prädikat 16980411208
Weingut Toni Jost D-55422 Bacharach Gutsabfüllung

SOUTH-WEST GERMANY

Mosel

Some of Germany's (and the world's) most distinguished and elegant white wines originate in the precipitous vineyards lining the serpentine Mosel and its tributaries, the Saar and the Ruwer. The wines range in style from delicate as filigree to luscious and sensual, but all share a hallmark racy acidity. Even the sweetest of them are so well balanced that they leave the palate refreshed and eager for more.

Riesling reigns supreme, accounting for over half of the planted vineyards and all the best wines. Müller-Thurgau has been grown for many years in sites away from the valleys, making abundant, innocuous, semi-sweet wines for the mass market. In the Obermosel and Moseltor in the south, Elbling is widely planted, but its wines are of little interest.

Middle Mosel

Most of the greatest vineyards are concentrated in the stretch between Schweich in the south-west and Pünderich in the north-east – the Mittelmosel or Bereich (district) Bernkastel.

Here the famous wine villages, such as Trittenheim, Piesport, Brauneberg, Bernkastel, Wehlen and Zeltingen, tumble one after the other. Vineyards occupy the right or left bank depending on the best exposure to precious sunlight, while the wide expanse of the river operates as a mirror, reflecting more ripening rays to the vines.

The vineyards, originally planted by the Romans, rise from the valley floor to almost 200 m/600 ft in places. Devonian slate soils readily whisk away rainfall and retain the heat of the day into the cool evening. They are ideal for viticulture, although vineyard work can be perilous after rain.

BELOW *The south-facing Goldtröpfchen (Golden [rain] drops) vineyard in Piesport is one of the most famous on earth, an amphitheatre of vines perfectly exposed to the sun.*

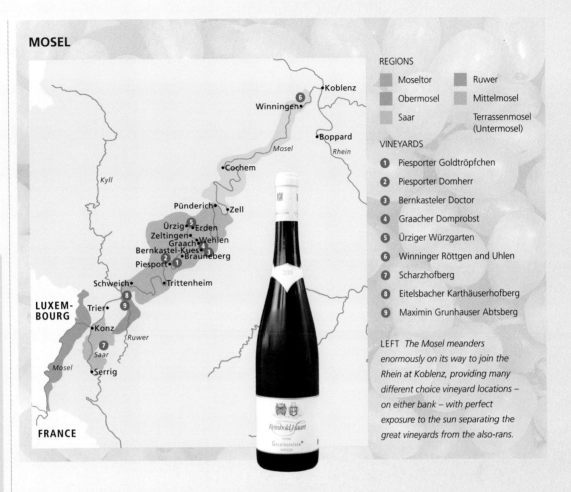

MOSEL

REGIONS

- Moseltor
- Obermosel
- Saar
- Ruwer
- Mittelmosel
- Terrassenmosel (Untermosel)

VINEYARDS

1. Piesporter Goldtröpfchen
2. Piesporter Domherr
3. Bernkasteler Doctor
4. Graacher Domprobst
5. Ürziger Würzgarten
6. Winninger Röttgen and Uhlen
7. Scharzhofberg
8. Eitelsbacher Karthäuserhofberg
9. Maximin Grunhauser Abtsberg

LEFT *The Mosel meanders enormously on its way to join the Rhein at Koblenz, providing many different choice vineyard locations – on either bank – with perfect exposure to the sun separating the great vineyards from the also-rans.*

Piesporter Goldtröpfchen Spätlese Reinhold Haart. Full and ripe, with spicy notes and minerality and a moderately sweet finish.

Brauneberger Juffer Kabinett Willi Haag. Excellent fruit with slatey minerality.

Graacher Domprobst Kabinett Weingut Willi Schaefer. Fresh, with intense flavours.

Wehlener Sonnenuhr Kabinett J.J. Prüm. Sensational aromatics with floral and citrus notes alongside ripe fruit, good acidity and a stony finish.

Zeltinger Sonnenuhr Kabinett Selbach-Oster. Fresh apple aromas with citrus notes; ripe yet clean on the palate.

A miraculous cure
Legend tells that, all medicines having failed the terminally ill Archbishop Boemund of Trier, he recovered after drinking a bottle of wine from Bernkastel. He named the vineyard 'the Doctor' in gratitude.

Piesport, with its *Grosslage* or area name of Michelsberg, was much maligned internationally from the 1970s onwards because of the vast quantities of lifeless wines that bore the name. They were seldom made from Riesling and were never touched by the locals. Yet some of Piesport's finest vineyards, such as Goldtröpfchen and Domherr, enjoy almost perfect southerly exposure and are capable of making world-class wines. Weingut Reinhold Haart's wines bear the true character of classic Riesling, with the telltale minerality associated with the great wines of Piesport. The nearby ruins of a Roman press house are testament to the long history of winemaking in the Mosel.

The fabled healing powers of the Doctor vineyard brought fame to the fairy-tale town of Bernkastel-Kues as long ago as the 14th century. This site, producing some of Germany's most expensive wines, lies just behind the town on a steep slope with a southerly exposure. Clay in the soil gives the wines rich notes with plenty of aroma. Dr Thanisch is one of only three owners, and the estate can claim that it produced the Mosel's first Trockenbeerenauslese in 1921.

Some of the Mosel's finest vineyards are found in quick succession from Graach, where the Domprobst vineyard gives delicious wines, to Wehlen and Zeltingen, where the Sonnenuhr vineyards – named after sundials on the site – also produce gorgeous wines, mostly in the Kabinett, Spätlese and Auslese catagories. Although excellent *trocken* wines can be found, the best ones generally have some degree of residual sugar. As Johannes Selbach of the distinguished Selbach-Oster estate in Zeltingen explained, 'Take a strawberry and eat it: it tastes of strawberry. Take another strawberry, cut it in two, put a touch of sugar on it, wait ten minutes and then eat it: it *really* tastes of strawberry.' Sugar helps carry the fruit flavours, and with the Mosel's lighter styles of Riesling it really intensifies those flavours.

Lower Mosel

The array of fine vineyards eventually dwindles after the villages of Ürzig and Erden, with the former's Würzgarten vineyard offering a spicy style. From Zell onwards the region becomes the Untermosel (Bereich Burg Cochem). It is less fashionable than its neighbour, but pleasant wines can be found, even some exceptional ones. The steep vineyards are mainly terraced: Reinhard Löwenstein, of the excellent Heymann-Löwenstein estate, coined the name Terrassenmosel, which seems to have stuck. This estate makes some of Untermosel's best wines, from vineyards in the village of Winningen close to the confluence with the Rhein at Koblenz. The vineyards of Röttgen and Uhlen are also consistently high performers.

Great wines of the Saar and Ruwer

In vinous terms the Mosel has two important tributaries, the Saar and the Ruwer. Over the 20 km/12 miles from Serrig to Konz the Saar produces some of the greatest bottles of Riesling in the world. The best sites are in the side valleys, where the slopes are sunniest. Arguably the top site is the Scharzhofberg, from which such estates as Egon Müller and Reichsgraf von Kesselstatt craft superb wines. Generally the microclimates of the Saar are cooler, and there are years in which the grapes cannot ripen. But good vintages give wines of exceptional freshness with bright, steely acidity, balancing the ripe fruit perfectly, especially in the sweeter wines. Other good sites include Ayler Kupp and Ockfener Bockstein.

Similar in style are the wines of the Ruwer Valley. Two supreme sites here are the Karthäuserhofberg vineyard in Eitelsbach and the steep Abtsberg vineyard behind the manor house of Maximin Grünhaus.

Ürziger Würzgarten Auslese Dr Loosen. Brimming with sweet apple fruit, notes of spice and perfect balancing acidity.

Winninger Uhlen 'Roth Lay' Trockenbeerenauslese Heymann-Löwenstein. Rich and complex with mineral and orange notes evident among luscious fruit and racy acidity.

Scharzhofberger Auslese Egon Müller. Delicate yet with a glorious combination of sweetness and steely acidity.

Maximin Grünhauser Abtsberg Spätlese von Schubert. Glorious Riesling with intense aromas and a fine acidity to balance the delicate sweetness.

RIGHT A head for heights is essential to work in many Mosel vineyards. This one, the Doctor vineyard overlooking Bernkastel-Kues, is perhaps the most famous of all.

SOUTH-WEST GERMANY

Rheingau, Rheinhessen and Nahe

Around the town of Bingen am Rhein, three great wine regions meet across the Rhein and Nahe rivers. Here the Rhein's northern banks boast a collection of southerly-facing slopes, sheltered by the Taunus Hills. These constitute the Rheingau, where some of Germany's finest and most famous vineyards are to be found. Across the river is Rheinhessen, Germany's largest wine-producing region, while the less productive Nahe is geologically and climatically diverse.

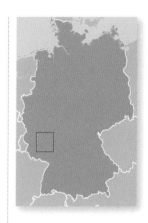

Rheingau

Names such as Schloss Vollrads and Schloss Johannisberg have, for centuries, represented the finest expression of the Riesling grape. Not every bottle produced is of the finest and, with varied soil structures, styles differ from vineyard to vineyard, but Rheingau wines are generally concentrated, with delicious ripe fruit balanced by a fresh acidity, which Riesling always maintains even at full ripeness. A recent designation of Erstes Gewächs (first growth) has been introduced for the finest sites but, as this covers around a third of all vineyards, it is far from specific.

These wines were once fermented dry, and this style has seen a renaissance recently. While dry by German standards, they can contain up to 9 g sugar per litre, sufficient to carry the delicious Riesling fruit and prevent their being austere or brittle, making them delicious as aperitifs and ideal with lighter foods. Proximity to the river brings autumn mists, perfect for the development of *Botrytis cinerea*, and, with it, incomparable Beerenauslesen and Trockenbeerenauslesen. Balancing acidity and succulent fruit, the wines are delicious in their youth yet they are capable of ageing divinely in the finest vintages.

Alongside Riesling, Spätburgunder performs well, especially around Assmannshausen. The resulting wines used to be so light they were almost rosés but, as in the Ahr, modern styles are much fuller and often barrel aged. They are good food wines and make excellent local drinking but, being so good, few escape for export.

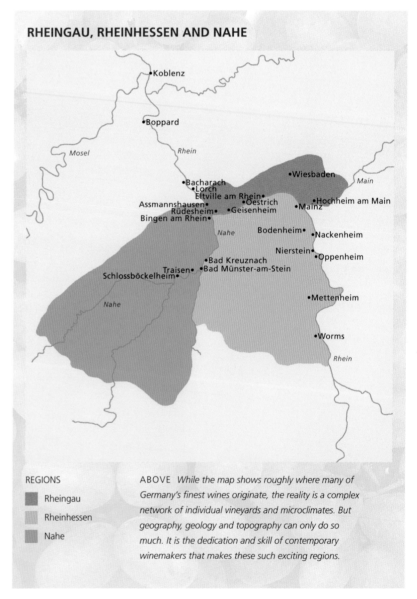

RHEINGAU, RHEINHESSEN AND NAHE

- Koblenz
- Boppard
- *Mosel*
- *Rhein*
- Bacharach
- Lorch
- Eltville am Rhein
- Wiesbaden
- *Main*
- Assmannshausen
- Oestrich
- Hochheim am Main
- Rüdesheim
- Geisenheim
- Mainz
- Bingen am Rhein
- *Nahe*
- Bodenheim
- Nackenheim
- Nierstein
- Oppenheim
- Bad Kreuznach
- Traisen
- Bad Münster-am-Stein
- Schlossböckelheim
- Mettenheim
- *Nahe*
- Worms
- *Rhein*

REGIONS

- Rheingau
- Rheinhessen
- Nahe

ABOVE *While the map shows roughly where many of Germany's finest wines originate, the reality is a complex network of individual vineyards and microclimates. But geography, geology and topography can only do so much. It is the dedication and skill of contemporary winemakers that makes these such exciting regions.*

Hochheimer Kirchenstück Riesling Spätlese Weingut Künstler, Rheingau. Soft, ripe and elegant with a silky finish.

Johannisberger 'V' Riesling Kabinett Weingut Johannishof, Rheingau. Fresh and well fruited with a dryish finish.

Kiedricher Gräfenberg Riesling Trocken Erstes Gewachs Weingut Robert Weil, Rheingau. Full flavoured and ripe with complex spicy fruit on the palate with stony minerality below. Dry but incredibly well fruited, this is a sensational wine.

RIGHT *Historically, Schloss Vollrads was one of the great Rheingau estates, but quality ebbed over the years. Serious investment and much hard work have begun to turn round the fortunes of this renowned vineyard.*

Rheinhessen

The Rheinhessen region accounts for around a quarter of Germany's vineyard area – and more in terms of production. It is the birthplace of Liebfraumilch, that bland, mass-produced white wine that almost singlehandedly damaged the reputation of Germany's fine wines in Britain and America. The blends were largely from early-ripening, high-cropping Müller-Thurgau, the region's most planted grape, which also dominated blends of Niersteiner Gutes Domthal. This *Grosslage* sadly appropriated the name of one of the region's finest wine towns, Nierstein. Above the river near here is a thin strip of vineyards capable of making wonderful wines, such as those of Hipping and Ölberg.

Collectively, the villages of the area from Bodenheim to Mettenheim make up the Rheinterrasse. Here the sloping vineyards benefit from good exposure and, in the north, from red slate (*Rotliegendes*), which imparts solidity and finesse. Riesling is the favoured grape. With a younger generation of winemakers at the helm, trocken wines are on the increase. Delicious Silvaner can also be found, the finest versions having a rich minerality. Weissburgunder and Grauburgunder also perform well in the hands of a skilled winemaker.

Although first-class Riesling thrives at Bingen and around Worms, almost a third of the region's wine is red, principally from the Dornfelder grape, which can provide flavoursome, well-fruited examples.

Schlossgut Diel

2006
Dorsheimer Burgberg
Riesling Kabinett

D-55452 BURG LAYEN
SCHLOSSABFÜLLUNG

Alc. 9 % by vol.   Nahe   750 ml

Nahe

The Nahe has never enjoyed the fame of the other great Rhine regions, yet its wines can be excellent. It is relatively small in terms of output but has a wide variety of soil structures across its scattered vineyards. The Soonwald and Hunsrück Mountains give shelter from cold winds and, with good sunshine and a low risk of frost, grapes can achieve good ripeness – late-picked versions are often made. Choice south-facing vineyards lie along the Nahe's tributaries and in the heart of the region, on the stretch of river that kinks and twists north from Schlossböckelheim to the spa town of Bad Münster-am-Stein. Around Schlossböckelheim the steep terraces make for spectacular scenery as well as being the source of many of the region's best wines. As in Rheinhessen, some of the most exciting developments are inland.

Another spectacular sight is the Traiser Bastei vineyard, where vines are planted beneath the Rotenfels Rock, said to be the highest cliff in Europe outside the Alps. The vineyard, planted in scree, produces excellent wines with varying degrees of sweetness.

Müller-Thurgau has lost its dominance in the Nahe. Riesling, although a relative latecomer by German standards, now accounts for a quarter of plantings and is predominant in the best sites. The finest wines have freshness with good, ripe fruit flavours, underpinned with mineral notes and spice, and good levels of acidity reminiscent of the best of the Mosel. Weissburgunder, Grauburgunder and Silvaner grapes are also found, especially in the north of the region. Lack of recognition often makes the region's wines good value and worthy of a search.

Riesling Trocken Weingut Keller, Rheinhessen. Clear apple fruit, stony minerality and refreshing acidity.

Nackenheimer Rothenberg Spätlese Weingut Gunderloch, Rheinhessen. Delicious fruit with tropical hints and pleasant sweetness on the palate with just the right level of acidity to balance.

Aulerde Riesling Trocken Grosses Gewächs Wittmann, Rheinhessen. Fresh fruit with tropical notes, hints of smoke in the clean, dry and mineral finish.

Traiser Rotenfels Riesling Spätlese Dr Crusius, Nahe. Honeyed peach fruit with spicy notes and fresh acidity.

Dorsheimer Burgberg Riesling Kabinett Schlossgut Diel, Nahe. Mouthwatering fruit with perfect levels of acidity and a sweet edge in the finish.

Schlossböckelheimer Felsenberg Riesling Spätlese Dönnhoff, Nahe. Glorious, spicy, tightly knit peach fruit, with gentle sweetness and good length.

LEFT *Looking south from Der Rote Hang over the town of Nierstein. On this 'red slope' beside the Rhein can be found four of the best vineyard sites in Rheinhessen: Hipping, Brudersberg, Pettenthal (in Nierstein) and Rothenberg (in Nackenheim).*

SOUTH-WEST GERMANY

Pfalz

The vineyards of the Pfalz run along the fringes of the Haardt Mountains (a continuation of the Vosges Mountains of France), making this a warm and dry area. For years the Pfalz was a source of bulk production, with the fertile soils producing large crops, especially in the south. Recently the region has developed dramatically and it is now providing some of Germany's most exciting wines.

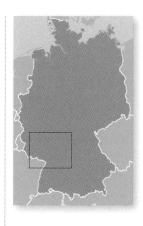

The great wines of the northern sector (the Mittelhaardt) have always been Riesling-dominated. Even in the Liebfraumilch days some growers remained resolute, making well-fruited and racy wines. The fashion for drier wines has been felt here, too, and with the warmer climate, more body can be achieved.

But it is in the south of the region that big changes have been made, with extensive plantings of Müller-Thurgau giving way to varieties such as Grauburgunder (Pinot Gris) and Weissburgunder (Pinot Blanc). Even oaked versions are to be found, adding a new dimension to spicy fruit. Riesling is on the increase here (as it should be) and traditional plantings of Traminer remain.

Almost 40 per cent of the region's wine is red, with Dornfelder, Blauer Portugieser and Spätburgunder making richer wines than in previous days, ranging in style from fruity with a gentle sweetness to dry and full flavoured.

Riesling Trocken Dr Bürklin-Wolf. Stylish and well-fruited with fine acidity.

Ungeheuer Grosses Gewächs Trocken Weingut Georg Mosbacher. Peach fruit with citrus notes and a mineral undercarriage.

Grauer Burgunder Kabinett Trocken Weingut O Rebholz. Gentle pear aromas lead to a soft and earthy palate with good balance and a long finish.

BELOW *Schloss Wachtenburg overlooks the Schlossberg vineyard at Wachenheim, a good, but not exceptional, source of Pfalz wine.*

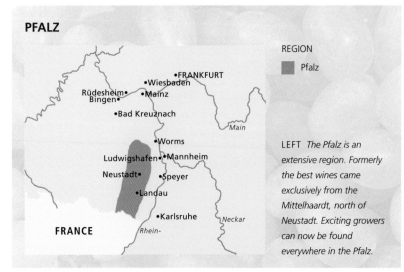

PFALZ

FRANKFURT
Wiesbaden
Rüdesheim• •Mainz
Bingen•
•Bad Kreuznach
Main
•Worms
Ludwigshafen• •Mannheim
Neustadt• •Speyer
•Landau
•Karlsruhe
Neckar
FRANCE
Rhein-

REGION
■ Pfalz

LEFT *The Pfalz is an extensive region. Formerly the best wines came exclusively from the Mittelhaardt, north of Neustadt. Exciting growers can now be found everywhere in the Pfalz.*

SOUTH-WEST GERMANY

Hessische Bergstrasse, Baden and Württemberg

Hessische Bergstrasse is a land of small growers with grapes only one of their crops. It is easy to see why, with its low production, its wine is seldom exported, but with Baden and Württemberg being third and fourth in terms of Germany's largest producers it is surprising that their wines are not easier to find. However, there is little that challenges the quality of the Mosel or Rhinelands.

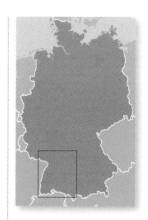

In Hessische Bergstrasse cooperatives dominate the wine scene. Riesling is usually fermented dry or *halbtrocken*, well fruited and elegant. Red wine accounts for around a quarter of production, with Spätburgunder the main variety.

Spätburgunder is also the main grape of Baden, occupying over a third of the vineyards. This is a long region with varied soils and climates and, therefore, a range of grape varieties. Müller-Thurgau, Grauburgunder and Weissburgunder are popular, with Riesling playing a minor role.

Spätburgunder Weingut Karl H. Johner, Baden. Plenty of berry fruit with more developed flavours beneath. Class act.

Malterdinger Bienenberg Weingut Huber. Elegant Weissburgunder with rich flavours of dried fruit in harmony with fresh acidity.

ABOVE *Terracing produces a practical solution for mechanization in the vineyard. Here vines grow in Baden, but where is the romance of the hand-worked vineyards of the Mosel?*

BERGSTRASSE, BADEN AND WÜRTTEMBERG

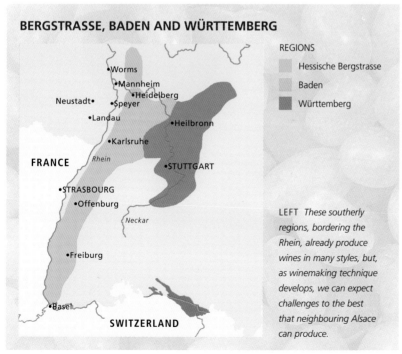

REGIONS
Hessische Bergstrasse
Baden
Württemberg

•Worms
•Mannheim
•Heidelberg
Neustadt•
•Speyer
•Landau
•Heilbronn
•Karlsruhe
FRANCE   *Rhein*
•STUTTGART
•STRASBOURG
•Offenburg
Neckar
•Freiburg
•Basel
SWITZERLAND

LEFT *These southerly regions, bordering the Rhein, already produce wines in many styles, but, as winemaking technique develops, we can expect challenges to the best that neighbouring Alsace can produce.*

Red wine truly dominates in Württemberg, weighing in with a huge 70 per cent of production. Although Spätburgunder is grown, the most popular varieties are Trollinger (Vernatsch) and Schwarzreisling (Pinot Meunier), and all three perform well in the mild climate, although sites are all-important in this landlocked region. Most reds are light, but some bolder versions are being fashioned. Weissherbst (rosé) wines are also made. Riesling remains the most planted white variety – almost 20 per cent.

CENTRAL GERMANY

Franken

Franconia is close to the Rheingau, yet its wines are totally different. While Müller-Thurgau remains the most planted variety, its popularity is declining. Riesling is also grown. A run of good Silvaner vintages has made excellent wines in this northern outpost of Bavaria. Bottled in the traditional *Bocksbeutel*, a short, round flask, these Silvaners have less aroma than many, but their full, dry flavours make them eminently suitable to partner food.

ABOVE *Würzburg is an extraordinary fusion of imposing buildings and humble dwellings, all intermingled with vineyards. Its distinctiveness is reflected in its individual wine.*

Most of the vineyards are on the hillsides that border the River Main and its tributaries as it flows to join the Rhein close to Hochheim in the Rheingau. The baroque city of Würzburg is at the heart of the region, with vineyards to both north and south. They are rich in limestone, which imparts a backbone to the wines. They are utterly distinctive. Here is the famous Stein vineyard, which gave its name to the region's wines – Steinwein. Red wines account for around 20 per cent of production, but in the west, where the climate is slightly warmer, some decent, sturdy Spätburgunder is being produced in the sandstone soils.

Silvaner 'Pur Mineral' Trocken Rudolf Fürst. Excellent apple fruit with a real grip on the palate.

Escherndorfer Lump Silvaner Trocken Grosses Gewächs Weingut Juliusspital Würzburg. Superb body with ripe apple fruit and silky palate.

FRANKEN

•Hochheim

•FRANKFURT

•Aschaffenburg

Main

①•Würzburg

•Mannheim

Nuremberg•

Neckar

REGION

Franken

VINEYARD

① Stein

LEFT *While the Franken wine region is extensive, prime sites for Silvaner are limited. Inferior Müller-Thurgau still persists on secondary land.*

EASTERN GERMANY
Saale-Unstrut and Sachsen

Both regions are in recovery from their time under the German Democratic Republic, when winemaking fell away. They are regions of extremes: Saale-Unstrut is the most northerly winemaking region in Germany and Sachsen (Saxony) the most easterly and smallest. Both suffer from a difficult climate, with frequent frosts at either end of the growing season, but the summers are warm. Winemaking is certainly possible, and there is a definite enthusiasm for wine.

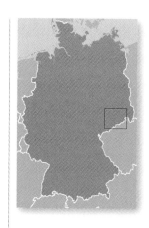

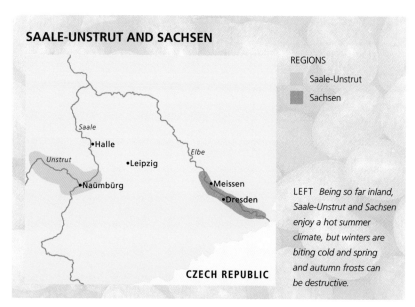

SAALE-UNSTRUT AND SACHSEN

REGIONS
Saale-Unstrut
Sachsen

LEFT *Being so far inland, Saale-Unstrut and Sachsen enjoy a hot summer climate, but winters are biting cold and spring and autumn frosts can be destructive.*

CZECH REPUBLIC

The area under vine in both regions has increased since unification, although neither is liable to return to its historical extent. Their vineyards are mainly on south-facing slopes in the proximity of rivers – the Saale, Unstrut and Saxony's Elbe – which help to temper the climate. The continental climate often brings magnificent summer weather, but the season is relatively short. Vines emerging from winter dormancy can be severely damaged by harsh spring frosts. Terraces can be steep, making work in the vineyards extremely difficult, and many have had to be repaired after years of neglect.

Riesling struggles to ripen in these northerly vineyards, as do red varieties, so the earlier ripening Müller-Thurgau is the favoured variety, approaching 20 per cent of the plantings in each region. Weissburgunder is also popular and Silvaner makes interesting wines in Saale-Unstrut. The wines are mainly dry, and only in the warmest of years are Spätlesen made. They have good depth of flavour but are generally quite tight in structure with decent acidity. Those of Saxony are slightly lighter in style. The higher levels of acidity are put to good use in the *Sekt* (sparkling wine) industry. Most wine is consumed in its region of origin, little being found outside Germany.

ABOVE *A great many of Germany's widespread vineyards are situated in attractive countryside. These pretty vineyards, overlooking the Elbe south-east of Meissen in Saxony, are no exception.*

Grauburgunder QbA Schloss Proschwitz, Sachsen. Baked pear aromas, good fruit on the palate with mineral notes and perfect balancing acidity.

●●● Regions 63–71

●●● Rest of Europe and Western Asia

With vineyards scattered from England and Wales to the eastern Mediterranean, the 'rest of Europe' is really a catch-all title embracing those other European countries which have some presence on the international wine scene. Their geographical diversity is remarkable. Politically there is an equal diversity, with change most apparent in those countries of the former Communist bloc that are now part of the EU.

It is claimed that global warming will produce riper grapes in the cool northern countries and that better winemaking knowledge and technique will improve wines from the hot south. This will happen only if the right level of investment is made in certain countries and there is the will to forsake quantity for quality. The results that can be achieved with such dedication and restraint are apparent in the best wines from all the countries in this chapter. Already a huge leap in quality has been achieved in Greece and Israel and the potential is there for an exciting future in the rest of the Balkans, particularly if good indigenous grape varieties are not lost to the international varieties.

EUROPE

Austria

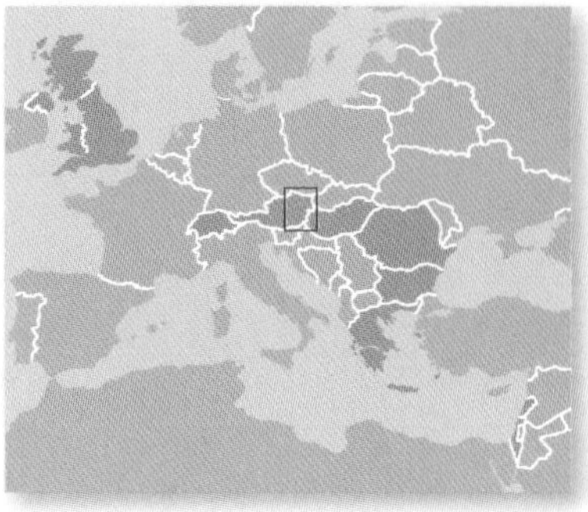

Austria's wine industry had to reinvent itself in the last two decades of the 20th century. After a damaging adulteration scandal in 1985, strict laws were introduced; a new wave of wines is now being produced, enjoyed at home and abroad. Attention has been paid to what grows best in each region, and winemakers have been sent abroad to learn their trade in other countries.

Growers no longer rely on local business but trade successfully in a variety of export markets. While the excellent late-harvest sweet wines are still made, the light, characterless offerings of the early 1980s have gone. First-rate dry whites are now the order of the day, together with fine, well-structured red wines. The widely differing soils and the climate contrasts between hills and plains ensure the wines, both white and red, are individual and full of character.

Lower Austria

Vineyards are located in the east of the country, mainly in the Niederösterreich surrounding Vienna. The various sub-regions have their own characteristics, with the steeply terraced Wachau area holding a prized place. Here both Riesling and Grüner Veltliner grapes reach perfection in vineyards bordering the Danube River. Even the lighter wines have good fruit.

Austrian wine classification
Wein: Ordinary table wine.
Qualitätswein (wine of quality) and Prädikatswein (certified wine): Quality designations governed by sugar content.
Landwein, Qualitätswein and Prädikatswein: Controlled origin and capped production.
DAC (Districtus Austriae Controllatus): Named wine regions for specific grapes.
Reserve: Full body and power.
Wachau: Quality levels governed by must weight and alcohol level – Steifeder, Federspiel, Smaragd.

LEFT *The Stadlmann family have owned their prized Mandel-Höh vineyard for over 175 years. These Zierfandler vines, which are a speciality of the Thermenregion, are approaching fifty years of age.*

WEINRIEDER

2007
Grüner Veltliner
Klassik

Riesling Smaragd 'Singerriedel' Weingut Franz Hirtzberger, Wachau.
Fine Riesling with power and luscious fruit held together with tight, fresh acidity.

Grüner Veltliner Smaragd 'Loibner Berg' Weingut F.X. Pichler, Wachau.
Intense and full flavoured, with mineral, spice and smoky notes.

Grüner Veltliner 'Klassic' Weingut Weinrieder, Weinviertel.
Light and fresh, with good fruit and hints of pepper.

Zierfandler 'Mandel-Höh' Weingut Stadlmann, Thermenregion.
Delicious fruit with mandarin and mango notes, mineral support and good balancing acidity.

Blaufränkisch Weingut Anita & Hans Nittnaus, Neusiedlersee.
Deep colour with full body, loaded with red fruit flavours.

Heurigen
The Austrian dialect word *Heuriger* means 'this year's', and the little taverns (*Heurigen*) scattered among the vineyards around Vienna, serving the new wine and regional food, have become an essential part of Viennese culture.

AUSTRIA

CZECH REPUBLIC

•Retz •Laa

Mistelbach•

Durnstein• •Krems •Stockerau

Danube

•St Pölten •VIENNA

•Baden

•Eisenstadt

Neckenmarkt•

•Oberwart

•Weiz

Fürstenfeld•

•Deutschlandsberg •Leibnitz

•Bad Radkersburg

SLOVENIA

SLOVAKIA

CENTRAL ALPS

HUNGARY

REGIONS
Niederösterreich (Lower Austria)
Wien (Vienna)
Burgenland
Steiermark (Syria)

SELECTED AREAS
1 Wachau
2 Kremstal
3 Kamptal
4 Traisental
5 Donauland
6 Weinviertel
7 Carnuntum
8 Thermenregion
9 Neusiedlersee
10 Neusiedlersee-Hügelland
11 Mittelburgenland
12 Wien (Austria)
13 Südburgenland
14 Südoststeiermark
15 Südsteiermark
16 Weststeiermark

In neighbouring Kremstal the valley opens out to a sunny plain that produces softer wines. The largest area is Weinviertel ('wine quarter'), dominated by Grüner Veltliner with its peppery fruit flavours, although pleasant reds are made from Zweigelt and Blauer Portugieser in the hotter areas.

The Thermenregion is noted for its Zierfandler and Rotgipfler grapes, giving wines with delicious fruit and fresh acidity in youth that age well, together with promising reds from St Laurent. Hearty Zweigelt reds are found in Carnuntum, which has both the Neusiedlersee and the Danube to regulate its climate. Carnuntum is the hottest wine region in Lower Austria and its wines are bold, with plenty of ripe fruit and tannins. Blaufrankisch also makes excellent reds. Wine is even produced within the city limits of Vienna: much of it slakes thirsts in local inns, or *Heurigen*.

Burgenland
South of the Thermenregion there is something of a change. The main variety is white Welschriesling (also known as Laski Rizling and unrelated to Riesling), which makes excellent botrytis-affected wines in Neusiedlersee and Neusiedlersee-Hügelland, when conditions are favourable. They are separated by the Neusiedler See, a long, shallow lake surrounded by reeds, encouraging the formation of mists in autumn, promoting the presence of botrytis, producing incomparable sweet wines. Fair Chardonnay (Morillon) and Sauvignon Blanc are also produced, plus good reds from Cabernet Sauvignon and Merlot.

In Mittelburgenland Blaufrankisch dominates, making sturdy, tannic reds. Steiermark produces spicy Sauvignon Blanc, well-fruited Chardonnay and delicious Traminers, rose-petal scented with just a hint of sweetness.

ABOVE *As can be seen from the map, Austria's vineyards are located in the east of the country, bordering the Czech Republic, Slovakia, Hungary and Slovenia. The recent success story of Austrian winemaking bodes well for its neighbours.*

EUROPE
Switzerland

Switzerland's chocolate-box image of high Alpine scenery might suggest that it is not a wine country. Until recently only visitors encountered its wines, as most production was consumed locally. With exports beginning to make an impact, quality is rising, though the country's varied climates and soils, not to mention a host of indigenous grape varieties, mean there is no unifying style.

The French-speaking area to the south-west of the country is the major producer, with the largest share coming from the Valais. South-facing slopes of the Rhône Valley are dominated by Chasselas (Fendant), giving light, gently fruited wines that are mainly dry and often have a touch of residual carbon dioxide. They reflect the terroir well, and fuller examples can be found. Pinot Noir is popular, too, and, when blended with Gamay, makes light and refreshing Dôle. These grapes predominate in the other areas in the region: Vaud, Geneva and Neuchâtel.

In the German-speaking east of the country, the red wines of Blauburgunder (Pinot Noir) proliferate, despite the harsh climate. Early-ripening Müller-Thurgau heads up the whites. In the warmer, Italian-speaking southern region (Ticino), Merlot makes good reds, from light and fruity to more serious, richly fruited styles. Pinot Noir is also found, especially at those altitudes where Merlot struggles.

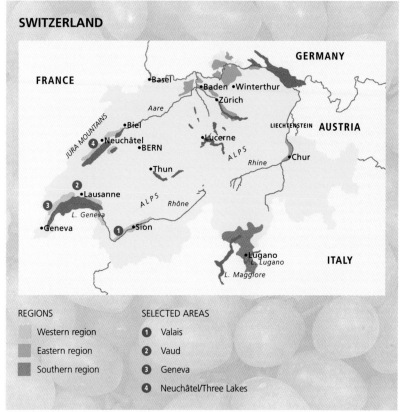

SWITZERLAND

REGIONS

◻ Western region
◼ Eastern region
◼ Southern region

SELECTED AREAS

❶ Valais
❷ Vaud
❸ Geneva
❹ Neuchâtel/Three Lakes

🍷🍷🍷 **Sassi Grossi Merlot, Ticino.** Big spicy, plummy fruit with floral notes. Bright fruit palate, hints of wild thyme and a long spicy finish.

🍷🍷 **Sept Dizains, Fendant de Chamoson, Valais.** Open, moderately fruited white. Drink young.

LEFT *These vines and an old wine press at Chamoson in the central Valais paint an idyllic picture but, in truth, Swiss wines have some catching up to do if they are to challenge those of their immediate neighbours, France, Italy, Austria and Germany.*

ABOVE *What the map can only hint at is the extent and enormity of Switzerland's mountains, totally unsuited to the growing of vines. They do, however, provide some shelter from the winds, and south-facing foothill slopes offer orientation to the sun.*

EUROPE

Luxembourg

The Grand Duchy of Luxembourg, considering its size, makes a reasonable amount of wine. In fact it has been making it for over 2,000 years. But its wines remain virtually unknown except by its inhabitants and those who have been there, for it is the home market that dominates sales. This is winemaking at the limits of its potential: Luxembourg lies even further north than Champagne.

🍷🍷 **Riesling 'Grevenmacher Fels' Clos des Rochers.** Clean and very dry, with citrus notes and good minerality.

🍷 **Crémant Poll-Fabaire Cuvée Brut.** Sparkling wine blended from several grape varieties, dry and refreshing with roundness and body when aged.

Müller-Thurgau, locally known as Rivaner, is the most widely planted grape variety, in vineyards concentrated along the stretch of the Moselle River that overlooks Germany's Obermosel and Moseltor. The wines it produces are genuine but innocuous. However, the most interesting wines are made from a clutch of white varieties more often associated with Alsace – Pinot Gris, Pinot Blanc, Auxerrois and, of course, Riesling. Most of the production is dry, refreshing and easy drinking. It should be ideal in favourable sites when production is limited and the weather kind.

The old Elbling vine is also grown, as it is in the higher reaches of the Mosel in Germany, and in both countries it produces a sharp, acidic wine in both still and sparkling forms. The only red grape grown in any significant quantity is Pinot Noir, but its production is best reserved for blending in the local sparkling wine, Crémant de Luxembourg, which is generally crisp and fresh and made by the méthode traditionelle. A small quantity of sweeter wine is made in vendange tardive, vin de glace or vin de paille styles when conditions are favourable.

RIGHT *Luxembourg is so far north that chaptalization (the addition of sugar to the grape must at fermentation to make up for the under-ripeness of the grapes) is standard practice. Acidic grapes are, of course, perfect for the production of sparkling wine.*

FAR RIGHT *Vineyards overlook the pretty town of Ehnen on the banks of the Moselle River. A wine museum, belonging to the Luxembourg state, was established here in 1978. Luxembourg is proud of its long winemaking tradition.*

LUXEMBOURG

BELGIUM

GERMANY

Echternach•

Mertert•
Grevenmacher•

Mosel

Wormeldange•

LUXEMBOURG•

Wellenstein•

Schengen•

FRANCE

Moselle

REGION

Moselle Luxembourgoise

EUROPE
England and Wales

Wine has been imported to Britain for over 2,000 years, yet the Romans maintained successful vineyards in Britain during their occupation. Only in the latter part of the 20th century did modern vine growing really take off. Commercial winemaking was re-introduced by Major-General Sir Guy Salisbury-Jones at his Hambledon vineyard in the early 1950s.

Since then almost 400 vineyards have been established, with around 100 producing wineries, some growers preferring to sell their crop to other winemakers. There is an unofficial regulatory system for English wines, with descriptions such as 'Quality Wine' or 'Regional Wine' seen on labels. 'British wine' is a concoction made from imported concentrate and should be avoided by serious wine drinkers!

The weather problem

Britain's climate is a perennial subject of conversation for its population, and it is without doubt on the edge of where grapes can ripen successfully. Original plantings were mainly of early-ripening hybrids such as Müller-Thurgau and Reichensteiner, more often associated with Germany, another marginal climate. But it is not just ripening that

Three Choirs Classic Cuvee. Light, fresh and balanced sparkling wine with clean apple/pear fruit.

Camel Valley Bacchus Dry. Open fruit aromas, clean fresh palate with grapefruit flavours dominant and a wonderful zesty finish. Excellent!

Pinot Noir/ Chardonnay Somborne Valley. Fresh with citric notes alongside touches of green apple to give a big finish.

Wickham Fumé Dry. Light with notes of pear drops in the mouth.

Stanlake Park 'Regatta'. Clean fruit salad aromas followed with notes of pear drops. Not huge but fine.

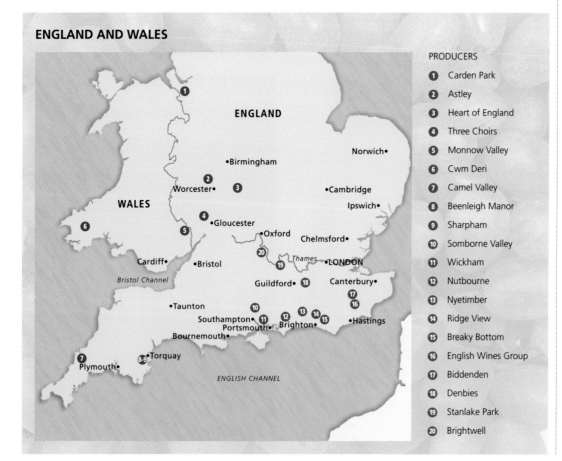

ENGLAND AND WALES

PRODUCERS
1. Carden Park
2. Astley
3. Heart of England
4. Three Choirs
5. Monnow Valley
6. Cwm Deri
7. Camel Valley
8. Beenleigh Manor
9. Sharpham
10. Somborne Valley
11. Wickham
12. Nutbourne
13. Nyetimber
14. Ridge View
15. Breaky Bottom
16. English Wines Group
17. Biddenden
18. Denbies
19. Stanlake Park
20. Brightwell

LEFT In 1086 there were 46 vineyards in England. By the early 16th century their numbers had grown to 139, owned by the Crown, the Church or the nobility.

RIGHT Stanlake Park vineyard was first established in 1979 but the house is much older and the estate older still, dating back to 1186.

bottle. Being priced similarly to Champagnes in the middle range of the market, they are not cheap and will always face competition from cheaper imports of lesser sparkling wines. Sparkling wines based on hybrids can be very drinkable at a moderate cost. Because the climate is so variable, harvests for still or sparkling wines can be lost, and this generally has to be factored in to prices.

Sparkling wine from England and Wales is impressing internationally, with Nyetimber's 1998 Blanc de Blancs scooping the Gold Medal and best in class at the 2009 Chardonnay du Monde competition. It is little wonder that major Champagne companies are paying the UK wine industry the compliment of seriously investing in it.

Boutique wineries
Most English and Welsh vineyards are small in comparison with those elsewhere. The biggest by area is Denbies in Surrey at 106 ha/260 acres, followed by Three Choirs in Gloucestershire. The largest producer by volume, however, is the English Wines Group based in Kent selling under the Chapel Down, Lamberhurst and Tenterden labels.

causes problems for growers. Rain at flowering brings uneven fruit set, and high humidity can lead to rot in the crop. Not surprisingly, most vineyards are found in the south-east corner of England where the climate is relatively warm and dry. Vines are also grown in south-west England and South Wales, and there is even a scattering of vineyards in the Midlands and North of England.

Production is mainly white, with an increasing amount of pink, and a little red is made from varieties such as Rondo and Dornfelder. A few producers grow grapes under cloche, such as the Cabernet Sauvignon and Merlot produced at Beenleigh Manor in Devon.

Sparkling wines

A small quantity of late-harvest wine is produced but, stylistically, white wines tend to be dry and fresh with gentle aromas of fruits and flowers. Acidity can be high but this adds to their refreshing quality. Such levels of acidity are excellent for the production of sparkling wine.

The limestone-rich soils in parts of the south of England are similar to those found in Champagne, and the climate is not dissimilar. Plantings of its three great grapes, Chardonnay, Pinot Noir and Pinot Meunier, are resulting in fine wines. Estates such as Nyetimber produce striking wines by the traditional method, making the secondary fermentation in

EUROPE

Hungary

Tucked away in the far north-east corner of Hungary lies one of the greatest wine-producing regions of the world, Tokaj. During decades of Communist rule, Hungarian winemaking seriously declined in quality. But memories remained of the delicious nectar that had once been made. After the fall of Communism there was a gold rush to acquire parcels of this precious land.

Tokaji

The wine of Tokaj (known as Tokaji) was the first to use botrytis-affected grapes in its production. Autumnal morning mists from the Bodrog River set up noble rot in predominantly Furmint grapes, gradually intensifying their natural sugar and acidity. Two other grapes complete the cast: Hárslevelű and Sárga Muskotály (Muscat à Petits Grains).

First a dry base wine is made. When the botrytis-affected grapes (aszú) are harvested – a job that was traditionally done using a hod called a puttonyo – they are piled together

for around a week. The unctuous, free-run juice that oozes out is called essencia. This is barely able to ferment, with the yeasts struggling to work in the presence of so much sugar, but its high level of acidity and syrupy consistency make it a heady, concentrated and mouth-watering essence of grapes. The remaining grapes are turned into a paste and added to the dry base wine to soak for a week or so before the wine is put in barrels to ferment and mature slowly.

Tokaji is classified according to the quantity of aszú grapes added to each barrel, measured in terms of the

BELOW Hungary's wine culture is centuries old. Although the growing season is shorter than in more southerly vineyards and average temperatures lower, autumns in Hungary are warm, ripening grapes successfully. In 1997 a total of 22 separate wine regions was recognized officially. There is considerable diversity in Hungary's wines.

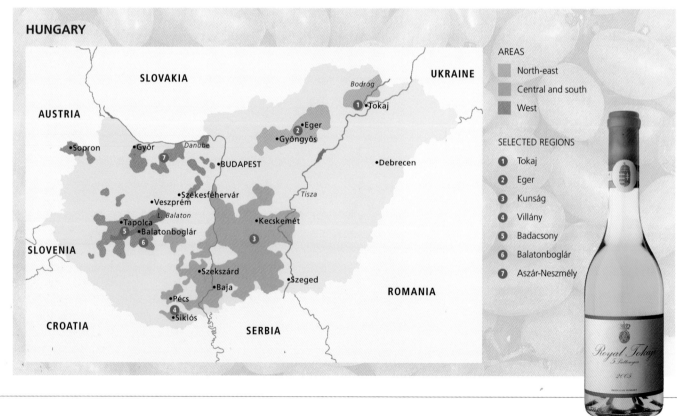

HUNGARY

SLOVAKIA

AUSTRIA

UKRAINE

•Sopron   •Győr   *Danube*   *Bodrog*

•Győr   **BUDAPEST**   ❶•Tokaj

❼   ❷•Eger
•Gyöngyös

•Debrecen

•Székesfehérvár
•Veszprém   *Tisza*
L. Balaton
•Tapolca   •Kecskemét
❺•Balatonboglár
❻   ❸

SLOVENIA

•Szekszárd
•Baja   •Szeged

•Pécs   ROMANIA
❹
•Siklós

CROATIA   SERBIA

AREAS

North-east
Central and south
West

SELECTED REGIONS

❶ Tokaj
❷ Eger
❸ Kunság
❹ Villány
❺ Badacsony
❻ Balatonboglár
❼ Aszár-Neszmély

ABOVE RIGHT *Some of Hungary's best and most characterful white wines originate in Badacsony, between Lake Balaton and the extinct volcano, Mount Badacsony. Here, sandy soils retain heat and drain well, their gentle slopes aiding exposure to sunlight. Traces of volcanic residue contribute to the flavour of the wines.*

number of *puttonyos* they would fill – three, four, five or six, or around eight for the intensely sweet *aszú essencia*. There is also a growing fashion for making late-harvest wines without oak ageing. This results in a fresher style. In addition there are *Szamorodni* ('as it comes') wines, either dry or sweet, which do not have *aszú* berries added – they are similar to sherry in style.

Other wine regions

Table winemaking flourishes throughout Hungary, using international and traditional varieties. The largest area under vine is in the central southern region of Kunság, but its wines are yet to achieve the quality of other areas. Fine reds originate across the Danube in the warmer climate of Villány, where Kékfrankos (Blaufrankisch), Cabernet Sauvignon and Cabernet Franc are the best varieties.

On the shores of Lake Balaton, in the Badacsony and Balatonboglár regions, Szürkebarát (Pinot Gris) gives flavoursome, spicy whites, and the local Kéknyelű makes a lighter, more floral style. Other good whites are found in Aszár-Neszmély, with Sauvignon Blanc and Chardonnay appearing. Hilltop is the market leader.

Bull's Blood, or Egri Bikavér, was once the most famous of Hungarian red wines and is still produced mainly in the Eger region. Although its style is now generally lighter, robust examples are still made.

EUROPE
Romania

Romania holds considerable promise. It has produced legendary wines: Cotnari was one of the world's great sweet wines. What went wrong? The dead hand of Communism. Wines were produced for quantity, many to the taste of alcohol-obsessed USSR, with little attempt to match grape varieties to soil, situation or climate. Europe's bargain basement became the obvious target.

Generally, Romania's climate is vine friendly: though winters can be harsh and summers hot and dry, good quality Cabernet Sauvignon, Merlot, Sauvignon Blanc, Chardonnay, Gewürztraminer and other international varieties can be grown. So too can a raft of indigenous grapes with inimitable names, such as Fetească Neagră, Băbească Neagră, Grasă, Frâncușă and Tămâioasă, the richly scented frankincense grape, though few of these are exported.

Happily, Cotnari is being revived in its traditional home, Romanian Moldova, where Romania's most extensive vineyards produce mostly white wines. In the higher temperatures of the hills of Muntenia red wines proliferate,

the vineyards of Dealul Mare being the best known. In neighbouring Oltenia it is much the same, with individual hills and valleys specializing in different styles of wine. Count Dracula's Transylvania, at a higher altitude, is cooler and produces crisper, fresher whites.

LEFT *A vineyard and church in the Dealul Mare area in the foothills of the Carpathian Mountains. South-sloping hills ensure perfect exposure to the sun in this, the hottest wine-growing area in Romania.*

BELOW *Romania is the sixth largest producer of wine in Europe. Most of it is consumed within the country, and two-thirds is white. As new wineries are built, the wines will improve and more will be seen in export markets.*

River Route Limited Edition Merlot Colinele Dobrogei. Old-vine Merlot with sweet fruit and a touch of oak, improving with exposure to the air.

ROMANIA

UKRAINE

HUNGARY

•Satu Mare

•Botosani

①

•Iasi MOLDOVA

•Oradea

•Cluj-Napoca

•Bacau

•Arad

③

•Timisoara

•Sibiu

•Brasov •Foscani
•Tirgu Mores

•Braila

②

•Ploiesti

SERBIA

•Craiova

•BUCHAREST

④

BLACK SEA

Danube

BULGARIA

REGIONS

Moldova

Muntenia and Oltenia

Dobrogea

Transylvania

Banat and Crisana-Maramures

SELECTED SUBREGIONS

① Cotnari

② Dealul Mare

③ Tarnave

④ Murfatlar

EUROPE

Bulgaria

Like Romania, Bulgaria is just emerging from the dark ages. The difference, however, is that Bulgaria was producing export-quality Cabernets and Merlots back in the 1970s, as well as pleasant Chardonnay. They were good enough – and cheap enough – to woo many drinkers from their traditional claret. Under troubled economic conditions Bulgaria promptly lost its way.

The potential for quality wine in Bulgaria has always been recognized. Since the demise of the Communist regime international investment has been an important element in the splitting up of the vast old wineries and the establishment of modern, quality-conscious (even boutique) wineries. Bessa Valley, Santa Sarah and Oriachovitza are among the leaders, mainly concentrating on the principal French varieties. Cabernet Sauvignon is the most widely planted grape in the country.

Native varieties are also, thankfully, thriving. Misket produces highly aromatic white wines in Rose Valley. Gamza-based reds are popular at home, while Mavrud and Melnik are capable of giving substantial reds with an ageing potential of 10 to 20 years.

To the wine lover, the name of the producer is of greater importance than that of the area from which the wine comes, but a Controliran system, similar to AC or DOC, was set up in expectation of Bulgaria's entry into the EU.

BELOW LEFT *Bulgaria's wineries are scattered throughout the country in no fewer than 47 designated regions. As yet the names of these regions have little significance in export markets.*

BELOW RIGHT *Traditional mule carts pass vineyards near Sliven in the East Thracian Valley. Vini Sliven are now employing the modern technique of ageing some of their wine in barriques.*

Bessa Valley Winery 'Enira', Pazarjik Region. Deeply coloured, attractively scented blend of several French varieties with a creamy flavour and balancing tannin.

BULGARIA

REGIONS

- Northern/Danube Plain
- Eastern/Black Sea
- Sub-Balkan/Rose Valley
- Southwest/Struma Valley
- Southern/Thracian Lowlands

ROMANIA
•Vidin
Danube
•Russe
2
DANUBIAN PLAIN
1
3
•Preslav •Varna
SERBIA
BALKAN MOUNTAINS
•SOFIA
3
•Karlovo 4 •Sliven
6 5
THRACIAN PLAIN •Burgas
7 •Plovdiv
Perushtitza• BLACK SEA
•Assenovgrad
9 8
MACEDONIA •Damianitza
•Melnik
TURKEY
GREECE

PRODUCERS

1. Suhindol
2. Stork Nest
3. Vini Sliven
4. Domaine Boyar
5. Oriachovitza
6. Santa Sarah
7. Bessa Valley
8. Vinzavod Assenovgrad
9. Damianitza

EUROPE

Greece

In recent years Greece has turned itself from a shameful underperformer into one of Europe's most exciting wine producers. While new technology and informed winemaking are transforming the wines, not everything has gone international. Many native grape varieties – some perhaps descended from the vines of the ancient Greeks – are revealing their inherent qualities.

First-time visitors to Greece may be shocked when they encounter Retsina, the extraordinary confection drunk copiously in the tavernas of Attica. Whatever the quality of its base wine, its Aleppo pine resin blots out all else. In contrast, find a Xinomavro from a good producer in Macedonia, from Náoussa or Amyndeo in particular, and the quality of this indigenous grape is abundantly clear: it makes a huge red wine with a wonderful bouquet.

Good producers can be found in most parts of Greece, on the mainland and the islands. Their wines range from delicate or powerful whites, through generally full-bodied reds to a host of sweet wines, often Muscats or Mavrodaphnes. The producers may be small and specialist, such as Gerovassiliou or Aivalis, or nationwide, such as the impressively consistent Boutari.

LEFT *The Kir-Yianni vineyards in Náoussa were planted with Merlot and Syrah in the 1980s. Greater emphasis is now placed on native Xinomavro, the grape used in their top wine, Ramnista.*

🍷 **Tsantali Cabernet Sauvignon Organic, Halkidiki.** Ripe, sweet Cabernet Sauvignon with cedar/mint nose.

🍷🍷 **Hatzidakis Assyrtiko, Santorini.** Crisp food wine with refreshing lemon acidity.

🍷🍷🍷 **Samos Anthemis Vin de Liqueur.** Alluring Muscat nose and flavours of raisins, nuts and orange, sweet yet not cloying.

GREECE

MACEDONIA · BULGARIA · THRACE · TURKEY · ALBANIA · Thessaloniki · Mt Olympus ▲ · EPIRUS · THESSALY · AEGEAN SEA · IONIAN ISLANDS · CENTRAL GREECE · Evia · ATTICA · AEGEAN ISLANDS · ATHENS · Tinos · CYCLADES ISLANDS · PELOPONNESE · MEDITERRANEAN SEA · Crete

SELECTED APPELLATIONS

1. Côtes de Meliton
2. Náoussa
3. Goumenissa
4. Amyndeo
5. Zitsa
6. Rapsani
7. Ankhíalos
8. Nemea
9. Pátras
10. Mantinia
11. Cephalonia
12. Lemnos
13. Sámos
14. Páros
15. Santorini
16. Rhodes
17. Archanes
18. Daphnes
19. Peza
20. Sitia

LEFT *Although Greece can be fiercely hot in summer, the moderating effects of the Mediterranean and Aegean are conducive to successful vine growing in many parts of the mainland and islands.*

WESTERN ASIA

Israel

In Biblical times vines were important in the Holy Land. Following the establishment of modern Israel in 1948, the country began to export mainly Kiddush wines, sweet and red, for religious ceremony. More recently Israel has found considerable success with high quality table wine. As with all of Israel's extensive agricultural industry, the supply of water is critical to success.

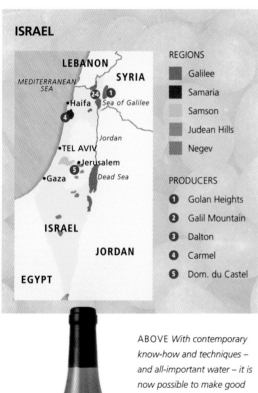

ISRAEL

LEBANON
SYRIA
MEDITERRANEAN SEA
•Haifa — Sea of Galilee
Jordan
•TEL AVIV
•Jerusalem
•Gaza — Dead Sea
ISRAEL
JORDAN
EGYPT

REGIONS
- Galilee
- Samaria
- Samson
- Judean Hills
- Negev

PRODUCERS
1. Golan Heights
2. Galil Mountain
3. Dalton
4. Carmel
5. Dom. du Castel

ABOVE *With contemporary know-how and techniques – and all-important water – it is now possible to make good quality table wines in many parts of Israel.*

ABOVE RIGHT *Ein Zivan vineyard provides grapes for Israel's third-largest winery, Golan Heights. The importance of wine in ancient times can be seen in the nearby Talmudic village, a reconstruction of life 2,000 years ago.*

The table wine revolution began in the Golan Heights, where the cooler climate suits Cabernet Sauvignon, Merlot, Sauvignon Blanc and Chardonnay. Good varietal wines are sold under the Yarden label of the Golan Heights Winery. Chardonnay and the Bordeaux varieties also thrive in the stony soils of the cool-climate Judean Hills, with Domaine du Castel foremost among producers. In Galilee, Galil Mountain and Dalton lead the way, and Carmel (founded by a member of the Rothschild family in 1882) has recently built a new winery here.

Samaria remains the largest region in terms of quantity. It and the more southerly Samson region were formerly known for their sweetish reds. Now both produce sound whites from Chardonnay and Sauvignon Blanc and well-rounded reds from Bordeaux varieties.

Domaine du Castel 'C' Blanc du Castel, Judean Hills. Full flavoured, barrel-fermented Chardonnay with yellow and white fruit dominant, with mineral notes behind.

Galil Mountain Winery Yiron, Galilee. Complex and well-flavoured blend with plenty of berry fruit alongside hints of vanilla and toast.

Golan Heights Winery Yarden Chardonnay, Galilee. Fresh open fruit dominated by apples and pears with a soft, full finish.

● ● ● Regions 72–76

South Africa

South Africa is a long-established wine-producing country. Its first Cape wine was made in 1659, and the famed Constantia vineyard was founded as long ago as 1685, making it an exact contemporary of composers Bach and Handel. The country was a major exporter of wine during the 19th century but the arrival of phylloxera and the Boer War heralded a decline in the trade, which was subsequently compounded by world reaction to apartheid.

As export markets reopened following the collapse of apartheid, South Africa almost started from scratch in the 1990s. This is basically a home-grown industry, with such black-equality initiatives as the Thandi Project – a unique partnership between the state, the community and private enterprise, whose aim is to create ownership, empowerment and a sustainable business entity for the community – now firmly established.

Virus has traditionally been the biggest problem for estates throughout the Cape, resulting in green and unripe flavours in some wines. Regular replanting of classic European varietal clones and careful vineyard management has this under control.

CAPE PENINSULA

Stellenbosch and Constantia

Without doubt, Stellenbosch is the major force in the South African wine industry and also one of the most beautiful – and most photographed – wine regions of the world. Although it is not the largest producer in terms of vineyard area, it is certainly the most significant for overall quality. At its centre is the beautiful university town of Stellenbosch, with its wealth of Dutch colonial architecture and a clutch of rugby Springboks.

Lying at the foot of the Simonsberg Mountain, just an hour's drive from Cape Town, Stellenbosch is rich in history and culture, and has become a leading centre for viticultural research, with undergraduate and postgraduate courses.

False Bay

The principal influence on wine production in the region is the cooling breeze emanating from False Bay, a huge Atlantic inlet south-west of Stellenbosch, bounded to the west by the Cape of Good Hope. Winds from here moderate what would otherwise be excessively high summer temperatures. Additionally, the variety of microclimates, soil structures and exposures on the flanks of the Stellenbosch, Simonsberg, Helderberg and Drakensteinberg Mountains gives birth to a diversity of wine styles. Irrigation can be used throughout the region, but with the winter rainfall well retained in the soil structure it is not such an important factor here as in many vineyards in other parts of the world.

'Today, praise be to God, wine was made for the first time from Cape grapes.'

JAN VAN RIEBEECK,
2 FEBRUARY 1659

BELOW *The Oude Nektar Estate is the principal source of Neil Ellis's red wines. Its deep, red, clay soils are irrigated by the area's notably high rainfall.*

Replanting

In the difficult years of the 20th century, when it was almost impossible to sell quality Cape wines, most grapes were grown for the table, grape-juice concentrate or distillation. Gradually, traditional plantings of Chenin Blanc and Colombard destined for the distillery have given way to fine red varieties such as Cabernet Sauvignon, Merlot and Shiraz, which are well suited to the water-retentive, decomposed granite- and clay-based soils found here. The cooler areas, notably the upper slopes, are prime sites for Sauvignon Blanc and Chardonnay; some plantings, such as Rustenberg Estate's Five Soldiers vineyard on the mid-slopes of the Rustenberg Mountain, are making exceptional wines to rival the world's finest Chardonnays. However, red wines are emerging as the kings here: in general, they possess depth and generosity while retaining their elegance.

Classification

As with other wine regions in South Africa, the Stellenbosch vineyard areas have recently been divided into subregions or wards, delineated according to soil type and climatic conditions. Where grape varieties have been matched to the characteristics of individual vineyard sites, this has resulted in more terroir-driven wines. But the names of these wards are infrequently seen on labels, largely because many wines are blended from different origins within Stellenbosch – and indeed the Cape – to create more homogeneous wines. However, the classification is a clear indication that we may see more distinctive examples arriving on the shelves in the coming years.

Tygerberg

The smaller district of Tygerberg is found at the very edge of Cape Town and, until recently, most of its production was sold off for blending. In wards such as Philadelphia, some great wines are now being made in the mineral-rich soils where the Atlantic breezes help temper the climate.

Estates such as Capaia and Havana Hills are already making excellent reds. Capaia is the result of international investment (French and German), and its Bordeaux Blend is receiving warm critical acclaim, as is Kobus from Havana Hills. Although they are still in their infancy, the Capaia Sauvignon Blanc vineyards seem set firm to produce classy wines in future.

Rustenberg Chardonnay, Stellenbosch. World-class barrel-fermented Chardonnay showing incredible fruit concentration and depth.

Rust en Vrede Merlot, Stellenbosch. Fabulous value, intense spicy plum fruit with hints of lead pencil and toast.

Neil Ellis Vineyard Selection Cabernet Sauvignon, Stellenbosch. Intense blackcurrant with touches of violet and eucalyptus. A real mouthful.

Vergelegen Shiraz, Stellenbosch. Elegant yet big (and alcoholic) Shiraz with notes of pepper and chocolate.

Guardian Peak Frontier, Stellenbosch. Complex fruit flavours, plum and berry notes dominant.

Vesuvian expansion
Philip van Zyl, editor of *Platter's South African Wine Guide*, once likened the expansion of the country's wine industry to a 'Vesuvian outpouring of energy and enthusiasm that pauses just long enough to siphon something of itself into a bottle before whooshing off again.'

RIGHT *Bartolomeu Dias discovered False Bay in 1488, calling it 'the gulf between the mountains', as if foretelling its influence on future South African wine growing.*

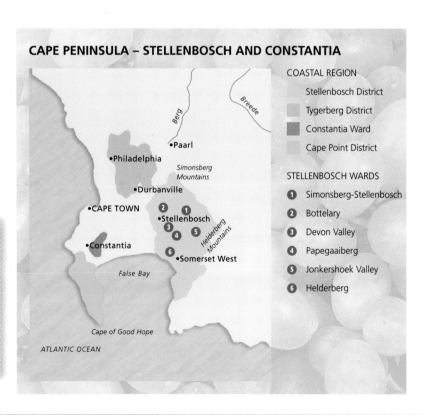

CAPE PENINSULA – STELLENBOSCH AND CONSTANTIA

COASTAL REGION
Stellenbosch District
Tygerberg District
Constantia Ward
Cape Point District

STELLENBOSCH WARDS
1 Simonsberg-Stellenbosch
2 Bottelary
3 Devon Valley
4 Papegaaiberg
5 Jonkershoek Valley
6 Helderberg

RIGHT *The Constantia vineyards lie within the Table Mountain National Park, in the pretty suburbs of Cape Town.*

BELOW *One of the world's great sweet wines is Vin de Constance, made from the same Muscat de Frontignan clone that was first planted in the 17th century.*

Historic Constantia

Constantia, one of the earliest wine areas of the Cape to be planted, is today an affluent suburb of Cape Town, and the property development of recent decades has meant that only a few estates remain. It does however produce quite exciting Sauvignon Blanc, thanks to the 'Cape Doctor', the south-easterly breeze that cools the vineyards. This wind is credited with giving the wines a definite grassy character, but the microclimate is such that rot can be a problem and careful vineyard management is essential for healthy fruit and the quality of the resultant wines.

These, of course, are dry wines, but it was a dessert Muscat that brought Constantia great fame. The Constantia vineyards are nowhere near as extensive as they once were, but there is still room for the production of a small amount of delectable Vin de Constance, the Emperor's Wine, from the Klein Constantia Estate, grown on the original 17th-century site.

CAPE PENINSULA

Paarl

Paarl, whose name derives from the Afrikaans for 'pearl', is one of the largest of South Africa's wine-producing regions. It lies over the Simonsberg Mountain from Stellenbosch and does not therefore benefit from the same cooling influences of the breezes from False Bay. Summers, then, are hot – although not excessively so – making it a difficult task for winegrowers and makers to select the perfect varieties.

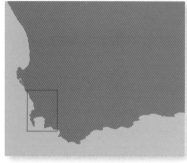

Wide variety

It is not only the climate that dictates the choice of grape varieties in Paarl. Soils vary throughout the region, and granite, sandstone and Malmesbury slate are all found. These, together with the differing altitudes and exposures of the vineyards, give rise to a wide variety of wine styles. The main reds come from Shiraz, Mourvèdre, Cabernet Sauvignon, Merlot and, of course, Pinotage (see page 166), but there are also pockets of Pinot Noir, such as at the Glen Carlou estate, that are attracting attention. Chenin is still the most widely planted white variety, but quality is being shown from Viognier, Sémillon and Chardonnay. Winter rains and water-retentive soils mean irrigation is required only in extreme years. Paarl is the home of the KWV cellars, formerly the powerful state cooperative but now in private hands. Also to be found here is a wealth of smaller producers.

A long history
The earliest European settlers in Paarl were the Dutch, who were first granted farms in 1687. Their aim was to be able to provide fresh food and water for the ships of the Dutch East India Company docking at Cape Town on their way to and from the East. French Huguenots followed shortly after this, bringing with them their useful knowledge of winemaking.

Franschhoek

Although Paarl is the catch-all designation for many of the wines, the wards of Franschhoek and Wellington are frequently seen as specific wine origins. Franschhoek ('French corner', named after the French Huguenot settlers) lies in a steep-sided valley resembling an elongated bowl. The central section on the sandy valley floor has never really produced wines of great note, but grapes grown on the hillside sites fare much better. Because of the topography, the vineyards are not exposed to full sun throughout the day, so they are best suited to varieties such as Sauvignon Blanc or grapes grown for the famous Cape sparkling wine Cap Classique, as at the Cabrière Estate, whose acclaimed Cuvée Reserve is blended from Chardonnay and Pinot Noir.

Massive investment has taken place in recent years to terrace the vineyards higher up the mountains. Although the vines are still too young to give definite results, it is hoped that this may be the source of good reds in the future. For the traveller, the charming, small town of Franschhoek is not to be missed and is becoming a gourmet's paradise.

Wellington

Further north in Wellington, temperatures rise and soil structures become quite complex. Known locally as Cartref soils, they are poor with a sandy surface and have a substructure of decomposed granite, with great variations even within 5 m/16 ft, yet this does not seem to cause problems for the wineries. Far from it, it adds complexity to the grapes from a single area, thereby enhancing the wine.

Vineyard techniques

Canopy management is essential here. Whereas in other regions leaf is taken away to expose grapes to the sun, here the vine is encouraged to bush out to protect the fruit from the sun's strong rays, thereby extending the growing season and allowing not only sugar/acid ripeness but also ripeness of tannins within the skins. Estates such as Mischa, which developed its huge vine nursery operation into wine production in the late 1990s, now make top class Cabernet Sauvignon and Shiraz varietals, while the results for white varietals Sauvignon Blanc and Viognier are also encouraging.

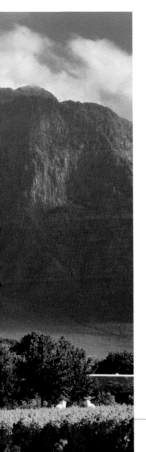

LEFT *Boschendal is an old estate with a Dutch colonial manor dating back to 1812. The Cape's biggest single estate, its vineyards cover 254 ha/628 acres.*

Glen Carlou Pinot Noir, Paarl. Juicy fruit aromas and palate backed by well integrated oak. Delicious.

Pierre Jourdan Blanc de Blancs, Cabrière Estate. Fresh Chardonnay style with vanilla notes and an underpinning minerality. A great aperitif.

Mischa Eventide Cabernet Sauvignon, Wellington. Fantastic Cabernet brimming with blackcurrant fruit, filling the mouth with a big, stylish finish.

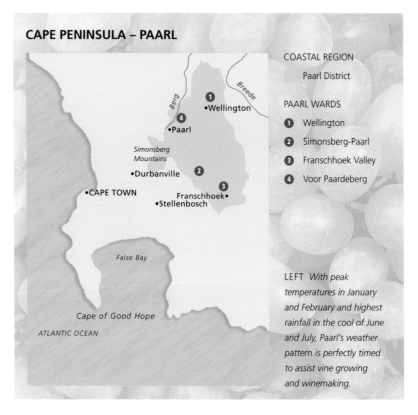

CAPE PENINSULA – PAARL

Berg
Breede
① •Wellington
④
•Paarl
Simonsberg Mountains
•Durbanville **②**
•CAPE TOWN **③**
Franschhoek•
•Stellenbosch
False Bay
Cape of Good Hope
ATLANTIC OCEAN

COASTAL REGION

Paarl District

PAARL WARDS
① Wellington
② Simonsberg-Paarl
③ Franschhoek Valley
④ Voor Paardeberg

LEFT *With peak temperatures in January and February and highest rainfall in the cool of June and July, Paarl's weather pattern is perfectly timed to assist vine growing and winemaking.*

WESTERN CAPE – SOUTHERN VINEYARDS

Overberg

Overberg is regarded as one of South Africa's most promising fine-wine regions. The more southerly ward of Walker Bay, with the major wineries of Hamilton Russell and Bouchard Finlayson, is pioneering high-class Pinot Noir and Chardonnay. Meanwhile, close to Africa's southernmost tip at Cape Agulhas, the small village of Elim has given its name to some of the Cape's newest vineyards, producing delicious cool-climate Sauvignon Blanc and Merlot.

Walker Bay

Here the soil is a mixture of clay and gravel with shale beneath, providing a source of moisture for the vines and a perfect ground for both Pinot Noir and Chardonnay. A climate of warm, rather than hot, summers and frost-free winters is ensured by the Atlantic Ocean: its breezes keep the vines cool and slow later development, giving grapes with more complexity for the winemakers to turn into classic examples. As well as the two great Burgundian varieties (Pinot Noir and Chardonnay), Sauvignon Blanc fares well, while the Italian varieties Sangiovese and Nebbiolo, developed by Peter Finlayson and used in his Hannibal blend, are also well suited to the terroir.

Vineyards share the area with the beautiful Fynbos, the diverse heathland landscape where the Cape's rich wild floral life is allowed to develop naturally, providing a dramatic backdrop for the vines.

Elgin

The Fynbos also surrounds the ward of Elgin in the Kogelberg Biosphere, a UNESCO World Heritage Site. This used to be apple country, and there is a saying that where apples grow well, vines do also, which is certainly true here. The decomposed shale soil with its underlying clay has a high mineral content, giving great underpinning to cool climate and aromatic varieties such as Sauvignon Blanc, Pinot Noir and Riesling. Cabernet Sauvignon, Shiraz and Merlot do well

– with correct canopy control – and produce wines that offer elegance as well as mouth-filling power. Irrigation is used sparingly here, and only to ensure the health of the vine – with too much irrigation vines can become lazy, not putting down deep roots, which in turn can lead to a lack of mineral complexity in the grapes.

It is from Elgin that some Stellenbosch producers are now sourcing a part of their Sauvignon Blanc requirement in order to gain the clean, natural acidity and bright gooseberry and green pepper flavours that can sometimes be lacking in fruit from a warmer climate.

> **Pinotage**
> Almost unique to South Africa, Pinotage is a hybrid of Pinot Noir and Cinsault (formerly known as Hermitage in South Africa) created in 1924 at the University of Stellenbosch. Initially, the wines tended to be unripe or overly alcoholic, but Hamilton Russell in Walker Bay have demonstrated the variety's potential, and their Ashbourne Pinotage is a flagship wine.

Hamilton Russell Chardonnay, Walker Bay. Top-class Chardonnay, elegant yet powerful with a wealth of fruit and good minerality. Long in the finish.

Bouchard Finlayson Galpin Peak Pinot Noir, Walker Bay. Rich meaty aromas with spice, loads of chewy red fruit and velvety texture. Not Burgundy, just fantastic Pinot Noir.

Iona Sauvignon Blanc, Elgin. Classic Sauvignon, with grassy aromas, clean fruity palate and perfect acidity. Brilliant!

Paul Cluver Chardonnay, Elgin. Bright peach fruit with well integrated oak flavours and tropical notes above. Long and true finish.

First Sighting Sauvignon Blanc, Elim. Highly aromatic with gooseberry fruit dominating and crisp refreshing acidity on the palate.

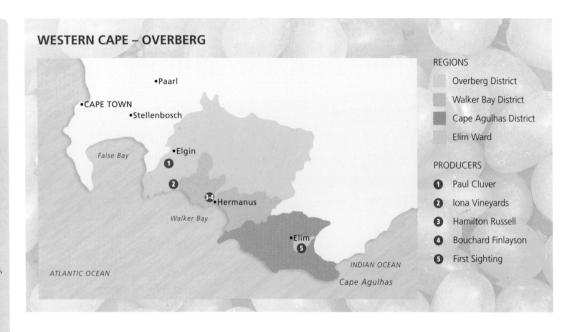

WESTERN CAPE – OVERBERG

• Paarl
• CAPE TOWN
• Stellenbosch
False Bay
• Elgin ❶
❷
❸⁴ • Hermanus
Walker Bay
• Elim ❺
ATLANTIC OCEAN
INDIAN OCEAN
Cape Agulhas

REGIONS
Overberg District
Walker Bay District
Cape Agulhas District
Elim Ward

PRODUCERS
❶ Paul Cluver
❷ Iona Vineyards
❸ Hamilton Russell
❹ Bouchard Finlayson
❺ First Sighting

Winemakers to watch

Two notable producers are Andrew Gunn of Iona Vineyards and Paul Cluver, both of whom make fine classical Sauvignon Blanc with grassy rather than tropical notes. The Cluver estate's range of aromatic varietals, including Gewürztraminer and Riesling, is also well worth searching out. (Dr Paul Clüver Snr was responsible for setting up the black empowerment initiative known as the Thandi Project.)

ABOVE *Temperatures in the Western Cape are moderated by the Benguela current that sweeps northwards up the Atlantic coast. This produces a Mediterranean climate with warm dry summers and mild, moist winters, conducive to healthy, flavoursome grapes.*

BELOW *Bouchard Finlayson established their vineyard in the aptly named Hemel-an-Aarde (Heaven and Earth) valley in 1989. A combination of clay shale soils and a frost-free climate is ideal for Pinot Noir, Chardonnay and Sauvignon Blanc vines.*

WESTERN CAPE – WESTERN VINEYARDS

Olifants River and Swartland

Long ago Olifants River was the source of grapes for distillation, while in Swartland wheat farming held the ascendancy. Both regions were too hot and dry for successful quality wine production. This is no longer the case, with contemporary grape-growing techniques permitting skilled winemakers to produce inexpensive, but good, wines.

Sauvignon Blanc is worth seeking out for its clean, steely acidity and elegant, dry fruit. Recent plantings of Shiraz promise well. There is potential, too, in the varied soils and elevations of the Tulbagh District, particularly for reds, such as Rijk's Private Cellar Shiraz, with big fruit and ripe tannins.

LEFT Harvest time at Contreberg Farm, Darling. The grapes are bought by Neil Ellis of Stellenbosch, who sources his grapes from dedicated growers.

Olifants River now produces many of the Cape's excellent value table wines. The Vredendal Cooperative (South Africa's largest producer of table wines) is based here. The Cederberg Ward, just to the east, today produces good wines, red and white, especially from vineyards at higher altitudes.

Swartland is home to a small number of growers making quite exceptional wines, notably Eben Sadie, whose family farm near Malmesbury produces two Cape gems. Columella, a Shiraz-based blend with Mourvèdre, is remarkably concentrated, spicy and complex. The white Palladius, from Viognier, Chenin Blanc, Chardonnay and Grenache Blanc, has peach and apricot scents balanced by clean acidity.

Darling and Tulbagh

In the Darling District, the Groenekloof Ward has built a reputation for Sauvignon Blanc thanks to the cooling influence of the Atlantic Ocean. Neil Ellis of Stellenbosch fame was one of the pioneers here, and his Groenekloof

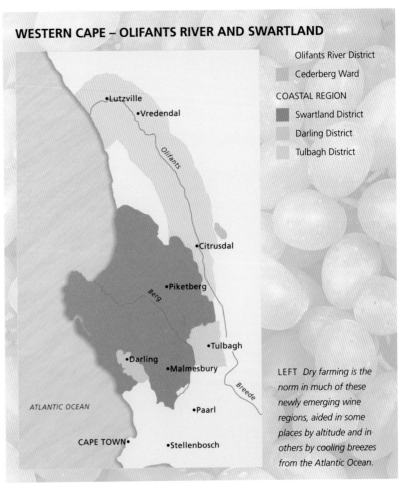

WESTERN CAPE – OLIFANTS RIVER AND SWARTLAND

Olifants River District
Cederberg Ward

COASTAL REGION
Swartland District
Darling District
Tulbagh District

•Lutzville
•Vredendal
Olifants
•Citrusdal
•Piketberg
Berg
•Tulbagh
•Darling
•Malmesbury
Breede
ATLANTIC OCEAN
•Paarl
CAPE TOWN•
•Stellenbosch

LEFT Dry farming is the norm in much of these newly emerging wine regions, aided in some places by altitude and in others by cooling breezes from the Atlantic Ocean.

WESTERN CAPE – EASTERN VINEYARDS
Breede Valley and Klein Karoo

The Breede River Valley is a powerhouse of wine production. In Worcester District alone a wealth of cooperatives produce over 20 per cent of the Cape's wine output. Although a fair proportion is still distilled into brandy, the recent expansion of the Cape wine industry has caused growers to aim higher. It is, then, a source of good quality, reasonably priced table wines.

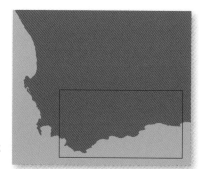

De Krans Vintage Reserve Port. Great class with oodles of sweet fruit and violets backed by a rich sweetness and ripe tannins.

Graham Beck 'The Ridge' Syrah. A single-vineyard Shiraz bursting with spicy plum aromas and flavours with smoky overtones.

RIGHT *Route 62, which passes through Breede River Valley and on to the Klein Karoo, is claimed to be the longest wine route in the world, with over 50 wineries.*

BELOW RIGHT *The success of Graham Beck's Robertson vineyard, established in 1983, led to the setting up of a second winery in historic Franschhoek region.*

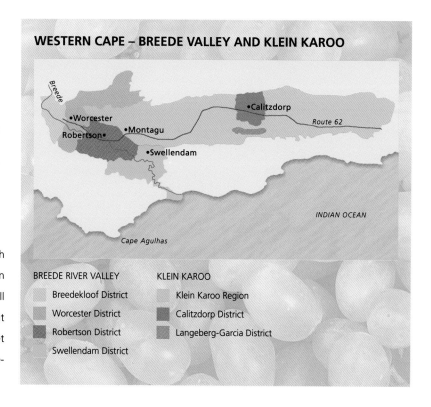

WESTERN CAPE – BREEDE VALLEY AND KLEIN KAROO

Breede
Worcester
Robertson
Montagu
Calitzdorp
Route 62
Swellendam
INDIAN OCEAN
Cape Agulhas

BREEDE RIVER VALLEY	KLEIN KAROO
Breedekloof District	Klein Karoo Region
Worcester District	Calitzdorp District
Robertson District	Langeberg-Garcia District
Swellendam District	

Further to the east, the Robertson District, with its lime-rich soils, is well suited to Chardonnay. Growers such as the Bon Courage Estate have been producing benchmark wines, still and sparkling. Their Cap Classique Jacques Bruére Brut Reserve Blanc de Blancs is most impressive. Cabernet Sauvignon and Shiraz reds also show class, as do some late-harvest and fortified wines from Riesling and Muscadel.

Traditional sweet wines

The intensely hot and dry Klein Karoo is home to some of South Africa's finest dessert wines. Irrigation is a must here, and most vineyards are situated close to rivers. Varieties such as Chenin Blanc, producing dry white wines, perform well, but it is chiefly Muscat – and the Portuguese varieties Barocca and Touriga Nacional – that have created the area's reputation for Port-style fortified wines. The Calitzdorp District, where the temperatures are tempered by afternoon breezes, is the most famous area for such production.

●●○ Regions 77–86

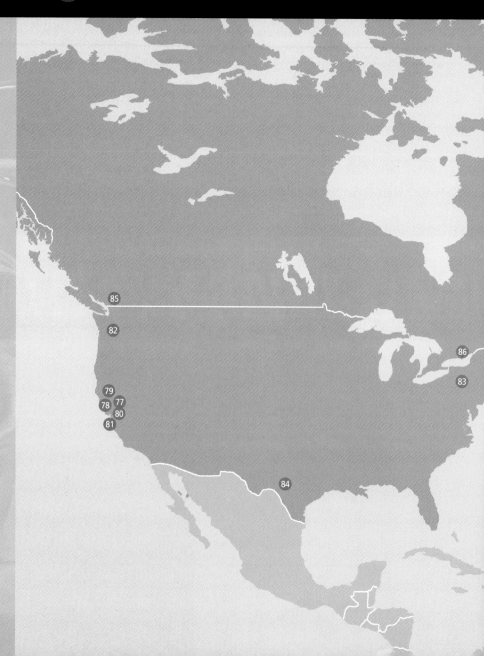

●●● USA and Canada

Wine has been made in North America for at least 300 years, and it is now produced in every single US state – even Alaska. The United States is the world's fourth largest producer of table wine, after Italy, France and Spain, yet all but a tiny fraction of its wines are consumed at home.

Commercial winemaking in the United States has had to survive the Civil War, a host of diseases, Prohibition and a sustained obsession with the notion that decent wine could be made from native varieties of vine. Today wineries flourish, in both the United States and Canada, making more than decent wines from European varieties. But while American winemakers frequently attempt to imitate the elusive, great wines of Burgundy, Bordeaux, Champagne or Piedmont, there is also a confidence in wines that directly reflect North America's climate and soil conditions – terroir – giving consumers a marvellous choice of individual wines to suit their particular tastes.

USA – CALIFORNIA NORTH COAST

Napa Valley

Heitz Martha's Vineyard, Opus One, Stony Hill Chardonnay, Dominus, Caymus Special Selection Cabernet Sauvignon, Grace Family Vineyard, Stags' Leap Cask 23, Cuvée J. Schram … Some of the most sought-after (and expensive) wines in the world originate in this most famous of California's wine-growing regions, little more than an hour's drive north of downtown San Francisco.

Napa is the jewel in the crown of the US wine industry. But, to put it mildly, Napa is complicated. It is an extraordinary collection of different microclimates, soil structures and exposures to the sun in a remarkably compact area. Quite frequently, however, this is irrelevant, because a Napa winery located in one part of the valley may well obtain some of the grapes it uses to make its wine from another part of Napa or even another part of California. Many wineries buy in some or all of their grapes. Others have vineyards in a number of places, making the most of the valley's variations to produce Zinfandel here, Cabernet Sauvignon there, and Chardonnay elsewhere. There are some single-vineyard wines, as there are throughout California, but these tend to be at the top end of a winery's output. Often a producer makes several grades of wine from the same grape variety.

There is a final complication: Napa is a small region producing only 4 per cent of California's wine. Most of it is bought by Californians, often at the cellar door. An eager export market simply cannot get hold of enough of the better wines and, even in California, these wines can never be inexpensive.

Mondavi – Napa's ambassador

Napa vineyards are historic. George Calvert Yount first planted vines here in 1836, and commercial winemaking appeared a couple of decades later, but it died in infancy with the first episode of phylloxera. Then came Prohibition in the 1920s. Although the industry was redeveloped afterwards, it really came to prominence only when the legendary Robert Mondavi opened his winery in Oakville in 1966. He was responsible for introducing modern winemaking to the region but also had a true passion for wine, becoming an ambassador for Napa Valley wines throughout the world. The area's vineyards have greatly expanded since, and production now exceeds 6 million cases a year, bringing in over US$1 billion in sales.

BELOW *The cool vineyards of the gentle hills of Los Carneros ripen grapes slowly, producing not only good Chardonnay and Pinot Noir but especially good sparkling wines. This attractive vineyard belongs to Robert Mondavi.*

Buyer beware
The Napa Valley is a wine lover's paradise, with some of the greatest bottles of Cabernet Sauvignon-based wines to be found here. But thanks to the area's high land values and the impressive amounts of new French oak that are used in making the wines, their prices can be astronomical.

CALIFORNIA NORTH COAST – NAPA VALLEY

REGION

Napa Valley

AVAs

1. Los Carneros
2. Wild Horse Valley
3. Oak Knoll
4. Yountville
5. Stags Leap District
6. Oakville
7. Rutherford
8. St Helena
9. Calistoga (pending)
10. Diamond Mountain
11. Spring Mountain
12. Mount Vedeer
13. Atlas Peak
14. Chiles Valley
15. Howell Mountain

ABOVE *The Napa Valley stretches for 50 km/30 miles between the Vaca Range to the east and the Mayacamas Mountains to the west. The diversity of the region's soils and climatic conditions is reflected in its clearly defined subregions or AVAs (American Victicultural Areas).*

AMERICAN VITICULTURAL AREAS

Wines in the United States are not classified by quality. Instead they are grouped geographically in American Viticultural Areas (AVAs), which can be huge or tiny. At least 85 per cent of the wine in a bottle bearing the name of an AVA on its label must originate in that AVA. The areas can cross state boundaries, and it is possible to have one AVA inside another; they are defined and granted by the Bureau of Alcohol, Tobacco and Firearms. Some producers do not agree with the system and do not use it.

'Drink what you like, and like what you drink.'

ROBERT MONDAVI,
FOUNDER OF THE
AMERICAN FINE WINE
INDUSTRY

Where Cabernet is king

Very little of the Napa Valley could be described as having a cool climate. The exception is Los Carneros at the southern end, which overlaps into neighbouring Sonoma County. This is the area closest to the ocean, where afternoon breezes from San Pablo Bay bring fog that helps to moderate the climate, allowing distinctive styles of Pinot Noir and Chardonnay to be grown in the thin soils. The little-known region of Wild Horse Valley further to the east also produces good Pinot Noir, but quantities are so limited it is rarely seen. Apart from this, Cabernet Sauvignon reigns supreme throughout the Napa Valley, with each specific area adding its own nuances. Other Bordeaux varieties such as Merlot and Cabernet Franc also perform well, and Syrah and Zinfandel produce some outstanding wines along with Chardonnay, Sauvignon Blanc and Riesling. The Italian grape Sangiovese is increasingly popular.

Valley floor

The regions of the central valley floor dominate production. Oak Knoll's lower elevations benefit most from the cooling breezes and coastal fogs of the afternoons, giving a moderate climate that favours Riesling and Chardonnay as well as the Bordeaux varieties, which can age well. Neighbouring Yountville makes concentrated Cabernet Sauvignon and Merlot with abundant tannins.

To the east is Stags Leap District, the first of three areas, running north-west, that are recognized for their outstanding wines. It was Stags' Leap Winery's 1973 Cabernet that brought Napa to prominence when – selling at US$6.00 – it took the top wine award at the now infamous Paris tasting of 1976, beating many Grands Crus of Bordeaux in the process. In Oakville the soils have more gravel and the style of Cabernet Sauvignon is more restrained, often with notes of spice and fine, silky tannins. Chardonnay and Sauvignon Blanc grow well, testament to which is the Mondavi Winery's Fumé Blanc from its old-vines To Kalon vineyard. The last of the three is Rutherford, where the ripe, majestic and long-lived Cabernet Sauvignon wines come from gravel- and sand-based loams that naturally restrict the yield. This is home to the famous Beaulieu Winery, which was able to survive through the years of Prohibition thanks to a contract for the supply of sacramental wines.

North of Rutherford, St Helena is cooled by breezes from the north rather than the south: its hotter climate intensifies and concentrates the fruit characters, giving an overall elegance to its wines. Just beyond is Calistoga, hemmed in by mountains, where the even hotter conditions and soils of a more volcanic nature give red wines of impressive stature with tightly knit fruit. Spring frosts are a threat, kept at bay by propellers, wind machines and sprinklers.

Higher ground

Some of Napa's most individual wines come from high ground, on either side of the valley, that is not cooled by afternoon fogs. Diamond Mountain, Spring Mountain, Mount Veeder, Atlas Peak and Howell Mountain are all renowned for the quality of their fruit. Zinfandel in particular thrives here, as it does also in the sheltered Chiles Valley adjoining Howell Mountain.

Dominus, Napa Valley. Wonderfully rich, Cabernet-dominated blend with powerful black fruit and incredible structure that is built to last.

Stags' Leap Wine Cellars 'Cask 23' Estate Cabernet Sauvignon, Napa Valley. Produced only in the finest years, a well-built wine packed with extraordinary levels of blackcurrant fruit, underpinned with complex nuances that can include truffle and violets.

Neyers Zinfandel 'High Valley Vineyards', Napa Valley. Ripe, spicy and velvety Zinfandel, powerful yet elegant.

Etude Wines Rutherford Cabernet Sauvignon, Rutherford. Ripe and concentrated dark-berry fruit, often with tobacco notes. Built for ageing, but can be drunk after a couple of years in bottle.

Robert Mondavi Winery Fumé Blanc Reserve, Oakville. Barrel-fermented, Sauvignon Blanc-dominated white, with layer after layer of fine fruit and complex notes of blossom and tropical fruits.

Spottswoode Estate Cabernet Sauvignon, St Helena. Deep and expansive plummy fruit with hints of lead pencil and with fine, supple tannins.

LEFT *Vineyards fill the valley floor in Oakville. It was here that Robert Mondavi built his iconic winery in 1966.*

RIGHT *The Quintessa vineyard, in the heart of the Rutherford AVA, with Mount St Helena in the distance.*

USA – CALIFORNIA NORTH COAST

Sonoma County

Across the Mayacamas Mountains from Napa Valley, Sonoma County is another area of widely varied climates, elevations and soils, making grape growing and winemaking all the more fascinating. The Pacific Ocean to the west is influential, bringing morning and late-afternoon fog to moderate the inland climate in the growing season, and protecting the vines from frost in spring, when unhindered flowering is crucial.

Sonoma has a long history of winemaking. The first grapes were planted by Russian settlers in 1812, and subsequent plantings of European vine varieties by Hungarian-born Agoston Haraszthy in the 1850s and 60s earned him the title 'Father of Californian Wine'.

Russian River Valley

Chardonnay remains the most popular variety, and Pinot Noir has a growing reputation, some of the best being made in the Russian River Valley, especially in the cooler south. Here, Green Valley was developed by the Dutton family in the 1970s. Iron Horse soon followed, with the Gold Ridge soils producing excellent base wines for its sparkling wine industry. Chalk Hill, with its exposed hillsides of volcanic ash, is warmer, producing excellent, grassy Sauvignon Blanc, powerful Chardonnay and delightfully fruity Merlot. The climate is also warmer at the northern end of the Russian River. Excellent old-vine plantings of Zinfandel can be found, such as the Carlisle Winery's Montafi Ranch.

Zinfandel and Cabernet

One of the newest AVAs is Rockpile, whose name perfectly describes its harsh landscape, which harbours some of the region's finest Zinfandel. Another source of excellent Zinfandel is Dry Creek Valley, where the gravel- and clay-based soils of the hillsides suit it ideally. Alongside an army of small growers, the giant Gallo enterprise makes some good wines here. Nevertheless, Cabernet Sauvignon is the

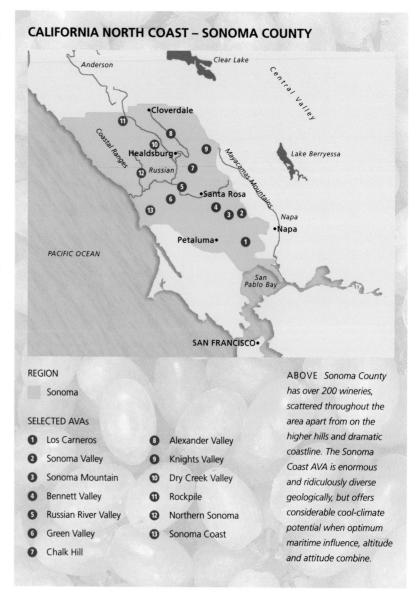

CALIFORNIA NORTH COAST – SONOMA COUNTY

REGION
Sonoma

SELECTED AVAs
1 Los Carneros
2 Sonoma Valley
3 Sonoma Mountain
4 Bennett Valley
5 Russian River Valley
6 Green Valley
7 Chalk Hill
8 Alexander Valley
9 Knights Valley
10 Dry Creek Valley
11 Rockpile
12 Northern Sonoma
13 Sonoma Coast

ABOVE *Sonoma County has over 200 wineries, scattered throughout the area apart from on the higher hills and dramatic coastline. The Sonoma Coast AVA is enormous and ridiculously diverse geologically, but offers considerable cool-climate potential when optimum maritime influence, altitude and attitude combine.*

Zinfandel

For many years Zinfandel was thought of as California's own grape. It is in fact of Croatian origin and identical to Italy's Primitivo. Producing enormous crops of commercial wine in the Central Valley, Zinfandel also makes superb blackberry-flavoured wines from precious ancient vines in Sonoma.

Kistler Vineyards Dutton Ranch Chardonnay, Russian River Valley. Full-flavoured, peachy and buttery Chardonnay with well-integrated oak.

La Crema Chardonnay, Russian River Valley. Fresh, lively Chardonnay with bright fruit over oak and clean acidity.

Mauritson Cemetery Vineyard Zinfandel, Rockpile. Intense, dense and spicy with an abundance of ripe fruit and full-on tannins.

Hartford Court Arrendell Vineyard Pinot Noir, Russian River Valley. Loaded with raspberry fruit and great depth of flavour that gives a big finish.

J. Rochioli Estate Pinot Noir, Russian River Valley. Hard to find, early-drinking Pinot with cherry-dominated aromas and plenty of ripe berry fruit on the palate.

RIGHT *Home to La Crema Winery, the Russian River Valley is one of Sonoma's coolest regions, providing ideal growing conditions for Pinot Noir and Chardonnay.*

most widely planted variety, and it also thrives in Alexander Valley, especially in the gravelly soils of the valley floor. Full-flavoured Chardonnay, fresh Sauvignon Blanc and parcels of Merlot are found close to the river here, as well as in the hottest of all AVAs, Knights Valley. Here, Sauvignon Blanc tends to be more tropical in style, but once again Cabernet Sauvignon is the greatest performer, making wines rich in blackcurrant fruit with notes of tobacco and ripe yet firm tannins. The other red Bordeaux varieties, Cabernet Franc, Petit Verdot and Malbec, are also planted here.

Bordeaux varieties similarly flourish on Sonoma Mountain, its well-drained slopes giving wines combining power and elegance. Bennett Valley is gaining a reputation for concentrated Merlot and Syrah. Pinot Noir and Chardonnay are generally sourced from Los Carneros, the region shared with the Napa Valley.

LA CREMA

2007
Chardonnay
RUSSIAN RIVER VALLEY

USA – CALIFORNIA NORTH COAST

Mendocino and Lake

Mendocino is the most northerly vine-growing area in California. Clear Lake exerts a tempering influence on this hot area, which prior to Prohibition grew more grapes than any other county. Re-establishment was slow, and only recently has commercial production reached a significant scale; it is now attracting domestic and international investment. Organic wine production is more popular here than elsewhere in the state.

Mendocino County

A few venerable rows of Zinfandel vines, grown in the sun high above the fog line on the Mendocino Ridges, survived Prohibition and are now making rare, majestic wines. Not all Mendocino's vines enjoy such favourable growing conditions – it can be too cold. The lower-lying north-west area of Anderson Valley is often shrouded in fog and much cooler. Here Pinot Noir and Chardonnay are grown, often for sparkling wine production, importantly attracting Roederer from Champagne to set up in the region. Perfumed Riesling and Gewürztraminer benefit from the crisp acidity imparted by such a climate.

BELOW *The sparkling wines produced from Roederer's Anderson Valley vineyards are consistently among the best made in California. All the grapes used for the winery's whole range of wines are grown on the estate.*

CALIFORNIA NORTH COAST – MENDOCINO AND LAKE

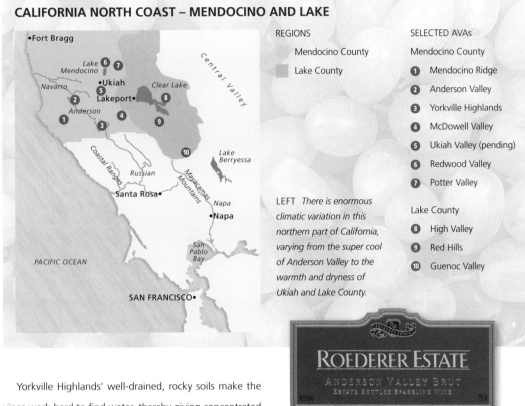

REGIONS

Mendocino County

Lake County

SELECTED AVAs

Mendocino County

① Mendocino Ridge
② Anderson Valley
③ Yorkville Highlands
④ McDowell Valley
⑤ Ukiah Valley (pending)
⑥ Redwood Valley
⑦ Potter Valley

Lake County

⑧ High Valley
⑨ Red Hills
⑩ Guenoc Valley

LEFT There is enormous climatic variation in this northern part of California, varying from the super cool of Anderson Valley to the warmth and dryness of Ukiah and Lake County.

Roederer Estate Brut N/V, Anderson Valley. Stylish Chardonnay/Pinot Noir blend with fresh pear aromas and nutty notes to the palate.

McDowell Valley Vineyards Syrah, McDowell Valley. Concentrated fruit with floral notes and hints of bacon fat. Great expression of Syrah.

Littorai Wines Savoy Vineyard Pinot Noir, Anderson Valley. Berry fruit and undergrowth dominate this complex, early-drinking Pinot.

Yorkville Highlands' well-drained, rocky soils make the vines work hard to find water, thereby giving concentrated flavour within the grape. Sauvignon Blanc does well, as do Cabernet Sauvignon, Merlot and Syrah. Syrah, Grenache and Viognier also flourish in the McDowell Valley.

Mendocino's largest production area is Ukiah Valley, where Chardonnay and Sauvignon Blanc thrive near the Russian River while higher-lying vineyards produce good Cabernet Sauvignon and Zinfandel. Further upstream, the slightly higher Redwood Valley vineyards produce some excellent Cabernet Sauvignon plus Petite Sirah and Italian varieties such as Barbera. In the late 1960s, the Fetzer family planted vineyards here that they farmed organically, a practice that has developed throughout the county and is now used in a significant number of vineyards.

Potter Valley produces a good range of varietals, with Pinot Noir and Chardonnay of increasing importance. The higher water table here increases humidity, which in some vintages encourages the formation of noble rot, giving some exquisite sweet wines from Riesling and the great Sauternes variety, Sémillon.

Lake County

Sauvignon Blanc was the first variety of significance here, performing very well in the High Valley. It grows best in the lower-lying vineyards, while the warmer hillside sites favour Cabernet Sauvignon. The latter also succeeds in Red Hills, where the differing air temperatures over land and water assist in creating wines rich in fruit with spicy notes.

Distant Guenoc Valley has only one winery. It produces some good Cabernet Sauvignon and Petite Sirah, but perhaps its greatest claim to fame is for the vines planted by its one-time owner Lillie Langtry, mistress of King Edward VII.

Central Valley and Sierra Foothills

After the scenic beauty of Northern California, a visit to the Central Valley shatters the mystique surrounding winemaking with a shock encounter with factory farming. Over half of the United States' wine is produced here on the flat, scorched plains of this arid region, where irrigation is essential. While it is easy to grow grapes in the fertile Central Valley, the foothills of the Sierra Nevada challenge the hardiest of producers.

Central Valley

If you see 'California Wine' on an inexpensive bottle, you can bet that a very high percentage of its contents originated in the Central Valley, the 'fruit basket of the world', where fruit, nuts and other crops are grown in vast quantities on its 2.8 million ha/7 million acres of irrigated agricultural land. Many different varieties of grape are grown, producing bulk wines of little character but with soft, fruity flavours for young, easy and inexpensive drinking.

Search hard, however, and you can find wines with individuality and style from Clarksburg and Lodi. Clarksburg benefits from the cool winds and fogs off San Francisco Bay. Although soils here are fertile, excellent Chenin Blanc with good floral aromas is made, and decent Petite Sirah. Lodi's soils, on higher ground, have better drainage and produce terrific Zinfandels, especially from older vines.

CENTRAL CALIFORNIA – CENTRAL VALLEY AND SIERRA FOOTHILLS

Sacramento
Clear Lake
Lake Tahoe
NEVADA
③
Sacramento
④ ⑤
Yountville
⑥ ⑦
Napa ①
②
Lodi
SAN FRANCISCO
Modesto
SIERRA NEVADA
Santa Cruz
San Joaquin
Salinas
Fresno
Coastal Ranges
PACIFIC OCEAN
Bakersfield
San Luis Obispo
Santa Barbara

REGIONS

Central Valley

Sierra Foothills

SELECTED AVAs

Central Valley

① Clarksburg

② Lodi

Sierra Foothills

③ North Yuba

④ El Dorado

⑤ Fair Play

⑥ California Shenandoah

⑦ Fiddletown

LEFT *California's flat Central Valley, bounded by the Coastal Ranges to the west and the Sierra Nevada to the east, runs for nearly 600 km/400 miles north to south. It is divided into two major regions: the Sacramento Valley in the north and the San Joaquin Valley in the south.*

ŶŶŶ **Terre Rouge Syrah, Sierra Foothills.** Smoke and spices over black fruits with hints of white pepper.

ŶŶŶ **Renwood 'Grandpère' Zinfandel, Amador County.** Big wine with high alcohol and loads of cherry fruit with leather and white pepper on the nose.

ŶŶ **Amador Foothill Clockspring Vineyard Zinfandel, Shenandoah.** Organically farmed, moderately intense berry and cherry flavours with spice leaving a good finish.

Ŷ **Holly's Hill Vineyards Viognier, El Dorado.** Fresh peach and apricot blossom with notes of citrus lead to a clean, peach-dominated palate and crisp finish.

TOP RIGHT *In the hills east of Sacramento, Amador Foothill Winery is known particularly for its range of Zinfandels. It is also creating excitement with Sangiovese (seen here) and – unusually for California – Aglianico, the temperamental grape of Taurasi and Vulture in Southern Italy.*

Sierra Foothills

The Sierra Foothills AVA takes in the western foothills of the Sierra Nevada, from Yuba County in the north to Mariposa County in the south. The warmest part is the Shenandoah Valley, where vineyards were planted to satisfy thirsty prospectors in the Gold Rush of the mid-1800s. Its relatively infertile, unirrigated soils yielded Zinfandel wines of great flavour. Even today many vineyards are not irrigated, and Zinfandel gives impressive wines that can be low in cost and high in flavour.

Although Italian grapes such as Nebbiolo and Barbera are being planted, Zinfandel – some of it very old – remains the standard-bearer, as it does in adjacent Fiddletown, where increased altitude helps with acidity levels, giving the wine a fresher feel in the mouth. Even higher in altitude is Fair Play, where acidity levels become yet more pronounced. Syrah could be a variety to watch here; likewise in El Dorado, another Gold Rush territory where the mountain vineyards are cooled by the winds of the Sierra Nevada.

Some aromatic varieties produce good wines in El Dorado, such as Viognier, which can have distinct floral notes, and Gewürztraminer, which enjoys the higher altitudes. In the lower, warmer areas, Zinfandel gives wines of dense colour and intense flavours but has recently been challenged by Syrah plantings.

TERRE ROUGE
SIERRA FOOTHILLS

SYRAH

PRODUCED & BOTTLED BY DOMAINE DE LA TERRE ROUGE
PLYMOUTH, CALIFORNIA. ALC. 14.5% BY VOL.

USA – CENTRAL CALIFORNIA

Central Coast

While it is geographically convenient to bring together the wine-growing areas that form the Central Coast, they could hardly be more different climatically. The cooling effects of San Francisco Bay and winds from the Pacific, humidity, dryness, heat and a wealth of differing geological factors affect vineyards in a multitude of ways. This is, then, an area of extremes, with wines of every style, quality and price.

San Francisco Bay

The influence of that huge expanse of water, San Francisco Bay, channelled through the narrow straits of the Golden Gate, is enormous. Leaving aside its major impact on all aspects of daily life – not least the persistent fog that keeps the climate cool – in vinous terms it leads to a wealth of microclimates, each suited to different grape varieties.

Cooler regions such as Ben Lomond produce excellent Chardonnay and Pinot Noir. The Santa Cruz Mountains vineyards enjoy warm sunshine and low rainfall, intensifying their delicious fruit qualities. On the warmer east-facing slopes, Syrah, Cabernet Sauvignon and Zinfandel are impressive; the latter two also make good wines in the gravel-based soils of the Livermore Valley, along with the

 **Wente Vineyards 'Louis Mel' Sauvignon Blanc, Livermore.** Fresh, grassy aromas with some tropical flavours on the palate and a crisp acidity to balance.

Calera 'Mount Harlan' Chardonnay. Creamy, well-balanced and with clear apple fruit.

Chalone Vineyard Estate Chardonnay, Chalone. Medium-bodied, barrel-fermented Chardonnay with nutty overtones and good mineral background.

Talley Vineyards Rincon Pinot Noir, Arroyo Grande. Blackberry and cherry aromas give way to a full and generous palate with earthy notes typical of the area and with big tannins and acidity to balance.

Garretson Winery 'The Aisling' Syrah, Paso Robles. Packed with spicy cherry fruit with Provençal and pepper overtones: Old World flavours in New World style.

Stolpman Vineyards Estate Syrah, Santa Ynez. Wonderfully meaty Syrah with spice, pepper and smoky notes. Long and savoury.

CENTRAL CALIFORNIA – CENTRAL COAST

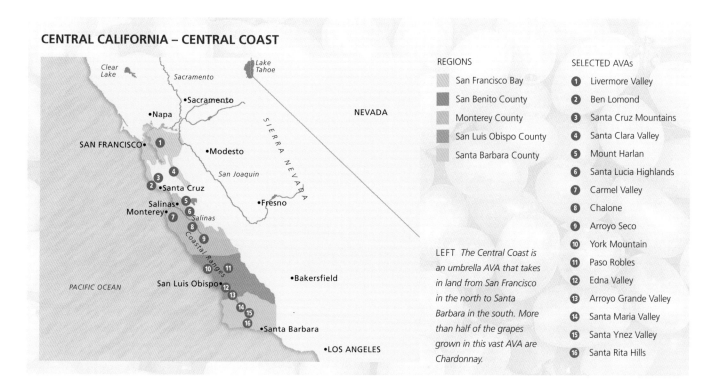

REGIONS
- San Francisco Bay
- San Benito County
- Monterey County
- San Luis Obispo County
- Santa Barbara County

SELECTED AVAs
1. Livermore Valley
2. Ben Lomond
3. Santa Cruz Mountains
4. Santa Clara Valley
5. Mount Harlan
6. Santa Lucia Highlands
7. Carmel Valley
8. Chalone
9. Arroyo Seco
10. York Mountain
11. Paso Robles
12. Edna Valley
13. Arroyo Grande Valley
14. Santa Maria Valley
15. Santa Ynez Valley
16. Santa Rita Hills

LEFT *The Central Coast is an umbrella AVA that takes in land from San Francisco in the north to Santa Barbara in the south. More than half of the grapes grown in this vast AVA are Chardonnay.*

white Sauvignon Blanc and Sémillon. Here proximity to the Central Valley gives elevated temperatures, which are moderated by winds off the Bay later in the day.

San Francisco's urban sprawl has claimed a few vineyards, not least at the northern end of the Santa Clara Valley. However, the southern end, where vines enjoy a warm climate in sandstone-based soils, is home to varieties such as Petite Sirah and Carignane (Carignan).

San Benito

The name of San Benito County is rarely seen on wine labels. Much of its wine ends up in the cellars of larger producers outside the area, under the Central Coast appellation. Towards the Gabilan Mountains soils contain limestone, which encourages good acidity levels, keeping freshness in their flavoursome Zinfandel wines. Cienega Valley produces some good Bordeaux varieties, while Syrah, Mourvèdre and Grenache are important in the small subregion of Lime Kiln. The cooler parts of the valley make good Pinot Noir and Chardonnay, which are also excellent in the limestone soils of Mount Harlan, home to the Calera estate.

Monterey

Salinas Valley runs south-east from Monterey Bay. The valley floor is a wind tunnel that was planted with vines in the 1970s in an ill-conceived viticultural gold rush. Most of its huge production ends up mixed with that of the Central Valley in basic Californian blends. However, remarkable wines from Pinot Noir and Chardonnay are being produced in a handful of specialized areas. The limestone and granite soils of the Santa Lucia Highlands and Chalone areas are ideal for these Burgundian grape varieties, and both give Chardonnays with good mineral underpinning. Crisp apple fruit is imparted to the vines in the cooler north-west, while

ABOVE *The cool cellars of Chalone Vineyard in the hills above the Salinas Valley. Chalone was the first vineyard to be established in Monterey County, and it enjoys its own AVA.*

OPPOSITE *Bien Nacido Vineyards in Santa Maria Valley does not make its own wine. Instead the vines are cultivated according to the wishes of the customer, in this case Qupé and Au Bon Climat.*

the south-east favours Pinot Noir that is rich in fruit. In Chalone, Pinot Noir comes with intense cherry and raspberry characters reminiscent of the Côte de Beaune.

In inland, sheltered parts of the Carmel Valley Cabernet Sauvignon and Merlot prevail with good, grassy Sauvignons Blancs, while in Arroyo Seco the dry, windy climate produces Gewürztraminer and Riesling wines with pronounced fruit flavours. In the more humid southern reaches of the region noble rot appears on a regular basis to give delicious botrytis-affected Rieslings.

San Luis Obispo

Known for Chardonnay, San Luis Obispo County's east–west valleys allow cooling breezes to penetrate. The Edna Valley makes great Chardonnays, the long growing season giving them a richness and depth of flavour. Alban Vineyards have acquired a stellar reputation for their Rhône varietals, making some of the greatest wines in the state.

The western end of the Arroyo Grande boasts both Chardonnay and Pinot Noir. Here the Champagne house Deutz has 65 ha/160 acres under vine for premium sparkling wine production. These two varieties make interesting still wines further up the valley, such as at Talley Vineyards.

With the exception of the cooler York Mountain, Paso Robles has a distinctly hotter climate more suited to the production of beefy reds: Cabernet Sauvignon and Syrah are the most widely planted. The best wines exhibit chunky tannins and benefit from bottle age to soften.

Santa Barbara

Santa Barbara's vineyards are only recently established. Having had almost no vineyards in the 1960s, the area now has over 8,000 ha/20,000 acres under vine, with Chardonnay and Pinot Noir leading the way.

The Santa Maria Valley and Santa Rita Hills, together with the western end of the Santa Ynez Valley, benefit from the cooler, maritime influence in which grapes thrive. Chardonnay displays crisp acidity, and Pinot Noir ranges from vibrantly fruity to a lighter though no less interesting style. Syrah is also grown here, but the area's Rhône Rangers favour the warmer, eastern end of the Santa Ynez Valley. Stolpman Vineyards are making excellent wines here and include an unusual blend of Syrah with Sangiovese.

SOUTHERN CALIFORNIA

This once thriving area has seen much decline in its vineyards, with urban development and the dreaded Pierce's Disease. Some replanting with more resistant grape varieties is taking place, as in Temecula Valley, where Callaway Vineyards were established in 1969. In addition to Syrah, Viognier and Sauvignon Blanc, Italian varieties have made some impact: Sangiovese (red and pink) and Dolcetto. A small quantity of interesting fortified wine is made in the Cucamonga Valley, but generally wines from Southern California lack the interest of those born in the cooler regions to the north.

BELOW *Vines in the Edna Valley south of San Luis Obispo. Spanish missionaries first planted vines here in the early 19th century, while modern plantings began in the 1970s. Cooling breezes from the Pacific Ocean and frequent fogs ensure a cool climate, and the dark, clay-rich soils produce flavoursome wines.*

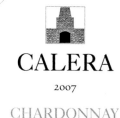

CALERA
2007
CHARDONNAY
MT. HARLAN

USA – PACIFIC NORTH-WEST

Washington, Oregon and Idaho

Winemaking in Washington State goes back to 1825, when the Hudson's Bay Company first planted vines for wine at Fort Vancouver. Today it is second only to California in production volume. Oregon features smaller, artisan wineries, while Idaho's high-altitude vineyards are fewer still. The best wines of all three states are distinguished by the care with which specific varieties have been matched to individual vineyard sites.

Washington

Despite early plantings, it was not until the 1960s that a commercial industry began to emerge in Washington, followed by major expansion in the late 1990s. Dry summers and autumns ensure healthy grapes, and the quality of the fruit has generated a significant export trade. While the major wineries are based in Seattle, the vineyards to the east of the Cascade Mountains are the main producers. This arid region, largely dependent on irrigation, is yielding exciting wines. Although Chardonnay is the most widely planted vine variety, red wine production dominates, with Cabernet Sauvignon and Merlot making a big impact, either as varietals or in blends. Riesling also enjoys the cool climate, and growers are having success with Syrah.

Columbia Valley is the appellation most likely to be encountered, as it covers six of the smaller subregions, allowing the larger wineries to blend fruit from various sources. The rise of smaller, boutique wineries has brought greater prominence to Yakima Valley, Red Mountain, Walla Walla, Wahluke Slope and Rattlesnake Hills. Columbia Gorge, which overlaps into Oregon, is becoming famous for its premium Pinot Noir production.

BELOW *Elk Cove's Roosevelt Vineyard, in Oregon, was planted in 1993 with Pommard Clone Pinot Noir grapes. The land is farmed organically and the vines are trained to single canes in order to restrict yield and maximize exposure to the sun in the growing season.*

Stevens Winery 'XY' Cabernet Sauvignon, Yakima Valley. Limited release, full-on Cabernet dominated by black fruit.

Columbia Crest Reserve Merlot, Columbia Valley. Spicy black fruit aromas and flavours, rich in tannins.

Ponzi Vineyards Pinot Noir, Willamette Valley. Delicious raspberry/blackcurrant fruit with ripe, soft tannins.

WillaKenzie Estate Pinot Noir, Willamette Valley. Open, early drinker with red fruit flavours.

Elk Cove Vineyards Pinot Gris, Willamette Valley. Clean pear fruit with tropical overtones.

The Winery at Eagle Knoll Riesling, Idaho. Fresh apple fruit with vibrant acidity.

PACIFIC NORTH-WEST – WASHINGTON, OREGON AND IDAHO

REGIONS
- Puget Sound
- Columbia Valley
- Yakima Valley
- Walla Walla
- Columbia Gorge
- Willamette Valley
- Umpqua Valley
- Rogue Valley
- Snake River Valley

LEFT *Agricultural land prices are lower in Washington, Oregon and Idaho than they are in California, attracting new winery investment. While the cooler climates are an advantage for the production of high-quality fruit, lack of water in certain parts necessitates expensive irrigation.*

Oregon

The wineries of Oregon tend to be on a small scale, as in Burgundy (the inspiration for many of the growers), and most are located in the cool northern part of the Willamette Valley. Domaine Drouhin of Beaune was so attracted to the climate's potential for Pinot Noir that it bought vineyards in the Dundee Hills subregion. Another investor is Brian Croser of Petaluma in Australia, while influential wine writer Robert Parker has taken a share in Beaux Frères, whose Pinots Noirs are among the market leaders. All were in search of something they could not find in California: a more European style of climate.

Pinot Noir clearly enjoys the conditions, but the trick for the growers is to ensure that ripe fruit can be harvested before the autumn rains arrive, which means planting clones that ripen sufficiently early. These wines have been compared to their Burgundian counterparts, yet they often display fruitier nuances. Other earlier ripening varieties are planted, with some excellent offerings from the aromatic Pinot Gris and Pinot Blanc. Wherever Pinot goes, Chardonnay follows, and fine examples are now emerging, such as at Ponzi Vineyards. The hotter and drier areas in the south of the region, notably Umpqua Valley and Rogue Valley, are now turning to Syrah, which gives fine, well-fruited wines, alongside Cabernet Sauvignon and Cabernet Franc.

Idaho

The highest vineyards in the Pacific North-west are in Idaho. This dry region, with its warm summer days and cooler evenings, generates wines with good fruit character and clean balancing acidity. With just over 30 wineries now in production, output is limited. The focus is on Chardonnay, Riesling and Cabernet Sauvignon, with good, well-priced wines coming from the likes of the Wood River Cellars.

USA – EASTERN UNITED STATES

New York State

East of the Rocky Mountains many states successfully produce commercial wine, principally Maryland, Michigan, New Jersey, North Carolina, Ohio, Pennsylvania, Virginia and the New England states. But it is New York State, the third most productive grape-growing state in the United States, where the main action is found. Traditionally much of its output was for grape juice, but conversion to wine grapes continues apace, with impressive results from its four main regions.

Long Island

New York City's local vineyards are on Long Island, mainly concentrated on the North Fork, where the modern industry began in the early 1970s. Sauvignon Blanc and Pinot Noir were favoured initially; recently a reputation has developed for Cabernet Sauvignon, Cabernet Franc and Merlot, with Chardonnay for whites. Their distinctive styles owe much to the climate, which is influenced by the Atlantic Ocean and Long Island Sound. Vintages can be ruined by autumn rainfall, but in favoured years the wines show great finesse with clean, elegant fruit flavours.

The cooler South Fork (the Hamptons) has only four wineries in operation. Atlantic breezes, often compounded by fog, cause the vines here to develop later, producing leaner and more restrained wines than those of its neighbour, with greater success for white varieties such as Chardonnay or Pinot Gris. The lesser-known Tocai Friulano shows good potential at the Channing Daughters Winery.

Hudson River

North America's earliest commercial winery still in production, Brotherhood, founded in 1839, is located at Washingtonville

Paumanok Vineyards Cabernet Franc Grand Vintage, North Fork Long Island. Violet aromas with floral notes, black fruit palate with good backbone.

Lenz Winery 'Estate Selection' Merlot, North Fork Long Island. Meaty and cherry dominated with savoury aromas.

Millbrook Vineyards 'Proprietor's Special Reserve' Cabernet Franc, Hudson River. Medium bodied with plum, vanilla and spice notes.

Dr Konstantin Frank Dry Riesling, Finger Lakes. Clean, crisp acidity backs bright apple/pear fruit with tropical notes.

Standing Stones Vineyards 'Vidal Ice', Finger Lakes. Apricot-dominated with juicy pineapple and clean acidity.

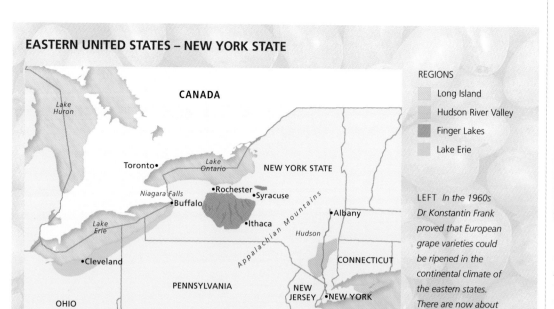

EASTERN UNITED STATES – NEW YORK STATE

CANADA

Lake Huron

Toronto

Lake Ontario

NEW YORK STATE

Niagara Falls

Rochester

Syracuse

Buffalo

Albany

Lake Erie

Ithaca

Appalachian Mountains

Hudson

Cleveland

CONNECTICUT

PENNSYLVANIA

NEW JERSEY

NEW YORK

OHIO

ATLANTIC OCEAN

REGIONS

Long Island

Hudson River Valley

Finger Lakes

Lake Erie

LEFT *In the 1960s Dr Konstantin Frank proved that European grape varieties could be ripened in the continental climate of the eastern states. There are now about 100 wineries in Finger Lakes alone.*

RIGHT *Vineyards and building of the Pleasant Valley Wine Company/Great Western Winery on the western side of Lake Keuka. Winegrowing in the Finger Lakes district dates back to the 1820s.*

Wine research
With the wine and grape industry annually contributing over US$6 billion to New York State's economy, the importance of research into all aspects of viticulture is recognized. Cornell University College of Agriculture and Life Sciences is located in Geneva, in the heart of Finger Lakes.

on the Hudson River. Small wineries prevail in this area. The hybrid Seyval Blanc and Vidal were once the most important varieties, but good Chardonnays and Cabernets Francs are now making an impact.

Finger Lakes

Vines benefit here from the influence of the lakes, which help to retain heat during the summer ripening months while also tempering the extreme cold of winter. Riesling has made the greatest mark. The Dr Konstantin Frank Winery makes delicious dry Riesling along with a host of other varietals. Gewürztraminer delivers good whites, while Pinot

Noir, Cabernet Franc and Merlot are successful red varieties. High levels of natural acidity enable good sparkling wines to be crafted, and clean and vibrantly fruity icewines can be outstanding, such as those of Standing Stone Vineyards.

Lake Erie

Extending into Ohio, the Lake Erie AVA is a prolific producer of grapes although much of the crop is for grape juice. The small number of wineries operating in this region produce pleasant wines from hybrid varieties such as Vidal Blanc, while Riesling, Chardonnay and Cabernet Franc are the best of the noble varieties.

SOUTHERN UNITED STATES
South-west States

In the hot, arid climates of the southern states, the growing season is generally too short for the development of the necessary flavour and acids within the grape to make interesting wines, unless the vineyards are planted in cooler, high-altitude sites. While the number of wineries is expanding in Missouri, Georgia, Arizona, Oklahoma, Utah and Nevada, it is in New Mexico, Colorado and particularly Texas that most wine production is found.

New Mexico

It is possible that New Mexico was the first place in North America where grapes were planted for wine production, as missionaries were making sacramental wine here as far back as the 1580s. Thanks to irrigation there are now more than 30 wineries, with Chardonnay and Riesling the most planted varieties and Cabernet Sauvignon, Merlot and Zinfandel representing the reds. Cold nights help maintain acidity, allowing excellent sparkling wines to be produced.

Colorado and Arizona

There are now some 60 wineries taking advantage of the altitude offered by Colorado's Rocky Mountains. The majority are in the Grand Valley, where there is a good

SACRAMENTAL WINE

Winemaking arrived in the western states through the explorations of Spanish missionaries. Every Spaniard who settled in Mexico was commanded by an order of 1522 to plant thousands of vines. And it was a Franciscan missionary, Junípero Serra, moving north from Mexico to found new missions, who established the first vineyard and winery in California, near San Diego, in 1769, to ensure a supply of sacramental wine. Later missionaries planted further vineyards, including Sonoma's first in 1805. Fortuitously, the making of sacramental wine offered several wineries a means of survival during Prohibition.

St Clair Reserve Merlot, New Mexico. Well coloured with ripe black fruit and soft tannins.

Gruet Brut N/V, New Mexico. Crisp and fresh with toasty notes above apple fruit.

Dos Cabezas Viognier, Arizona. Beautifully balanced with clear blossom fruit.

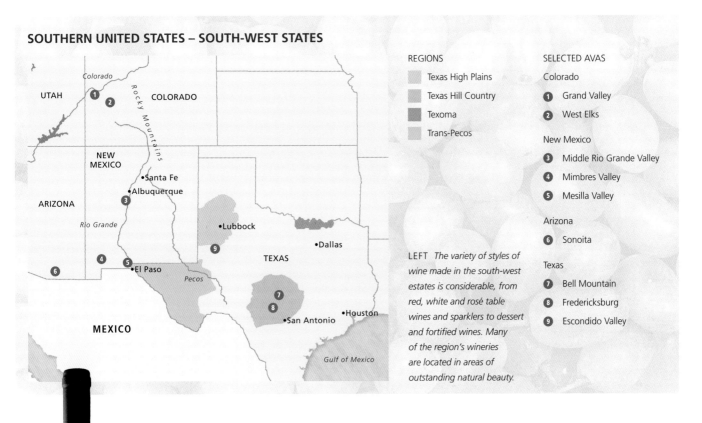

SOUTHERN UNITED STATES – SOUTH-WEST STATES

REGIONS

- Texas High Plains
- Texas Hill Country
- Texoma
- Trans-Pecos

SELECTED AVAS

Colorado
- ❶ Grand Valley
- ❷ West Elks

New Mexico
- ❸ Middle Rio Grande Valley
- ❹ Mimbres Valley
- ❺ Mesilla Valley

Arizona
- ❻ Sonoita

Texas
- ❼ Bell Mountain
- ❽ Fredericksburg
- ❾ Escondido Valley

LEFT *The variety of styles of wine made in the south-west estates is considerable, from red, white and rosé table wines and sparklers to dessert and fortified wines. Many of the region's wineries are located in areas of outstanding natural beauty.*

LEFT *Mount Garfield, icon of the Grand Valley, rises majestically over the vineyards of Palisade, where there are over a dozen wineries, forming – with Grand Junction – the epicentre of Colorado's wine country.*

differential between day and night temperatures, which slows ripening and protects acidity. Plantings of Chardonnay, Cabernet Sauvignon and Merlot have been joined recently by the Rhône varieties Syrah and Viognier. Some excellent Rhône varietals are already being made in Arizona's Sonoita AVA. Arizona, like New Mexico, has a long wine history, Jesuit missionaries having planted vineyards to make sacramental wine some 350 years ago.

Texas

The largest producer in the southern states, Texas has 1,500 ha/3,700 acres under vine, with over 150 wineries now producing over 2 million gallons of wine annually. As in Southern California, Pierce's Disease has affected some vineyards, leading to the planting of more resistant, hybrid grapes such as Blanc du Bois; traditional varieties survive in unaffected vineyards.

Many vineyards are located around Lubbock on a plateau some 1,050 m/3,400 ft above sea level in the Texas High Plains AVA. Refreshing breezes moderate the heat of the day, and cool evenings help with acidity. This is a varied agricultural area with Cabernet Sauvignon and Merlot vineyards growing alongside wheat and cotton.

The Bell Mountain and Fredericksburg appellations – subregions within the wider Texas Hill Country – produce attractive wines from Cabernet Sauvignon, Merlot and the less widely planted Syrah and Sangiovese grapes. Val Verde, the state's oldest winery, is still producing here and makes delicious fortified wines such as its Don Luis Tawny Port.

Found in the highest area of the Trans-Pecos region, the state's largest vineyard was planted by the University of Texas in 1981; it is now leased out on a commercial basis. The Trans-Pecos region accounts for a high proportion of Texan wine output.

In the Escondido Valley AVA there are no resident wineries, but the dry climate and well-drained soils are ideal for grape production, allowing some decent, inexpensive bottles to be made from Chenin Blanc, Chardonnay, Cabernet Sauvignon and Merlot, mainly under the Ste Genevieve brand.

CANADA

British Columbia

Canada is a land of great contrasts, particularly where weather is concerned. Bitterly cold in winter and seriously hot in summer, it might not, at first glance, seem to have the credentials for viticulture. But it does. A few dedicated winegrowers succeed against the odds in Quebec and Nova Scotia, and in British Columbia and Ontario there is a flourishing wine industry – provided it has a little help from geography.

LEFT *The extensive vineyards of Quails' Gate overlook Lake Okanagan. In good years their best wines are marketed under the Stewart Family Reserve banner: Pinot Noir, Foch and Chardonnay.*

British Columbia's principal geographical help comes in the form of Lake Okanagan. Its breezes moderate the summer temperature in the south while protecting the north from harsh winters. The hotter southern end produces excellent red Bordeaux varieties, with recent plantings of Syrah looking good. Chardonnay and Pinot Gris are the best whites. In the cooler north, Gewürztraminer, Riesling and Pinot Noir are successful.

The nearby Similkaneen Valley is at higher altitude. Here reflective mountain rocks intensify the sunlight and retain heat during the evening, assisting the ripening of Merlot, Gamay and Chardonnay in particular.

In Fraser Valley, Vancouver Island and the Gulf Islands, where the rainfall is higher, the mild climates suit Pinot Noir and Chardonnay together with aromatic Gewürztraminer, Riesling and Pinot Gris.

Cedar Creek Winery 'Platinum Reserve' Pinot Noir, Okanagan Valley. Medium bodied with spicy cherry fruit and clean balancing acidity.

Prospect Winery 'Birch Canoe' Pinot Blanc, Okanagan Valley. Pineapple dominated with fresh, vibrant acidity.

Mission Hill Winery Reserve Riesling, Okanagan Valley. Rich, well-flavoured with clean, peach-style fruit.

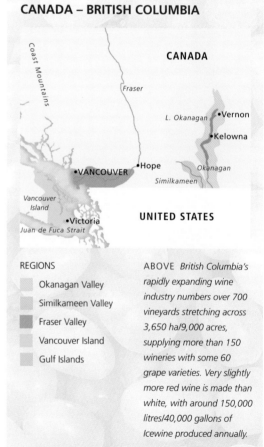

CANADA – BRITISH COLUMBIA

CANADA

Coast Mountains
Fraser
L. Okanagan • Vernon
• Kelowna
• VANCOUVER • Hope
Okanagan
Vancouver Island
Similkameen
• Victoria
Juan de Fuca Strait

UNITED STATES

REGIONS
Okanagan Valley
Similkameen Valley
Fraser Valley
Vancouver Island
Gulf Islands

ABOVE *British Columbia's rapidly expanding wine industry numbers over 700 vineyards stretching across 3,650 ha/9,000 acres, supplying more than 150 wineries with some 60 grape varieties. Very slightly more red wine is made than white, with around 150,000 litres/40,000 gallons of Icewine produced annually.*

CANADA

Ontario

Canada's largest wine-producing region, Ontario supplies about 75 per cent of the country's grapes, which is just about enough to provide for the domestic market. Internationally, it has become renowned for the production of luscious Icewines. As in British Columbia, geography is a significant factor: Lakes Ontario and Erie provide cooling summer breezes and stave off harsh winters, regulating vine growth.

This is particularly so in the Niagara Peninsula, the principal production area. Chardonnay produces excellent still wines, as does Riesling. But Riesling really stars, with Vidal, in the production of Icewine. Pinot Noir and Cabernet Franc make good reds with recent Syrah plantings showing well.

Promising reds

Pelee Island was the home of Canada's first winery, established in the 1860s. It and Lake Erie North Shore are hotter during the growing season, giving red wines of greater structure. Even Cabernet Sauvignon can ripen here – with Cabernet Franc, it makes up the lion's share of red-wine production. Chardonnay is the favoured white variety, Vidal Blanc being used for Icewine.

Prince Edward County is a newcomer on the Ontario wine scene and could be worth watching for the future.

CANADA – ONTARIO

Lake Huron

CANADA

ONTARIO

•TORONTO
Lake Ontario
•Hamilton

•Buffalo

•DETROIT

Lake Erie

Pelee
Island

•Cleveland

UNITED STATES

REGIONS

Prince Edward County

Niagara Peninsula

Lake Erie North Shore

Pelee Island

ABOVE *Lakes Ontario and Erie act as hot water bottles for the Ontario vineyards. The 'Lake effect' ensures fewer frosts in spring and a longer ripening in autumn. It may seem hard to believe, but Ontario's southern vineyards are on a more southerly latitude than Bordeaux.*

🍷🍷 **EastDell Estates Barrel Fermented Chardonnay, Niagara Peninsula.** Fresh pear fruit with a crisp finish.

🍷🍷🍷 **Dan Aykroyd Winery 'Signature Reserve' Vidal Icewine, Niagara Peninsula.** Ripe tropical fruits with honey and toffee notes and good balancing acidity.

🍷🍷🍷 **Magnotta Winery Riesling Icewine, Niagara Peninsula.** Apricots dominate with citric notes and hints of honey.

VQA system
Canadian wines are regulated under the Vintners Quality Alliance appellation system. The regulations govern the origin and type of grapes, sugar content, wine style, vineyard designation and vintages, and wines are blind tasted by an expert panel.

LEFT *Harvesting for Icewine can start only when the temperature drops to -8°C/18°F. Artificial freezing of the grapes is prohibited by VQA rules. Inniskillin, one of the top producers, now exports to 59 countries.*

●●● Chile and Argentina

South America is a vinous sleeping giant. Argentina may be one of the largest wine producers in the world, yet only recently has it become a big player on the international stage. Chile, although not as prolific, is highly active in the export market, while Brazil and Uruguay (see pages 234 and 235) have burgeoning wine industries, with Uruguay in particular gaining recent plaudits.

The Andes Mountains provide Argentine vineyards with the altitude to ensure hot days and cold nights – encouraging the grapes to develop good aroma and colour profiles during the long growing season – and water from melted snow to irrigate them. Water from the Andes also irrigates Chilean vineyards. Here the quality-producing factor is the cooling effect of winds from the Pacific Ocean, providing the ideal climate in inland valleys.

Both countries have gained justified reputations for making honest, fruit-driven wines at realistic prices. A wide selection of noble grape varieties is to be found, and winemakers are increasingly quality conscious in selecting the ideal terroir for each of them. There are also two national specialities: the Carmenère grape in Chile and the Malbec in Argentina.

NORTHERN CHILE

Coquimbo and Aconcagua

These are exciting times for those involved in the Chilean wine industry. Expansion is the order of the day, with new vineyards being created in previously untapped regions of the hot, dry north, where cooling Pacific breezes are a key factor and irrigation is paramount. Most are planted by the big companies, but a few small boutique wineries are setting a new trend in Chile.

Coquimbo

Chile's most northerly vineyards are in the Elqui Valley, 600 km/360 miles north of Santiago. As yet Elqui is quite a small-scale undertaking, but its granitic soils show clear potential for growing the Syrah grape. Viña Falernia is the first significant winery to be established in the area, with vines planted at a heady altitude of over 2,000 m/6,600 ft.

The Limarí Valley is one of Chile's most recent quality wine discoveries, with several big players already established here, notably Concha y Toro. A number of fashionable boutique wineries are also making names for themselves,

particularly with Chardonnay and Syrah. Among them is Viña Tabalí, a newish addition to the Viña San Pedro portfolio, which is making a good barrel-fermented, citric-style Chardonnay, and Casa Tamaya, which produces the award-winning 'Pink Goat' Syrah Rosé from 10-year-old vineyards. This favoured coastal region, with its clay and limestone soil, is especially suited to Chardonnay, although the morning mist that rolls in from the ocean, known locally as the *camanchaca*, requires a vigilant eye in the vineyards.

Further south, the rocky soils of the small Choapa Valley are proving conducive to Syrah and Cabernet Sauvignon.

BELOW *The Don Maximiano vineyard of Errázuriz in the Aconcagua Valley is 550–600 m/ 1,800–2,000 ft above sea level. It is mostly planted with Cabernet Sauvignon.*

Aconcagua

The long-established Aconcagua Valley vineyards were once a bastion of Cabernet Sauvignon, but recent plantings of Syrah suggest that there may be even greater potential for this popular grape variety, particularly on granitic hillside sites. Refreshing breezes temper the warm, dry climate to give Aconcagua vineyards the ideal conditions for growing really healthy grapes.

Most of the big companies are in residence here: Errázuriz was founded in the valley as long ago as 1870, and Agustinos, San Esteban, and Swiss-owned Viña von Siebenthal are prominent. Errázuriz has expanded into the cooler coastal part of the valley, nearer to Valparaiso, with new plantings of Chardonnay and Sauvignon.

Water into wine

Cool-climate Casablanca Valley underwent major expansion in the 1990s, but the lack of a major water source means that water for irrigation must be drawn from wells, and restricted water rights may well limit further development.

Casablanca is well represented in the export market. It has a justified reputation for the quality of its white wines, with Sauvignon Blanc generally considered the best, but its Pinot Noir is also worth seeking out. The long growing season here ensures a good expression of terroir.

New kid on the block

Although vineyard planting in the San Antonio Valley did not begin until 1998, it has already attracted critical acclaim for its Sauvignon Blanc, Pinot Noir and Shiraz wines. It is another cool-climate region, and the differing soils and microclimates in the individual vineyards spread among the hills produce wines with distinctive styles, with particular success in the case of Sauvignon Blanc. These wines are fresh, spicy and complex with good acidity and minerality, displaying a variety of fruit nuances.

BELOW To be viable, vineyards need a reliable source of water. Wells supply some of Chile's vineyards, but meltwater from the Andes is highly prized. Rich in calcium, it is very vine-friendly.

NORTHERN CHILE – COQUIMBO AND ACONCAGUA

COQUIMBO
- Elqui Valley
- Limarí Valley
- Choapa Valley

ACONCAGUA
- Aconcagua Valley
- Casablanca Valley
- San Antonio Valley

PRODUCERS
1. Viña Falernia
2. Concha y Toro
3. De Martino
4. Viña Tabalí
5. Casa Tamaya
6. Agustinos
7. Errázuriz
8. Viña von Siebenthal
9. San Esteban

De Martino Single Vineyard Chardonnay, Limarí Valley. Produced only about 15 km/9 miles from the coast, this is a fairly rich, barrel-fermented Chardonnay with mineral notes from terroir in the finish.

Tabalí Special Reserve Chardonnay, Limarí Valley. Fresh and complex with crisp citric acidity and stony minerality to underpin.

Viña von Siebenthal 'Carabantes', Aconcagua Valley. Creative Syrah-dominated blend with small percentages of Cabernet Sauvignon and Petit Verdot. Aromas and flavours of deep black fruit with suggestions of bacon fat, herbs and pepper.

CENTRAL CHILE

Central Valley

Chile's most extensive vineyards are found around and to the south-west of the capital, Santiago, in valleys stretching towards the Pacific. Some date back to the 19th century, and there is an abundance of native winemaking wisdom to be found here. The majority of wines are fruit-driven reds, and the standard is high, but cool-climate Sauvignons Blancs and Chardonnays can be excellent, too.

Maipo Valley – shades of Bordeaux

When the earliest vineyards in the Maipo Valley were planted in the 19th century by the likes of Concha y Toro, it was with cuttings brought from Bordeaux. Hardly surprisingly, then, Cabernet Sauvignon is the king here, accounting for over 60 per cent of the grapes grown. Merlot, Carmenère and Syrah – often, but by no means always, in classic blends – also contribute to the roster of fine reds for which the region is noted. Although particular microclimates and soils influence individual wines, a quality of intense colour is common to most of them, and the characteristic Cabernet blackcurrant and mint is usually prevalent, with greater complexity achieved in cooler areas where the growing season is longer. While red wines predominate, quality whites can also be found, especially Sauvignons Blancs.

As the city of Santiago expands, encroaching on the old vineyards, new plantings have been made higher into the Andean foothills of the Maipo Alto, where the cooler climate and poorer soils are producing red wines of some distinction. Almaviva, Domus (especially Aurea) and Santa Rita (Casa Real) are among the stars taking the name of Maipo Alto around the world. While the flatter central part of the valley is warmer, cool conditions prevail in the coastal reaches in the west and southwest, and the low rainfall here is another factor in producing wines of greater quality.

Maipo's proximity to Santiago has ensured that almost all the major companies are present in the region. Foreign investment has been significant, and one of the most interesting outcomes has been the success of Odfjell Wines, produced in the Maipo Valley by a Norwegian-owned company, with notably impressive Carmenère and Cabernet Sauvignon heading up a red wine list that ranges from the inexpensive entry level to pricey boutique wines.

RIGHT *La Palmería vineyard of Viña la Rosa is named after the ancient palm forest, next to which it is planted, in the Cachapoal Valley.*

CENTRAL CHILE – CENTRAL VALLEY

REGIONS

- Maipo Valley
- Rapel/Cachapoal Valley
- Rapel/Colchagua Valley
- Curicó Valley
- Maule Valley

PRODUCERS

1. Almaviva
2. Cousino Macul
3. Domus Aurea
4. Concha y Toro
5. Santa Rita
6. MontGras
7. Montes
8. Cono Sur
9. San Pedro

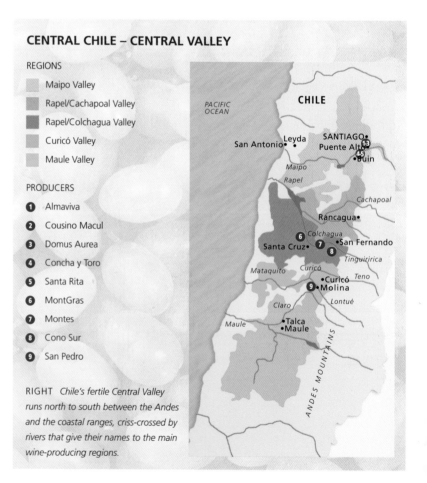

RIGHT *Chile's fertile Central Valley runs north to south between the Andes and the coastal ranges, criss-crossed by rivers that give their names to the main wine-producing regions.*

Rapel Valley

The gifted *huasos*, or Chilean cowboys, whose traditional home is the Rapel Valley, are proud of their reputation as upholders of Chilean equestrian skills, and their dedication to their art is rivalled by the disciplined cultivation of vines practised by the valley's winemakers. In fact the Rapel is really two valleys, the Cachapoal and Colchagua: both names are seen on wine labels, while the use of the term 'Rapel Valley' usually indicates that the wine has been blended from both. Red wines are to the fore here. Areas of clay soil in the more northerly Cachapoal Valley make it ideal for the Merlot grape. Merlot also flourishes in Colchagua, but in the mist-affected Andean foothills beside the Tinguiririca River Pinot Noir is particularly successful.

Both valleys are of considerable extent, ranging from the cooler Andean eastern side, down through the hottest, central part to the western stretches, which are very much influenced by cooling breezes from the Pacific. Yet, with modern irrigation techniques, hillside plantings in the poorer soils of the hot central area, aided by skilled winemaking, are producing a number of wines of remarkable quality.

Although it is a relative newcomer, having been established in 1987, Viña Montes has from the very start set exciting standards, with its 'Alpha' Cabernet Sauvignon an immediate and continuing success. The winery has several vineyards in the Colchagua Valley, as well as further south in Curicó, and is now also among Chile's finest makers of Carmenère and Syrah. Other Rapel producers of note include MontGras, Apaltagua and Cono Sur, whose winery is in Colchagua, although it has vineyards in most of the main growing areas.

MEDITERRANEAN CLIMATE

Chile's predictable climate provides long periods of uninterrupted sunshine and a clean atmosphere for growing particularly healthy grapes. But it brings little rain, and the further north the vineyard the more the winegrower must depend on irrigation, either from wells or rivers. Chilean winemakers do not squander their valuable resource. Consequently, a high proportion of these wines are made conscientiously, giving Chile's wines a justified reputation in the export market at all levels, from cheap and cheerful to exceptional and expensive. And almost all Chilean wines also display varietal typicity and correctness.

Almaviva, Maipo. Chile (Concha y Toro) meets Bordeaux (Rothschild) in this Cabernet-dominated blockbuster, packed with sweet black fruit.

Santa Rita 'Medalla Real' Cabernet Sauvignon, Maipo. Spicy blackcurrant-rich red with good structure and concentration.

Viña MontGras Carmenère Reserva, Colchagua. Deeply coloured and richly flavoured with spicy black fruit, vanilla and toast on the full and generous palate.

Viña San Pedro 'Castillo di Molina' Cabernet Sauvignon, Curicó. Soft fresh berry fruit (cherry and vanilla) gives way to a complex, balanced palate.

De Martino 'Limavida Old Bush Vines', Maule. A Malbec, Carmenère, Carignan, Tannat blend from ancient vines – red/black fruits, silky tannins, fresh acidity.

Carmenère

This grape arrived in Chile in the 19th century, along with other Bordeaux varieties, but it was not until 1994 that it was recognized there as a separate variety from Merlot. Extensive plantings, encouraged by its suitability to the climate, have made it the flagship Chilean variety.

RIGHT *Harvesting Carmenère grapes in the vineyards of Luis Felipe Edwards. In 'Doña Bernada', the estate's top wine, 30 per cent Carmenère is used.*

Southern valleys – Curicó and Maule

Travelling south, the climate becomes wetter and the risk of frost higher. Nonetheless, winemaking is the major economic activity in the Curicó region, especially in the Lontué Valley, and a few vines can still be found dating back to the mid-19th century. Many of the major houses maintain vineyards here, and there has been much recent investment. As in the rest of the Central Valley, far more red wine is produced than white, but east of Molina, where the climate is cooler, Sauvignons Blancs (particularly from the boutique winery Echeverría) have acquired a reputation for their clean freshness, while the reds are deliciously fruit driven.

Even further south is Maule, where just about all the well-known grape varieties are planted and are gradually overtaking the table grapes that were formerly prevalent here. Cabernet Sauvignon leads in terms of quantity, but it is for Carmenère that the region is building a new and growing reputation. The valley is one of the oldest areas to be under vines, and there are many small parcels of old vines that give fruit of a stunning quality and make sensational wines – if you can find them. Because Maule is situated so far south its grapes tend to have a higher natural acidity,

making the wines good for ageing and also giving a fresher style to the young varietals. Not surprisingly, most of these wines can now be found in the export market. Viña Botalcura (from the town of that name in the valley) has established growing export sales of value-for-money wines, red and white, from the main grape varieties. Prominent among international investors has been Miguel Torres, the award-winning wine producer from Catalonia, who set up a winery in Curicó as long ago as 1979 and has since established another in western Maule.

ABOVE *Cabernet Sauvignon vines in the Clos Apalta vineyard of Lapostolle, in the Colchagua Valley, with the Andes in the distance.*

SOUTHERN CHILE

Itata, Bío-Bío and Malleco

Grapes were grown in the wetter southern regions in the days before irrigation systems allowed the hotter, drier regions further north to dominate the industry. Traditional varieties – Muscat of Alexandria and País – were the most planted, as grapes for the table or for bulk wine, but not for quality wine. They are still grown prolifically, but plantings of international grape varieties are ever increasing, with encouraging results.

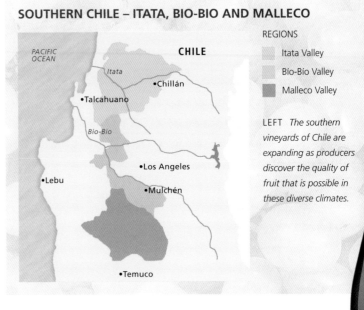

SOUTHERN CHILE – ITATA, BIO-BIO AND MALLECO

PACIFIC OCEAN

CHILE

Itata
•Chillán
•Talcahuano
Bío-Bío
•Los Angeles
•Lebu
•Mulchén

•Temuco

REGIONS
Itata Valley
Bío-Bío Valley
Malleco Valley

LEFT *The southern vineyards of Chile are expanding as producers discover the quality of fruit that is possible in these diverse climates.*

ABOVE *Cono Sur's Bío-Bío vineyard, where the pollution-free climate is conducive to growing healthy grapes.*

Cono Sur Gewürztraminer, Bío-Bío Valley. This stylish Gewürztraminer shows good fruit with notes of spice. Typical varietal aromas of lychee and cumin give way to a full and luscious palate that lingers in the finish.

Already the big companies such as Cono Sur have invested in the area, with most wine production being concentrated in the Itata and Bío-Bío Valleys. However, in the southernmost of the regions, Malleco, Chardonnay is producing wine of some quality, suggesting that more vineyards will be following soon.

A region of contrasts

Although they are contiguous, Itata and Bío-Bío enjoy markedly different climates. In Itata, which has a particularly large thermal range, the area around Chillán is one of the hottest in Chile. The cooler Bío-Bío Valley is proving well suited to aromatic varieties such as Riesling and Gewürztraminer, with good-value examples coming from Zarcillo and Cono Sur. There are also successful plantings of the notoriously tricky cool-climate grape Pinot Noir, and the widespread producer Viña Porta specifically chose the Bío-Bío Valley in which to establish its Pinot Noir vineyard. The climate is in fact quite similar to that of Bordeaux, where the addition of sugar to the fermenting must is considered normal. In Chile, however, this practice is outlawed, which explains the lack of plantings of Chile's most popular variety, Cabernet Sauvignon.

NORTHERN ARGENTINA

Salta and La Rioja

Two of Argentina's northerly outposts, Salta and La Rioja, are setting standards that suggest great potential. Although they are comparatively remote, the quality of their wines is sufficiently high to attract the kind of investment that will ensure their promise is fully realized. What sets the wines of Salta apart, however, is the altitude at which the grapes are grown: the vineyards here are among the highest in the world.

Torrontés

Argentina's star white grape, Torrontés, is an aromatic, fruity grape that produces a crisp, refreshing wine. It is planted in many areas, but finds its greatest expression in the high-altitude vineyards of Salta, around the mountain resort of Cafayate. Here the high summer temperature is moderated by cooling afternoon winds, providing perfect conditions for developing the heady perfumes that characterize this grape, as exemplified by the Colomé Torrontés of Donald Hess. Good Malbec and other red varieties, such as Etchart's Cafayete Cabernet Sauvignon, demonstrate the region's potential.

Of the three varieties of Torrontés, the finest flavoured is Torrontés Riojana, named after La Rioja province, roughly halfway between Salta and Mendoza. This is a dry, almost desert region, where irrigation is essential to produce wine. While Torrontés flourishes here, the future for La Rioja may actually lie in its red wines.

Geographically separating Salta and La Rioja, the Catamarca region is yet to reveal its potential, while in low-level San Juan, where around a quarter of Argentina's grapes are grown, few make it as far as the bottle. However, investment in the higher-altitude Pedernal Valley is producing promising red and white wines.

Colomé Torrontés 'Vino Blanco de Gran Altura', Salta. Bright floral aromas with notes of roses dominating, well flavoured in the mouth with refreshing acidity to balance.

RIGHT *Felix Lavaque produced his first wine in Cafayate as long ago as 1889. The vineyards, at an altitude of over 1,500 m/5,000 ft, enjoy hot days and cool nights, producing good colour and flavour in the grapes.*

NORTHERN ARGENTINA – SALTA AND LA RIOJA

REGIONS	PRODUCERS
Salta	❶ Felix Lavaque
La Rioja	❷ Colomé Amalaya
Catamarca	❸ Etchart
San Juan	

CHILE

ANDES MOUNTAINS

•Salta
①-③•Cafayate
•Catamarca
•Chilecito
•La Rioja
•San Juan
•Mendoza **ARGENTINA**

LEFT *Although the dry Argentine climate generally promotes healthy grapes, they can be severely damaged by winds, with the powerful Zonda threatening at flowering time. The temperature fluctuations of El Niño occasionally bring devastating rains.*

CENTRAL ARGENTINA

Mendoza

Mendoza is one of the world's great wine cities. Vineyards are to be found in its suburbs, while wineries line the roads leading from the city. But this is a vinous crossroads, with altitude a major factor in determining which of the outlying regions produce fine wines and which are better left untouched. Rainfall is low, so irrigation – with the crystal-clear waters from melting snow in the Andes – is key.

Wine has been produced in Mendoza since the arrival of the early Spanish settlers. They inherited a network of irrigation channels devised by the area's previous inhabitants, the Huarpe Indians, to provide a water supply for their crops of potatoes and corn.

Mendoza River – star region

With the soaring Andes as a magnificent backdrop, the upper Mendoza River (particularly the area around Luján de Cuyo) is where many of Argentina's flagship wines originate. Almost all offer great value for money, such as the Reserva range of Terrazas de los Andes, a 1999 still-wine subsidiary of Champagne giant Moët & Chandon. The award-winning

'Privada' is the icon of Bodega Norton, now in Austrian ownership, and its entire range offers good value. The French-owned Alta Vista winery has vineyards in Luján de Cuyo, as well as the Uco Valley and Salta's Cafayate Valley. It produces superb Malbec from its Alizarine vineyard.

Another yardstick is Luigi Bosca's tasty Malbec Reserva DOC. This old winery, dating back to the late 1800s, has been at the forefront of developing the Luján de Cuyo DOC. It is the combination of cloudless skies coupled with little risk of frost that provides ideal growing conditions for the Malbec grape, which has found an ideal second home in Argentina. It is by no means alone, however, with many red varieties adding to the prestige of the region.

BELOW *Nicola Catena planted his first Malbec vines in Mendoza in 1902. The present-day Catena Zapata vineyards in the Andean foothills are located around Agrelo and San Carlos, at altitudes ranging from 860 m/2,850 ft to 1,500 m/5,000 ft.*

High-altitude vineyards

Altitude is a major factor in the quality of Argentine wines. An elevated vineyard position brings large temperature swings between day and night, allowing the grapes to develop excellent aroma profiles, plus good levels of acidity. At lower, hotter levels, as in Northern and Southern Mendoza, the grapes often lack acidity, producing flat, flabby wines, and it is a common practice to acidify musts.

Hail is an ever-present threat, and vineyards can be devastated in a matter of minutes. Netting is now widely employed to protect the crop.

Mendoza's powerhouse

The hotter climate of eastern Mendoza's lower altitudes potentially leads to grapes ripening prematurely. To combat this the vines are trained on *parrales* (trellises), so that the leaf canopy shades the grapes from sunlight, keeping them cooler. Red wine grapes predominate, but the white Viognier, star of the northern Rhône Valley, is showing signs that it is well suited to this huge winegrowing region.

Uco Valley – star in the making

Argentina's most promising wine region is without doubt the Uco Valley, especially around Tupungato. Here, in the cooler climate, the high-altitude vineyards (ranging from 1,000–1,500 m/3,300–5,000 ft) are proving notably successful for a wide range of grape varieties. The poor soils and naturally high levels of acidity achieved in the grapes allow flavoursome wines with good backbone and character to be produced.

Under these conditions the ubiquitous Malbec does well, but so does the temperamental Pinot Noir. Syrah, Cabernet Sauvignon and Chardonnay are the predictable stalwarts, but no less successful are the more aromatic varieties of Riesling and Pinot Gris. They more than justify the recent investment in modern vineyards and wineries. Bodegas

Fabre Montmayou Malbec 'Gran Reserva', Mendoza, Luján de Cuyo. Elegant yet intense Malbec, packed with spicy, dark cherry aromas wrapped in an overcoat of ripe, silky tannins.

Bodega Norton 'Privada', Mendoza. Intense blend of Malbec, Merlot and Cabernet Sauvignon with a concentrated fruit nose and palate, hints of espresso and a big velvety finish.

Malbec Bodegas Catena Zapata, Mendoza. Full, creamy and loaded with spicy black fruits.

Pulenta Estate Chardonnay, Mendoza, Luján de Cuyo. Judicious blend of tank- and barrel-fermented wines offering fresh fruit aromas, a lively and complex palate and a zesty acidity leading to an elegant finish.

CENTRAL ARGENTINA – MENDOZA

Mendoza
Mt Aconcagua
Mendoza
1-6
Luján de Cuyo
Medrano
Desaguadero
CHILE
Tupungato
Tunuyán
7
Diamante
San Rafael
Atuel
Villa Atuel
General Alvear
ARGENTINA

REGIONS
- Northern Mendoza
- Eastern Mendoza
- Mendoza River area
- Uco Valley
- Southern Mendoza

PRODUCERS
1. Alta Vista
2. Catena Zapata
3. Fabre Montmayou
4. Luigi Bosca
5. Norton
6. Terrazas de los Andes
7. O. Fournier

ABOVE *Though linked by their proximity to the city itself, the five subregions of Mendoza have distinctive characters. Just as in Bordeaux, the region may have a generic style, but geography and geology create subtle vinous variations.*

Trapiche produces a range of pricey but award-winning single-vineyard Malbecs, demostrating how well this variety has adapted itself to the climate and soils. They are full bodied and powerful, with delicious fruit and spice. Another producer making single-vineyard wines here is Alta Vista. Its Temis Malbec is made from vines over 40 years old, displaying great fresh fruit aromas and flavours against a backbone of ripe, soft tannins. The Spanish-owned O. Fournier is one of those Uco bodegas proving successful with Syrah.

RIO NEGRO

This most southerly area of Argentina, bordering Patagonia, is renowned for fruit production thanks to the Alto Valle irrigation channel. Wine production is on the increase here and, although red varieties dominate, it should certainly be watched in the future for some crisp, fresh whites and fruit-driven Pinot Noir.

BELOW *Malbec is a rich, tannic grape variety producing deep ruby-hued wines. In Argentina its rustic qualities are best tamed to make ripe, damson-flavoured wines.*

RIGHT *Alta Vista's 60-year-old Malbec planted in its Alizarine vineyard is producing superb wine. Its 'Grande Reserve' Malbec offers a massive, affordable mouthful.*

●●● Regions 92–101

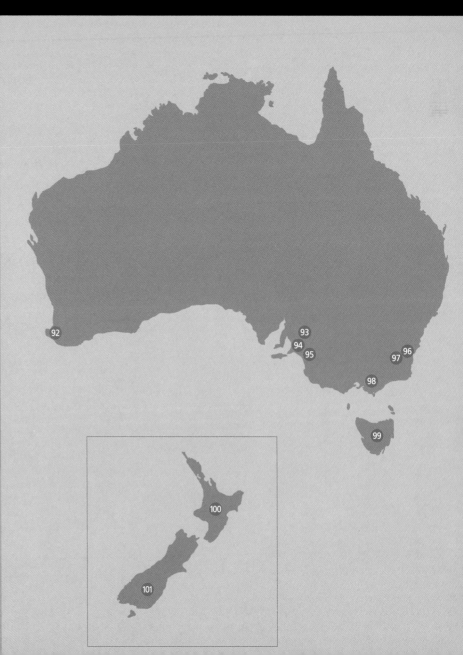

Australia & New Zealand

Although vines were planted in Australia by the earliest European settlers, its wines were rarely encountered outside the country – until the last quarter of the 20th century, that is, when exports rocketed. The rapid success of Australian wines throughout the world gave the old wine-producing countries a much-needed wake-up call.

What is more, Australia also began to export its winemaking skills, as winemakers trained there found themselves in demand as consultants to producers throughout the world, even in France. They brought with them a wholly scientific approach to winemaking and a thorough understanding of the importance of cleanliness and hygiene in every facet of wine production, the cellar in particular.

New Zealand has been another comparative latecomer to the world wine market. It does not produce anything like the huge quantities that Australia does, but it has created quite a stir with its high-quality, fruit-driven Sauvignon Blanc, Chardonnay and, latterly, Pinot Noir.

WESTERN AUSTRALIA

Margaret River and beyond

Western Australia's wineries produce less than 10 per cent of the country's output but around 20 per cent of its quality wine. This is premium wine country, focused on the coastal areas around and to the south of Perth. The flagship Margaret River region, with its Mediterranean climate, glorious coast and beautiful vineyards, has become one of Australia's top tourist destinations.

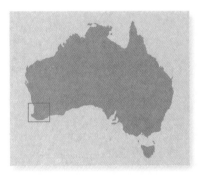

Millbrook Limited Release Viognier, Perth Hills. Big, alcoholic wine offering spicy and floral fruit with a rich palate.

Cape Mentelle Chardonnay, Margaret River. Intense and generous Chardonnay with big tropical fruit underpinned by mineral notes and well-integrated oak.

Vasse Felix Semillon, Margaret River. Classy, barrel-fermented wine with a wonderful, creamy texture balancing delightful citric fruit flavours.

Leeuwin Estate 'Art Series' Chardonnay, Margaret River. Sometimes acclaimed as Australia's top Chardonnay. Peach-dominated fruit, perfectly integrated with oak, gives way to a finish that lasts an eternity. Stunning!

Voyager Estate Cabernet-Merlot, Margaret River. Incredible structure supporting ripe, black-fruit aromas and flavours. Great potential for cellaring yet delightful short-term drinking.

Brookland Valley 'Verse 1' Merlot, Margaret River. Generously fruity wine with plums dominant, an earthy character, great balance and delicately oaked.

WESTERN AUSTRALIA – MARGARET RIVER AND BEYOND

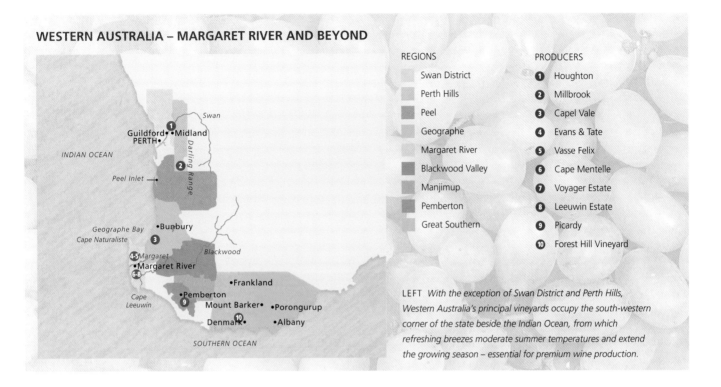

REGIONS

- Swan District
- Perth Hills
- Peel
- Geographe
- Margaret River
- Blackwood Valley
- Manjimup
- Pemberton
- Great Southern

PRODUCERS

- ❶ Houghton
- ❷ Millbrook
- ❸ Capel Vale
- ❹ Evans & Tate
- ❺ Vasse Felix
- ❻ Cape Mentelle
- ❼ Voyager Estate
- ❽ Leeuwin Estate
- ❾ Picardy
- ❿ Forest Hill Vineyard

LEFT *With the exception of Swan District and Perth Hills, Western Australia's principal vineyards occupy the south-western corner of the state beside the Indian Ocean, from which refreshing breezes moderate summer temperatures and extend the growing season – essential for premium wine production.*

'You can exist without wine but you cannot live . . .'

JACK MANN

Swan Valley fortified wines
Fortified wine production continues, with the Muscat Gordo Blanco and Muscadelle varieties excelling. To experience the great style of these fortified wines, try the Talijancich Reserve Muscat from a solera started in 1961. It is like drinking liquid Christmas cake.

LEFT *Black Angus cattle graze beneath red gum trees beside the vines and winery of Vasse Felix. Established in 1967, the estate ferments its entire range of wines in this winery, to maintain consistently high standards.*

Since the mid-1990s the number of producers in Western Australia has more than trebled; there are now over 350 wineries. With varied soil structures and climates, a wealth of different wines is being produced, from the cool-climate Pinots Noirs of Pemberton to the blockbuster reds and fortified wines of the Swan District.

Swan District

Commercial winemaking in Western Australia started in the mid-1800s at the Houghton estate in the Swan Valley. With its hot climate and dry summers, the area was known for its fortified wines until pioneering winemaker Jack Mann started producing quality white table wines from the Chenin grape. His first vintage, in 1937, was likened to white Burgundy, and thus a name was born for one of Australia's biggest-selling white wines: Houghton's White Burgundy. Today, most of the district's wineries are concentrated around the Swan Valley towns of Midland and Guildford; they produce excellent whites made from Verdelho, Chardonnay, Chenin Blanc and Sémillon, together with full-on reds made from Shiraz and Cabernet Sauvignon.

Perth Hills and Peel

A long, scattered region with a number of valleys running through it, Perth Hills offers a wealth of differing microclimates, thereby ensuring numerous styles of wine. Smaller boutique wineries thrive, their makers showing individual flair in exploiting the varied topography and soil structures. With a change in altitude of some 300 m/1,000 ft, night-time temperatures can vary by several degrees. This slows grape development in the higher-lying vineyards and gives longer ripening time to other varieties planted nearer the valley floors. The climate is generally Mediterranean, with cool, wet winters and hot, dry summers. Major varieties here are Viognier, Chardonnay, Sauvignon Blanc, Chenin and Verdelho for white wines; for reds, Shiraz (Syrah), its traditional Rhône partner Grenache, and Bordeaux varieties Cabernet Sauvignon and Merlot.

To the south of the city of Perth, the region of Peel, one of Western Australia's youngest and smallest regions, was first developed in the 1970s and now has over 200 ha/500 acres under vine. Peel is known for its quality Shiraz and Chenin Blanc production.

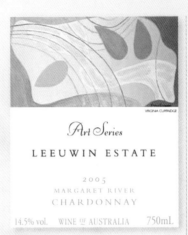

RIGHT AND BELOW *The best potential sites for planting the vineyards of Leeuwin Estate were identified by California's Robert Mondavi in 1972; planting followed from 1975 to 1979. Rapturous reviews of the 1980 'Art Series' Chardonnay immediately put the estate on the map. Matching Leeuwin's commitment to excellence in its wines is its commitment to art, with a series of concerts bringing some of the world's great musicians to Australia and commissions for original artworks from Australian artists for its wine labels.*

Geographe

Some of the finest fruit in Western Australia is grown in Geographe. Much of it ends up in regional blends, but there are small wineries now producing wines solely from this area. With 1,200 ha/2,965 acres under vine, it is a significant region, accounting for around 11 per cent of total state production. It has diverse soil types, but it is its proximity to refreshing coastal breezes that has the greatest effect.

Chardonnay grows particularly well in Geographe. Peter Pratten, one of the pioneers in the region, planted vineyards here in the 1970s. His Capel Vale Winery today makes excellent wines, notably the barrel-fermented Geographe Chardonnay, which has wonderful peachy fruit with tropical and nutty overtones.

Margaret River

Western Australia's best-known region runs some 90 km/ 56 miles between Cape Naturaliste in the north and Cape Leeuwin in the south. It is bordered to the east by a ridge opening into rolling hills and to the west by the stunningly beautiful Indian Ocean coastline.

Margaret River is home to some of Australia's pre-eminent names, such as Vasse Felix and Cape Mentelle, which established their wineries in the 1960s and 1970s respectively. Since the mid-1990s, vineyard plantings and the number of producers have grown tremendously.

The region's reputation was first established for Cabernet Sauvignon, but today numerous varieties are found here. Its Shiraz came to fame when the Evans & Tate Winery won the trophy for Best Red Wine at London's International Wine Challenge in 2000. Chardonnay also holds a deservedly elevated status, making highly regarded wines such as the 'Art Series' Chardonnay from Leeuwin Estate.

Three regions for the future

To the east of Margaret River, Blackwood Valley is a small region initially acclaimed for its white wines. Growers have more recently been attracted to the loam- and gravel-based soils for Cabernet Sauvignon and Shiraz.

Pemberton has attracted both major players and boutique wineries and is rapidly gaining a reputation as one of Australia's great cool-climate terroirs. Site selection is imperative for Pinot Noir and Chardonnay. More recent plantings of Cabernet Sauvignon and Merlot show potential, while Sauvignon Blanc is admirable.

Manjimup – slightly warmer than neighbouring Pemberton – offers hope to the Chardonnay and Pinot Noir brigade, with multinationals such as Cape Mentelle investing in the region. The best results have been from Pinot Noir and Merlot grapes, which thrive in the cold winters and moderate late-summer temperatures. Soils with less fertility than in Pemberton help to intensify the flavour in the grape.

Great Southern

Great Southern embraces five subregions, which between them offer a complete spectrum of soils and conditions for talented winemakers to exploit. Albany offers good possibilities with Pinot Noir and Chardonnay, Mount Barker with excellent Shiraz, Cabernet Sauvignon and Riesling. Denmark is providing wonderful Sauvignon Blanc and Pinot Noir, Frankland River weighs in with some incredible Riesling, and in Porongurup numerous varieties are successful, including Sémillon and Verdelho.

SOUTH AUSTRALIA

Clare Valley and Riverland

Being responsible for about half the country's total production, South Australia is clearly the force behind the Australian wine industry. Its name appears as the catch-all area on many of the good-value bottles that have taken Australian wine to prominence in world markets, thanks mainly to the multinational companies based here. The first vineyards were established as long ago as the late 1830s.

Beside Riverland, which is responsible for a quarter of the nation's production, other famous winegrowing areas in South Australia include the country's biggest quality wine region, Barossa Valley (see page 216), and remote Coonawarra (see page 219), while two of Australia's iconic wines – Penfolds 'Grange' and Henschke's 'Hill of Grace' – originate here. There is a great variation in climate between the regions, from areas of intense heat such as Riverland to cooler-climate sectors such as Clare Valley and Adelaide Hills. Drought is an increasing problem, making irrigation essential for vine health and wine quality.

Clare Valley

The most northerly of the state's classic wine regions is the delightful Clare Valley. Here the hotter daytime climate is tempered by refreshing afternoon breezes, and the valley (actually a series of valleys) has carved out a name for itself for the production of mouth-watering Rieslings, with fresh, citric acidity and great minerality.

Widely ranging vineyard aspects, soil types and exposures allow a wealth of varieties to be grown successfully, and both the cool-climate Sauvignon Blanc and heat-seeking Grenache are found here. Because of the popularity of the flagship Riesling other varieties are occasionally dismissed, yet Clare Valley also produces fine and distinctive reds. Shiraz here can have an elegance that takes nothing away from the intense berry flavours, while Cabernet Sauvignon gives wines of concentration and juicy fruit.

Screw cap

To ensure the retention of the fine, steely acidity and delicious fruit that makes Riesling so enjoyable, Clare Valley producers pioneered the use of the Stelvin closure in 2000. Where they led, others have followed.

🍷 **Pikes 'The Merle' Riesling, Clare Valley.** Intensely flavoured with citric notes interwoven with racy acidity. Quite delicious!

🍷 **Annie's Lane 'Copper Trail' Riesling, Clare Valley.** Bags of lemon/lime flavours with a clean clip of acidity. Good for ageing as well as immediate drinking.

Riverland

The Murray River gave this region its name and is the source of irrigation, vital not only for grape growing but also for fruit production in general. For the most part the land is flat, allowing economical mechanized pruning and harvesting. The hot, dry climate quickly ripens the grapes without much fear of disease – ideal for producing well-priced bottles for export. That is not to say that the wine is of low quality: far from it. Modern vinification techniques ensure that the generous, fruit-filled styles match the demands of the consumer. Chardonnay is the most widely planted variety, with Shiraz, Cabernet Sauvignon and Merlot also making a considerable contribution. Alongside the large, multiple producers, some smaller wineries coexist.

LEFT *Clare Valley wineries are, for the most part, small – independent of the big companies. They are, therefore, able to make the most of terroir differences to enhance each wine's individuality.*

SOUTH AUSTRALIA – CLARE VALLEY AND RIVERLAND

Spencer Gulf

•Clare
❶
❷

❸ •Renmark

Murray

Mt Lofty Ranges

ADELAIDE•
Piccadilly•

Gulf of St Vincent

•McLaren Vale

REGIONS

Clare Valley

Riverland

PRODUCERS

❶ Pikes

❷ Annie's Lane

❸ Angove's

ABOVE *While the Riverland climate is hot and dry all day long, Clare Valley is cooled by afternoon breezes, and its colder nights help to preserve acidity and natural flavours.*

SOUTH AUSTRALIA

Barossa and Adelaide surrounds

Mention Barossa and wine lovers immediately think of Shiraz, the grape that put Australia's most famous wine region on the map. Fortunately, the phylloxera that wiped out many vineyards in the 19th century never reached here, leaving parcels of old bush vines to produce majestic bottles of black-fruit-driven, velvety wine. Today, most major players are found in the region.

Barossa Valley

Wine was first produced in this hot region north-east of Adelaide in the mid-1800s, by a mix of German, British and Silesian settlers. Little did they know of the future fame and fortune they were bestowing on the area.

As with most Australian regions, the landscape is varied, with numerous differing soil types and microclimates, so it is not just Shiraz that performs well. The world demand for Chardonnay saw an expansion of white wine production here, which can be anything from full-on and mouth-filling to lean and clean, depending on its origin. But, in truth, it is reds that fare best, with Rhône varieties such as Grenache and Mourvèdre, together with the ubiquitous Cabernet Sauvignon, making wines of distinction.

Eden Valley

Part of the so-called Barossa Zone, Eden Valley's cooler-climate vineyards are planted at higher altitude in rugged terrain. Here Riesling is at home, regularly vying with that of Clare Valley as Australia's finest. It reigns supreme in the windswept subregion of High Eden, where it makes wines with a distinct lime characteristic and great acidity, giving good ageing potential.

SOUTH AUSTRALIA – BAROSSA AND ADELAIDE SURROUNDS

BAROSSA
- Barossa Valley
- Eden Valley

ADELAIDE SURROUNDS
- Adelaide Hills
- McLaren Vale
- Langhorne Creek

PRODUCERS
1. Wolf Blass
2. Penfolds
3. Peter Lehmann
4. Yalumba
5. Grant Burge
6. Henschke
7. Pewsey Vale
8. Petaluma
9. Shaw + Smith
10. Hardys

Penfolds Grange
First produced in 1951, Penfolds Grange has been acclaimed as Australia's greatest red wine. Named after Dr and Mrs Penfold's cottage, and formerly known as Grange Hermitage, this is not a single-vineyard wine, but is blended (according to the vintage) from fruit from some of Penfolds' best parcels of vines, mainly Shiraz but sometimes with a little Cabernet Sauvignon. It is a hugely structured wine, capable of ageing for many years.

ABOVE *Each of the wine-producing regions close to Adelaide has carved a name for itself and a distinctive identity in the export market. Wolf Blass, Penfolds and Yalumba are among the big names present, while Henschke leads in quality.*

LEFT *Biodynamic and organic practices are employed in Henschke's vineyards, with mulching to avoid mechanical disturbance of the soil. Water retention is improved, as a result of which over a third of Henschke's vines are grown without irrigation.*

Grant Burge 'The Holy Trinity', Barossa Valley. A blend of Shiraz, Grenache and Mourvèdre old vines (up to 110 years old), rich in floral, spicy and herbaceous red and black fruits backed by fine-grained tannins.

Hare's Chase Red Blend, Barossa Valley. Inexpensive, Shiraz-dominated blend with great body and complexity.

Pewsey Vale 'The Contours' Riesling, Eden Valley. Big, mineral and citric Riesling with sweet fruit and a crisp finish.

Henschke 'Mount Edelstone' Shiraz, Eden Valley. Old-vine Shiraz bursting with ripe blackberry fruit backed by spice and chocolate notes. Powerful yet elegant.

Shaw + Smith Sauvignon Blanc, Adelaide Hills. Grassy Sauvignon with tropical overtones, elegant purity and a clean acidity.

Coriole Cabernet Sauvignon, McLaren Vale. Dark, ripe fruit with good intensity and hints of chocolate. Supple with an ample finish.

Bleasdale Vineyards Shiraz/Cabernet Sauvignon, Langhorne Creek. Full of plum and black-fruit flavours with a hint of mint and spice. Great value!

Johann Christian Henschke founded vineyards around Keyneton in the 1860s, and today his great-great-grandson Stephen Henschke produces one of Australia's greatest reds, Hill of Grace, from Shiraz vines dating from this time. Rare and expensive, this is an incredibly concentrated wine, rich in fruit, with the capability of ageing for decades.

Adelaide Hills

Thanks to their altitude, Adelaide Hills enjoy a distinctly cool climate, and vineyards were established along with orchards in the 1830s and 40s. Then in the 1970s Brian Croser of Petaluma came here to plant Chardonnay, a variety relatively unseen at the time. Its success was immediate. Other cool-climate grapes such as Sauvignon Blanc and Pinot Noir also produce well. The subregions Lenswood and Piccadilly are at even higher elevations. Lenswood produces Sauvignon Blanc, Pinot Noir and Riesling grapes of good, natural acidity; Piccadilly makes admirable sparkling wines.

McLaren Vale

In 1839 John Reynell planted South Australia's first vines at Chateau Reynella (as it became), which continues to produce wine to this day. The area developed rapidly and parcels of vines surviving from the 19th century today make excellent wines. King of the crop is Cabernet Sauvignon, producing wines rich in blackcurrant fruit and soft, ripe tannins.

Langhorne Creek

Shiraz and Cabernet Sauvignon predominate, often as part of blends from multinational wineries. The region has also attracted smaller growers making excellent boutique wines, and the white Verdelho has made something of an impact.

SOUTH AUSTRALIA

Limestone Coast

The Limestone Coast Zone covers a group of vineyards in the south-east of South Australia, all of which share the limestone subsoil on which vines thrive. Much of the topsoil is *terra rossa*, a mixture of clay and sand over the limestone base, which has made Coonawarra – so popular for its fine Cabernet Sauvignon – one of Australia's classic wine regions.

Mount Benson

Promoting itself as 'Terra Rossa by the Sea', Mount Benson's first viable vineyard was planted in 1989. Vineyards have since expanded to over 500 ha/1,250 acres, with locals, national wine companies and even the Rhône wine specialist Chapoutier making investments. With immediately attractive wines, this is definitely an area to watch.

Padthaway

Originally a source of good Chardonnay, Padthaway is also noted for Cabernet Sauvignon and Riesling, especially for botrytis-affected, late-harvest wines with their ripe fruit flavours and hints of orange. Seppelt first established a vineyard here in 1964; other major wine companies followed, notably Hardys, whose Stonehaven Winery, built

BELOW *The red soil so characteristic of Coonawarra can be seen in the hilltops of neighbouring Wrattonbully.*

SOUTH AUSTRALIA – LIMESTONE COAST

•Keith

SOUTH AUSTRALIA

VICTORIA

•Naracoorte

Robe•

Coonawarra

•Penola

•Mt Gambier

REGIONS

Mount Benson

Padthaway

Wrattonbully

Coonawarra

PRODUCERS

① Stonehaven

② Tapanappa

③ Penley Estate

④ Wynns

LEFT Wine communities of the Limestone Coast have soils in common, but the ocean has differing effects on local climates.

Shades of Italy
The *terra rossa* soils that characterize Coonawarra resemble those found in parts of southern Europe. The topsoil of sand and clay allows drainage while the sublayer of limestone retains moisture, giving the vines much-needed water even in dry conditions. When the soil is exposed to air, iron oxide forms within the clay to give it its distinctive red hue.

in 1998, is now one of Padthaway's major producers. Much of the fruit grown here is used to add class to blends from other areas and those labelled simply 'Limestone Coast'.

Wrattonbully

The gentle undulations of the *terra rossa* vineyards and the moderate climate, slightly cooler to that of Coonawarra, make this an excellent source of good red wines, with Cabernet Sauvignon and Shiraz topping the list. Small wineries such as Redden Bridge, Tappanappa and Malone Wines sell their excellent wines by mail order.

Coonawarra

John Riddoch was the first to plant vines here back in 1890, but it was not until the arrival of Wynns and Penfolds in the 1950s that Coonawarra's reputation for quality wine emerged. From that time it has become synonymous with high-quality red wines, first for Shiraz and latterly for Cabernet Sauvignon, some of which are among Australia's best. Coonawarra's major contributory factors are its fabled *terra rossa* soil running over a limestone ridge, ideally suited to Cabernet Sauvignon, and its maritime climate. This provides cloud cover during the critical ripening season, giving rise to an extended growing season that allows complex flavours to develop within the grape. From good fruit comes good wine.

Other varieties flourish here too, ranging from Pinot Noir to Malbec for red wines and Sauvignon Blanc, Chardonnay, Sémillon and (especially) Riesling for whites. The growers are committed to the region and speak of it with reverence.

Today there are over twenty cellar-door tasting venues to visit, where the passion and dedication of producers such as Koonara in Penola can clearly be seen.

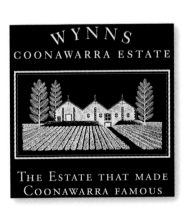

Tapanappa 'Whalebone Vineyard' Cabernet Shiraz, Wrattonbully. Ripe black fruits with complex notes of eucalyptus and liquorice supported by fine, ripe tannins.

Penley Estate 'Phoenix' Cabernet Sauvignon, Coonawarra. Loaded with ripe fruit with blackcurrant dominant. Wonderful!

Katnook Estate 'Odyssey' Cabernet Sauvignon, Coonawarra. A hefty price but a hefty wine. Ripe, berry fruit and plum-filled wine with layer after layer of complexity.

Wynns 'Michael' Shiraz, Coonawarra. A rarity in that it is produced only in exceptional years and then using only a fraction of the very best Coonawara Shiraz available from the estate. If you see a bottle, grab it.

AUSTRALIA – NEW SOUTH WALES

Hunter Valley

Vineyards were first planted in New South Wales in the 1780s, soon after the arrival of the First Fleet. Within 40 years, what is now known as the Lower Hunter Valley – one of Australia's most famous wine regions – had been established. It was perhaps a further 150 years before a true wine industry developed here, but by then it was exporting to most corners of the world.

Lower Hunter Valley

Traditionally, the Hunter Valley has been considered as two regions, divided by the great Hunter River, although today's official zoning couples them together. It was the Lower Hunter Valley that achieved international recognition for table wines and it was here that Australia's commercial industry originated when George Wyndham planted vines on the Dalwood Estate around 1830. This, the oldest Australian winery in continuous production, was later renamed Wyndham Estate in honour of its founder. Hunter Valley (just

BELOW *Englishman Edward Tyrrell established his Ashmans Estate at Pokolbin in 1858, producing his first vintage in 1864. It quickly became a Hunter Valley standard-bearer.*

a two-hour drive north of Sydney, and to the north-west of the coastal town of Newcastle) was the earliest Australian wine region to gain fame abroad, thanks to Wyndham, who showed his wines at exhibitions in Europe and the United States. The wines were frequent prize winners, and were exported in quantity to Britain and India.

Sémillon was responsible for the region's early fame. Here it produces wines light in alcohol and body, with a crisp, zesty acidity in youth, that age over the ten years or more of their lives into rich, honeyed and luscious examples with notes of toast and vanilla. Cabernet Sauvignon, despite the summer rains, also does well here, but Shiraz is the more noted variety – it can be traced back to the 1830s, when William Kelman, brother-in-law of James Busby (who is credited with introducing wine grapes to Australia), first planted vineyards here. It makes wines that can last in bottle for decades, undergoing a metamorphosis to become complex and silky with notes of leather and earth.

Upper Hunter Valley

The Upper Hunter Valley is a more recent development in commercial terms, Penfolds having been the first to enter in a major way in 1960. Irrigation is essential, and white varieties such as Chardonnay and Verdelho fare well. Sémillon is also popular, although it can lack the depth obtained further south in the Lower Hunter Valley. Chardonnay gives full-bodied wines with chewy, peachy fruit more suitable for younger drinking, and the heat-resistant Verdelho makes well-endowed, fruity wines with a tropical edge for pleasant quaffing.

Broke Fordwich

Among the subregions, Broke Fordwich has over seventy small estates and now makes around a quarter of the region's wine. The Brokenback Range makes a superb background for this delightful region on the edge of the Yengo National Park, where new varieties such as Dolcetto and Barbera, natives of Italy's Piedmont region, are to be found.

Tyrrell's 'Vat 1' Semillon, Hunter Valley. A showstopper with a few years' age on its back, starting with delicious citrus fruit in a lean structure and becoming a golden nectar with loads of toasty, honeyed layers.

Brokenwood Semillon, Hunter Valley. Clean, crisp and citric in youth with underpinning minerality, luscious and rich in age with honey and nutty notes.

Pepper Tree Limited Release Shiraz, Hunter Valley. Medium bodied with good berry fruit and earthy undertones ageing to develop typical Hunter earthiness.

ABOVE At Hope Estate in the Hunter Valley, red basalt soils support Shiraz and Merlot vines. The estate also owns the famed Rothbury Estate in the Hunter Valley.

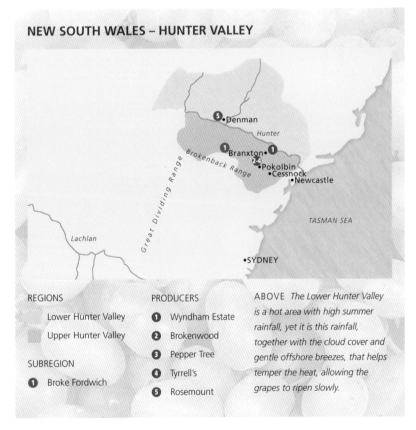

NEW SOUTH WALES – HUNTER VALLEY

REGIONS
Lower Hunter Valley
Upper Hunter Valley

SUBREGION
1 Broke Fordwich

PRODUCERS
1 Wyndham Estate
2 Brokenwood
3 Pepper Tree
4 Tyrrell's
5 Rosemount

ABOVE The Lower Hunter Valley is a hot area with high summer rainfall, yet it is this rainfall, together with the cloud cover and gentle offshore breezes, that helps temper the heat, allowing the grapes to ripen slowly.

AUSTRALIA – NEW SOUTH WALES
Central and Southern

New South Wales is not just about the Hunter Valley. From the cool high vineyards of Orange to the heat of the plain of Riverina, a wealth of wine styles can be found, made from a full range of varieties: clean, crisp Sauvignon Blanc; round, full-flavoured Chardonnay; honeyed Sémillon; deep, earthy Shiraz; luscious 'stickies' and clean sparklers.

Mudgee

Picturesque Mudgee (Aboriginal for 'nest in the hills') is a collection of gently rolling hills and interwoven valleys on the edge of the Great Dividing Range. Its warm, dry summers suit the vine ideally, and the stars are fine, concentrated Cabernets Sauvignons and full-flavoured, peachy Chardonnays grown by small, family producers. Although long established, Mudgee has only recently become known.

Orange and Cowra

Established as a convict settlement in the early 1800s, Orange is Australia's highest vineyard region, based on the basalt-rich slopes of Mount Canobolas. Chardonnay, Sauvignon Blanc and Riesling thrive in the cool climate, as do the red varieties Cabernet Sauvignon and Merlot.

Heading south, Cowra was first planted with vines by settlers in the 19th century, but it was not until the 1970s

BELOW *While Riverina, on the hot plain, has been largely a quantity wine producer, the other regions represented on the map are mostly cool climate. Their vineyards are planted at altitude, particularly those of Orange and Canberra.*

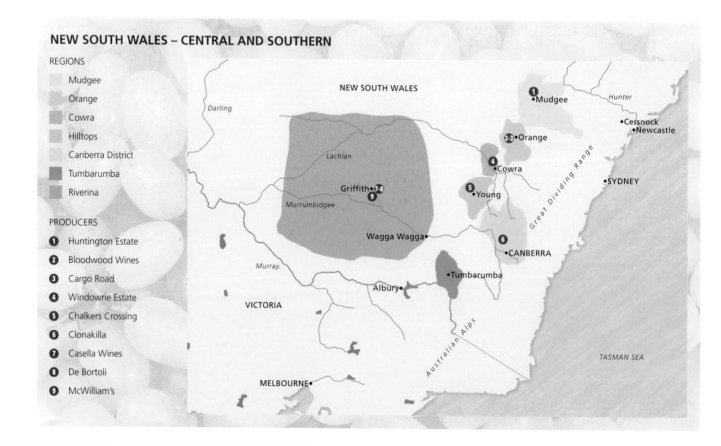

NEW SOUTH WALES – CENTRAL AND SOUTHERN

REGIONS
- Mudgee
- Orange
- Cowra
- Hilltops
- Canberra District
- Tumbarumba
- Riverina

PRODUCERS
1. Huntington Estate
2. Bloodwood Wines
3. Cargo Road
4. Windowrie Estate
5. Chalkers Crossing
6. Clonakilla
7. Casella Wines
8. De Bortoli
9. McWilliam's

that its modern wine industry was created. Over 2,000 ha/ 5,000 acres have now been planted, and Chardonnay, Shiraz and Cabernet Sauvignon are successful, especially from the more mature vineyards.

Southern NSW Zone

Hilltops, once renowned for its cherry orchards, is fast becoming a hot property in the Australian wine industry. Vines were originally planted to satisfy the thirst of the gold rush pioneers in the 1850s. Today, HIlltops is noted for good Cabernet Sauvignon, Shiraz, Riesling and Chardonnay, with McWilliam's one of the major players.

Vines were planted in the Canberra District back in the 19th century, but its wine industry remains in its infancy, with numerous small producers leading the way. The scattered vineyards are planted at high altitude, making this a cool-climate region where Chardonnay, Riesling, Viognier and Shiraz flourish. The Tumbarumba region is another recent high-altitude development, primarily known for sparkling wines from Chardonnay and Pinot Noir.

Riverina

The hot, dry plain of Riverina is Australia's second largest producer of table wines, thanks to its well-developed irrigation systems. It is home to some of the country's best-known wineries, including McWilliam's (pioneers of commercial winemaking here) and Casella Wines.

Despite the low rainfall, some rain does fall in summer, raising the humidity level and encouraging the formation of noble rot for the production of Riverina's flagship sweet wines. The De Bortoli winery was first to present a botrytized Sémillon in 1982, since when numerous producers have crafted similar styles of wine. Aside from these, good Chardonnay, Sémillon, Shiraz, Cabernet Sauvignon and Merlot are made.

Cargo Road Sauvignon Blanc, Orange. Wonderfully clean with crisp gooseberry fruit and overtones of passion fruit and a fresh, vibrant acidity.

Windowrie Estate 'The Mill' Chardonnay, Cowra. Full flavoured tropical style of Chardonnay with notes of oak.

Chalkers Crossing Cabernet Sauvignon, Hilltops. Deeply coloured wine with great intensity of blackcurrant fruit and fine, silky tannins to support it.

Clonakilla Shiraz Viognier, Canberra. Beautifully crafted, with cherry and bramble fruit flavours and loads of spice and pepper above.

De Bortoli 'Noble One' Botrytis Semillon, Riverina. Honeyed, peachy nectar with notes of orange above luscious fruit.

Yellow Tail
Casella Wines' Yellow Tail brand has become the greatest success story of the Australian wine industry. First imported into the United States by W. J. Deutsch & Sons in 2001, sales rapidly grew to over five million cases by 2005.

RIGHT *The vineyard of Bloodwood Estate, Orange, was the pioneer in the area, first planted in 1983. There are now over 20,000 vines on the estate, producing mostly varietal wines, red and white. Its notorious pink is called 'Big Men in Tights'.*

AUSTRALIA

Victoria

In wine terms Victoria is the most exciting of all the mainland Australian states, simply because of the diversity of its vineyards, aided as they are by a comparatively cool climate. New vineyard sites are constantly sought, and the most promising are in the coolest parts of the state, either in the hills or close to the sea. Quality, not quantity, is the watchword.

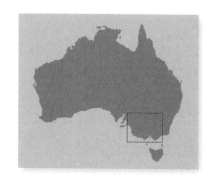

North West Victoria

The North West Victoria Zone, comprising the Murray Darling and Swan Hill regions, is Victoria's equivalent to neighbouring NSW's Riverina region, with over 23,000 ha/56,800 acres in production, making around a quarter of Australia's wine. All the major companies are present, producing huge quantities of immediately attractive – though not for keeping – Chardonnay, Shiraz and Cabernet Sauvigon, in wineries that resemble small towns. Brown Brothers' famous Orange Muscat & Flora comes from here.

Grampians, Pyrenees and Henty

Charles Pierlot pioneered the production of traditional-method sparkling wines in Grampians. Great Western Winery, now owned by Seppelt, continues to make excellent examples. Good still wines are also produced by it and many smaller wineries. Of these, Mount Langi Ghiran is well known internationally. Its Langi Shiraz is noteworthy, and it makes a well-priced Pinot Gris. Cool-climate Riesling and Chardonnay impress, while Shiraz and Cabernet Sauvignon give intensely flavoured reds, as they do also in the Pyrenees. The Henty region is one of Victoria's smallest producers, with only a handful of growers, yet the quality is amazing. Vibrant Riesling, fruity Shiraz and spicy Pinot Noir stand out.

RIGHT *There is huge diversity in the style of wines produced in Victoria, with a wealth of different influences on the climate, and wineries ranging from giant to boutique.*

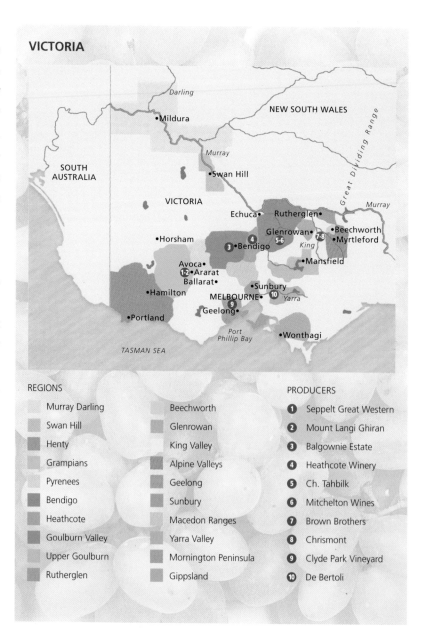

VICTORIA

REGIONS

Murray Darling	Beechworth
Swan Hill	Glenrowan
Henty	King Valley
Grampians	Alpine Valleys
Pyrenees	Geelong
Bendigo	Sunbury
Heathcote	Macedon Ranges
Goulburn Valley	Yarra Valley
Upper Goulburn	Mornington Peninsula
Rutherglen	Gippsland

PRODUCERS

1. Seppelt Great Western
2. Mount Langi Ghiran
3. Balgownie Estate
4. Heathcote Winery
5. Ch. Tahbilk
6. Mitchelton Wines
7. Brown Brothers
8. Chrismont
9. Clyde Park Vineyard
10. De Bertoli

Bendigo and Heathcote

In Central Victoria, Shiraz gives wines of generous style with considerable ageing potential, notably in Bendigo's Mediterranean climate. Well-structured Cabernet Sauvignon and a few stylish whites from Chardonnay and Sauvignon Blanc are made by small, boutique wineries. Heathcote's Shiraz is some of the greatest in Australia, and David Anderson's 'Duck Muck' is quite celebrated. Ron and Emily Laughton are making intense red wines and a delicious, powerful Riesling at Jasper Hill. .

Goulburn Valley

In the Goulburn Valley, Tahbilk is Australia's second oldest continuously producing winery: its Shiraz (from 1860) and venerable Marsanne vines are reputed to be the oldest in the world. Roussanne and Viognier also flourish in Goulburn, where the Mitchelton estate makes terrific wines at affordable prices from Rhône varieties. David Traeger also produces delicious Verdelho. At high altitude, Domaine Chandon grows Pinot Noir and Chardonnay with high acidity, suitable for the production of quality sparkling wine.

ABOVE *Brown Brothers' Whitlands Vineyard, south of their Milawa winery, is up in the cool alpine climate of the Great Dividing Range.*

BELOW *Chateau Tahbilk, with Swiss-French origins, is the oldest winery in Victoria. Some of its vines date back to its foundation in 1860.*

Gippsland
Around thirty wineries are located in widespread Gippsland, producing good Chardonnay, Cabernet Sauvignon and Pinot Noir depending on the vineyard site.

North East valleys

The North East Victoria Zone embraces Alpine Valleys, Beechworth, Glenrowan, King Valley and Rutherglen, its epicentre. Rutherglen and Glenrowan survived the phylloxera plague, rapidly re-establishing their vineyards on resistant American rootstock. Both hot-climate areas are renowned for great fortified dessert wines from Muscat and Muscadelle, plus powerful reds from Shiraz and Durif (Petite Sirah).

Beechworth is producing some excellent wines from family-run estates, albeit in small quantities. Its cool climate suits Pinot Noir and Chardonnay, making elegant wines with delicious purity of fruit. Another cool-climate region is the King Valley, where Brown Brothers was established in 1855 and purchases much of the region's crop. Chardonnay grown at higher altitudes is excellent for the production of sparkling wines. Growers of Italian descent are succeeding with the Italian varieties Barbera, Nebbiolo and Sangiovese.

A long growing season at altitude in the beautiful Alpine Valleys produces wines with intense fruit flavours and good natural acidity, particularly from Chardonnay and Pinot Noir.

Port Phillip

Centred on Melbourne, the Port Phillip Zone takes in Geelong, Yarra Valley, Mornington Peninsula, Sunbury and Macedon Ranges. Geelong is making top-class wines from Cabernet Sauvignon, Shiraz, Pinot Noir and Chardonnay, and recent plantings of Riesling and Viognier promise much. Good Shiraz is found in Sunbury, while Australia's coolest wine region, the Macedon Ranges, grows Chardonnay and Pinot Noir with the natural acidity required to make high-quality sparkling wines.

Another of Australia's coolest regions is the Yarra Valley, where more than 3,500 ha/8,650 acres of vines are cultivated. It has become famous for its Pinot Noir, delivering elegant wines with staying power. Here Chardonnay gives wines that age gracefully, as does Cabernet Sauvignon.

Mornington Peninsula wines are rich in fruit flavour, with the generally light Pinots Noirs showing typicity. Chardonnay is distinguished by fig and melon fruit flavours with nutty overtones. The best Cabernets Sauvignons are quite intense with pronounced berry fruit.

Brown Brothers Orange Muscat & Flora. Fresh with bright aromas of citrus fruits and blossom with clean refreshing acidity to balance the gentle sweetness.

Balgownie Estate Shiraz, Bendigo. Deeply coloured with concentrated black fruits and velvety finish. Good in youth but holds up well in the bottle.

Mitchelton 'Print' Shiraz, Central Victoria. Well-priced, powerful, yet elegant Shiraz, packed with ripe berry fruit with spicy overtones, all wrapped up with chocolaty tannins. Fantastic!

Chrismont Chardonnay, King Valley. Peach/melon fruit dominate this well-balanced, round and moderately intense offering with oak integrated but evident.

Clyde Park Vineyard Shiraz, Geelong. Black cherries in abundance with notes of cloves and pepper and soft, ripe tannins.

De Bortoli Reserve Release Pinot Noir, Yarra Valley. Burgundian-priced, spicy, plum-fruited Pinot Noir with great intensity and silky texture.

LEFT *Coldstream Hills, overlooking the Yarra Valley, was set up by wine writer James Halliday, producing its first vintage in 1985. Almost every operation in the wine production is done by hand. Halliday had previously established Brokenwood in the Hunter Valley.*

AUSTRALIA

Tasmania

The planting of Pipers Brook Vineyard in 1973 heralded the rebirth of the Tasmanian wine industry, which subsequently developed a reputation for excellent wines based on Chardonnay and Pinot Noir – and, more recently, quality sparkling wines – produced in its cool, maritime climate. White Alsatian varieties also impress. Site selection is vital to maximize exposure to sunshine, reduce the risk of frost and protect against cold winds.

TASMANIA

UNOFFICIAL REGIONS

1. North West
2. Tamar Valley
3. Pipers River
4. East Coast
5. Coal River
6. Derwent Valley
7. Southern

RIGHT *Tasmania is on the same latitude as the southern tip of New Zealand's North Island and the wine-growing areas of South Island. With comparable maritime influences, its wines have a similar purity of fruit.*

Pinot Noir is the most-planted variety and produces a wide range of styles, from light and gentle to full bodied. The best examples are wines of great depth of fruit and complexity. Chardonnay is the next most prolific, with a similar range of styles. However, the clean, clear fruit quality it gives here is not always enough to handle the big oak flavours common to many of the hotter-climate mainland wines, so barrel fermentation must be carefully managed if it is used.

Some of the more aromatic grape varieties, such as Riesling, Gewürztraminer and Pinot Gris, can make very

ABOVE LEFT *Pipers Brook is one of several Tasmanian vineyards owned by the Belgian Kreglinger Estate. The coastal influence on Pipers Brook makes it one of its cooler vineyards, ideally suited to the production of Pinot Noir, Chardonnay, Riesling and sparkling wines.*

appealing wines here, with their high natural acidity imparting a steely character.

There are over two hundred individual producers on the island, but most of these operate on a very small scale, simply selling their wines to eager customers at the winery door.

Tamar Ridge 'Devils Corner' Pinot Noir. Attractively priced Pinot with a delicious red fruit and spice palate with silky tannins.

Bay of Fires 'Tigress' Chardonnay. Well-made, barrel-fermented wine with peachy fruit, citrus notes and judiciously integrated oak.

NEW ZEALAND

North Island

Until the mid-1970s, New Zealand's wine production was concentrated in North Island, with Hawkes Bay carrying the flag. It has since been eclipsed by South Island, but is still a major contributor to the export market. The generally warmer climate is well suited to the red Bordeaux varieties, while the worldwide demand for Pinot Noir has seen the development of the Wellington region, to great acclaim.

Northland and Auckland

Grapes were planted in Northland by English missionaries as long ago as 1819; some years later, the first wine was produced from a vineyard planted by James Busby, a British government official, who subsequently founded the wine industry in Australia. Serious wine production began in Northland only in the late 20th century, when Cabernet Sauvignon, Merlot and Chardonnay were planted, achieving full ripeness in the warm summer conditions.

Further south in the Auckland region, the same varieties produce well in Henderson and Waiheke Island, with recent plantings in the Matakana area rapidly gaining recognition. Pinot Gris is well thought of there, too. Major companies with worldwide reputations, such as Montana and Villa Maria, are based in Auckland, processing wines from throughout the country, but smaller, boutique wineries are exploring new areas such as the Clevedon Valley, where Italian varieties including Arneis are being planted.

BELOW *Most of Craggy Range's Pinot Noir and Sauvignon Blanc vines are planted in this vineyard on Te Muna Road. It also has a small number of Pinot Noir vines in Bannockburn and Pinot Gris in the Waitaki Valley, in each case matching vines to soils.*

Waikato, Bay of Plenty and Gisborne

Good Chardonnay emanates from Waikato and Bay of Plenty, but this is becoming overtaken by production in Gisborne, where New Zealand's most easterly vineyards benefit from fertile soils and many hours of sunshine.

Hawkes Bay

By far the most important region of North Island is Hawkes Bay, with a continuous tradition dating back to missionary plantings in the the mid-1800s. It is the home of the Te Mata winery, the oldest in the country. A wide variety of soil types, long hours of sunshine and a dry climate make for excellent growing conditions. The region has more than doubled in vineyard area since the mid-1990s; much of this is in the Heretaunga Plains, away from the coastal influence, where temperatures are higher.

Cabernet Sauvignon and the earlier-ripening Merlot are the standard-bearers for the region and account for over half the island's production. Together they produce blends of world class, with good depth of flavour and predominantly berry fruit. Syrah is now attracting attention for its intense fruit characteristics. Chardonnay also grows well here but requires careful management. Sauvignon Blanc and Riesling tend to a riper, fuller style than those from South Island.

Wellington

Some of New Zealand's finest Pinots Noirs originate in the Wellington region, particularly around the village of Martinborough, which is similar in both climate and soil structure to Burgundy, with a long growing season, warm days and cool nights. Pinot Noir now accounts for almost 40 per cent of the plantings in this region. Sauvignon Blanc also performs well, and recently planted Pinot Gris has a bright future.

Craggy Range 'Te Kahu Gimblett Gravels Vineyard', Hawkes Bay. A Bordeaux blend packed with ripe plum and dried berry fruit, with great structure and clean balancing acidity.

Martinborough Vineyard Pinot Noir, Martinborough. Richly fruited and savoury with notes of game and spice and good concentration.

Escarpment Pinot Gris, Martinborough. Rich and generously flavoured with juicy pear fruit and a round yet fresh finish.

NEW ZEALAND – NORTH ISLAND

North Cape

PACIFIC OCEAN

TASMAN SEA

1 Waiheke Island

Auckland

2

Bay of Plenty

Hamilton

NORTH ISLAND

Lake Typo

▲ Mt Egmont

Gisborne

Napier Hawkes Bay
Hastings 3-4

Palmerston North

WELLINGTON Martinborough 5
Blenheim

SOUTH ISLAND

REGIONS

Northland

Auckland

Waikato/Bay of Plenty

Gisborne

Hawkes Bay

Wellington

PRODUCERS

1 Matakana Estate

2 Villa Maria

3 Te Mata

4 Craggy Range

5 Martinborough

LEFT *Despite strong westerly winds and a high rainfall, North Island enjoys a climate not unlike that of Bordeaux.*

NEW ZEALAND

South Island

South Island's vineyards are relative newcomers that have shot to stardom in a remarkably short time, principally, though not solely, for their production of some of the world's finest Sauvignon Blanc. Plantings have increased dramatically since the mid-1990s, and South Island seems set fair to develop its reputation still further.

Nelson

This small region at the northern tip of the island has vineyards scattered over the Waimea Plains, where stony, alluvial soils yield fruity wines with good acidity. The Moutere Hills, with their clay and gravel base, produce richer, more structured wines. Chardonnay, Sauvignon Blanc, Riesling and Pinot Noir are the main contenders. Autumn rainfall can be a hindrance here, which may explain the relatively small area of land under vine.

tropical overtones. Chardonnay and Pinot Noir are making excellent wines, too, with a proportion of the crop going for premium sparkling wine production, such as the Pelorus brand of Cloudy Bay. Riesling and Pinot Gris complete the picture, but it will be hard to surpass the reputation of the Sauvignon Blanc.

Sauvignon Blanc
Sauvignon Blanc is one of the world's great grapes. Highly aromatic, its style varies according to where it is grown. France's Loire Valley, around Sancerre and Pouilly, is premium territory, giving wines of great intensity. Good Sauvignons Blancs are produced in all the New World regions, with Marlborough arguably the best of them all.

Marlborough

The leading light in Sauvignon Blanc production is the Marlborough region. It first came to attention in 1980, when Montana unveiled its Sauvignon Blanc to much acclaim. Other producers soon followed, such as Cape Mentelle, which established its New Zealand winery, Cloudy Bay, in 1985. Cloudy Bay wines have enjoyed cult status ever since. From the mid-1990s Marlborough has more than quadrupled in size, thanks to the worldwide clamour for its wines, and it is now the largest of all New Zealand regions, accounting for more than half of the land under vine.

The alluvial soils of the Wairau and Awatere Valleys have proved to be a perfect source of Sauvignon Blanc. With long hours of sunlight and a refreshing maritime climate, vineyards here can produce stunning results in years that are not affected by early frosts or excessive autumn rainfall. These unusually complex wines are characterized by their refreshing acidity and cool, green pepper/gooseberry/ passion fruit aromas and flavours, sometimes with more

NEW ZEALAND – SOUTH ISLAND

NORTH ISLAND

TASMAN SEA

WELLINGTON
Blenheim 1 3 Cloudy Bay

SOUTH ISLAND
4 Waipara
Christchurch

Southern Alps
Mt Cook

Waitaki
Queenstown 5 6

Dunedin

PACIFIC OCEAN

Stewart Island

REGIONS
Nelson
Marlborough
Canterbury
Central Otago

PRODUCERS
1 Cloudy Bay
2 Montana
3 Saint Clair
4 Pegasus Bay
5 Rippon Vineyard
6 Felton Road

RIGHT *Machine-harvesting Sauvignon Blanc grapes in a Cloudy Bay vineyard, Marlborough.*

Canterbury

South of Marlborough, around the beautiful city of Christchurch, the Canterbury region is another rising star. Once considered too cold for wine production, Canterbury now has almost 1,000 ha/2,470 acres under vine. The more northerly Waipara region, which is protected from the cool east winds and enjoys slightly higher average temperatures, does particularly well.

Riesling and Pinot Noir are the leading lights here. Rieslings are vibrant and steely with deliciously clear fruit, and Pinot Noir gives wines of clean fruit, fresh acidity and ripe tannins that can age well.

Central Otago

Set in glorious alpine country, Central Otago – New Zealand's most southerly wine region – is another area producing terrific Pinot Noir. Experimental vineyards were planted in the 1970s but by 1997 only 135 ha/350 acres were under vine; subsequent successes, mainly the boutique production of Pinot Noir, have led to a tenfold increase in plantings.

At such latitudes frost is a major risk, so vineyards tend to be planted on warmer, north-facing hillsides. With low rainfall and humidity, the conditions encourage healthy, disease-free grapes. Water for irrigation is readily available, cloudless skies provide ripening sunshine, and cool nights subdue the process, to build intense flavours in the grape.

There are four subregions here, each affected by the microclimates and varied soils of the mountainous landscape. For the most part, they produce long-lived, black-cherry-dominated wines with good levels of alcohol. As the vineyards age their regional differences should develop and become more distinct, but even today wines from Central Otago are certainly worth seeking out, even if high production costs and the possibility of losing the crop to an early winter mean that these will always be expensive.

Saint Clair 'Wairau Reserve' Sauvignon Blanc, Marlborough. Pungent gooseberry and passion fruit aromas lead to a clean, crisp palate with lingering fruit flavours in the finish. Delicious!

Cloudy Bay Sauvignon Blanc, Marlborough. Fresh peach and passion fruit aromas with slight tropical notes, a rich, fresh palate and a crisp, zingy acidity that lingers in the finish.

Pegasus Bay Riesling, Waipara. Delicious ripe fruit aromas balanced by racy acidity and underpinning minerality.

Felton Road Pinot Noir, Central Otago. Complex berry fruit and violet aromas, full juicy palate and a dark and complex aftertaste.

Rippon Pinot Noir, Central Otago. Cherry fruit with floral notes, intense fruit on the palate and a glorious, ripe finish.

LEFT *Rippon Vineyard, overlooks Lake Wanaka, with the snow-covered Buchanan Mountains of the Southern Alps beyond.*

FELTON ROAD
ESTABLISHED 1991

PINOT NOIR
CENTRAL OTAGO
2008

PRODUCED AND BOTTLED BY
FELTON ROAD WINES LTD
BANNOCKBURN

GRAPES GROWN AT OUR BANNOCKBURN VINEYARDS

750 ml   *Wine of New Zealand*   Alc. 14.0% Vol.

Other wine-producing countries

Winemaking is undertaken in every continent except Antarctica. In countries such as China and Japan there is an ever increasing demand for home-produced, Western-style wine, despite largely unhelpful climates. There is real opportunity for such countries as Uruguay, Brazil and Mexico to emulate the export successes of Argentina and Chile. But it is to the former Balkan states and North Africa that we should look for signs that their undoubted potential is at last being fulfilled.

ALBANIA

Albanian winemaking has not yet recovered from years of national repression, but it has attracted foreign investment hoping to capitalize on opportunities for the future.

ALGERIA

Once a very important source of wine (a lot of it sold under French appellations), Algeria is currently trying to re-establish its industry.

BOLIVIA

Bolivia's humid climate is not conducive to the growing of grapes. The vineyards of its principal producer, Bodegas y Viñedos de La Concepción, are some of the highest in the world, at 1,700–2,100 m/5,500–7,000 ft above sea level.

BOSNIA AND HERZEGOVINA

Still rebuilding after the civil war in the 1990s, the region was an important producer of both red and white wines in the 19th century.

BRAZIL

Almost all of Brazil's considerable output of wine is consumed at home. Standards are rising in the face of stiff competition from imported wines.

CHINA

China's extremes of climate present serious difficulties to the success of traditional vineyards, but there is a ready and lucrative internal market for Western-style wines from the international varieties. Commercial vineyards have been planted in a number of different provinces, from Xinjiang in the north-west to Gansu and Ningxia in the west and Yunnan in the south. Grace Vineyard leads in quality, and the Rothschilds of Château Lafite have recently invested in a vineyard in Shandong province.

CZECH REPUBLIC

The bulk of Czech wines originate in Moravia, just north of Austria's Weinviertel. As yet quality is not on a par with that of Austria. Clean, archetypical Sauvignon Blanc is, so far, the pick of the wines. Many grape varieties are grown, both classic and indigenous. A few wines are made in Bohemia, close to the border with Germany.

CROATIA

Croatian wines have character, the best coming from vineyards close to the Adriatic coast. Almost every island and peninsula (and there are a lot) boasts its own local grape. Pošip from the island of Korčula and Bogdanuša from Hvar make robust white wines able to withstand the strong local cuisine. Cabernet Sauvignon, Merlot and Teran (Refosco) are producing promising red wine in Istria. Inland wines are insipid.

CYPRUS

An island with a vine-growing culture going back some 5,500 years, Cyprus's fame rests with its incredibly sweet Commandaria. Made from Mavro and Xynisteri grapes grown at the foot of the Troodos Mountains, much commercial Commandaria is simply too sweet and sickly, but the best retains a grapey freshness despite the enormously high sugar content. As a result of its joining the EU, Cyprus is transforming its formerly lacklustre table wine industry into a higher quality one based in the cooler climate of the Troodos Mountains.

GEORGIA

Traditional Georgian wines were rough and ready, made from grapes, pips, skins and stalks and immensely tannic. Russians loved Georgian Saperavi red wine, but its import was banned by Moscow in 2006. Foreign investment (notably from Pernod Ricard) should help realize the undoubted promise of this sleeping giant.

INDIA

India's wine industry is growing rapidly in size, expertise and significance. Because of the climate many wineries are located in the state of Maharashtra, with Château Indage first on the international scene with its popular sparkler Omar Khayyam. Sula makes good whites from Sauvignon Blanc and Chenin Blanc. Grover Vineyards near Bangalore produce very convincing Bordeaux-influenced reds with advice from Pomerol's Michel Rolland.

JAPAN

The climate and the enormous cost of land are the two main factors hindering winemaking in Japan. Most successful wineries are conveniently close to Tokyo and within sight of Mount Fuji. Four big companies lead the way: Suntory (which also has holdings in Europe), Mercian, Sapporo and Manns.

LEBANON

With thousands of years of winemaking history behind it, Lebanon today has a handful of fine producers in the Bekaa Valley. They have earned a high reputation for their excellent wines, a reputation enhanced by astonishing achievements during twenty years of civil war.

Although Lebanon produces some whites, it is the red blends that attract the greatest attention. The best vineyards are located at around 1,000 m/3,300 ft, with varieties such as Cabernet Sauvignon and Cinsault performing well. Serge Hochar's Château Musar is the best-known winery; excellent wines also come from Châteaux Ksara and Kefraya.

MACEDONIA

With its hot summer climate Macedonia should be able to produce red wines of the quality now being made in neighbouring Greece. So far it has not done so. White and red wines from the Tikveš winery are sometimes seen in export markets.

MALTA

As with Cyprus, Malta's entry to the EU may turn round an archaic winemaking industry. That Antinori, the Tuscan giant, has chosen to invest in the Meridiana Winery is sufficient proof of the island's potential.

MEXICO

Very promising wines are being produced in Mexico, given considerable foreign investment and American winemaking expertise. Baja California is the leading production area, where notable producers include Casa de Piedra, L.A. Cetto, Doña Lupe and Santo Tomas.

MOLDOVA

Moldova was a respected supplier of quality wines to the Tsars of Russia. Its ideal climate (tempered by the Black Sea) prompted the Soviet Union to plant mind-blowing quantities of vines here to satisfy its people's thirst. Quality sagged. But there are great possibilities if the country can attract the right sort of investment. At the economy end of the market its Firebird Legend varietals are enjoyable.

MONTENEGRO

The indigenous grape Vranac produces a powerful, well-structured red wine benefiting from a few years' ageing, which is exported. There is also a sweetish version, Duklja.

MOROCCO

Morocco is the current leader in North Africa in terms of volume and quality. Foreign investment, mostly by French companies, is bringing new technology and good growing techniques to the vineyards, and the Appellation d'Origine Garantie system has been put in place. Rhône-wine specialist Alain Graillot makes a particularly rewarding Moroccan Syrah.

PERU

Exports of Viña Tacama wines (red, white and sparkling) show that Peru holds considerable promise for the future.

RUSSIA

Under the Soviet regime, Russia had a huge wine industry, one of the biggest in the world. Today it is a mere minnow, as almost all the vineyards of the former USSR are in the hands of independent republics such as Georgia, Moldova and the Ukraine. Its surviving production areas of any significance are Krasnodar and Rostov-on-Don.

SERBIA

Serbia's vineyards are extensive but its wines are not yet fulfilling their promise. Reds and whites in styles similar to those of neighbouring Hungary and Romania are made from native grape varieties in addition to classics such as Pinot Noir, Cabernet Sauvignon, Merlot and Sauvignon Blanc.

SLOVAKIA

Mainly centred on Bratislava and extending along the Hungarian border, Slovakia's vineyards grow a selection of international grapes such as Riesling and Cabernet Sauvignon, plus a number of Hungarian varieties. J.E. Hubert sparkling wine has been made for almost two hundred years, but the big international success is Kastiel Belá Riesling, produced by Egon Müller, one of the Saar's most distinguished winemakers.

SLOVENIA

Slovenia is currently the top performer of the former Yugoslav countries. In Primorska, along the border with Italy, wines similar to those in Friuli are found, with well-focused whites and substantial yet refined reds, mostly from international varieties. Podravje is mainly a white wine area with Laški Rizling, Renski Rizling and Šipon the principal varieties, although Chardonnay and Sauvignon Blanc are on the increase. Radgona is the centre of Slovenia's sparkling wine industry. In general, Posavje produces lighter whites.

TUNISIA

With state encouragement, foreign investment is being sought to drag Tunisia's once important but run-down wine industry into the 21st century. The signs are promising.

TURKEY

Turkey has its own indigenous grape varieties, but it is imported varieties that are creating the greatest interest, particularly in Marmara, where Sarafin is the leading light (inspired by its founder's experience in Napa Valley). Doluca is another good Marmara producer. However, the Kavaklidere Winery, near Ankara, produces interesting wines from local varieties.

UKRAINE

Crimea was the source of sparkling and sweet wines for the cellars of the Tsars. It still holds the greatest potential but has not yet been significantly exploited.

URUGUAY

Uruguayan wines are becoming increasingly prominent in export markets. Many of the international grape varieties are cultivated to a high standard, but it is the Tannat grape that steals the show. This somewhat tannic variety is the main ingredient in Madiran from south-west France. Uruguayan Tannat is softer and rounder, also blending well with Syrah or Merlot. Pisano, Juanicó and De Lucca are among the country's leading producers.

Glossary

ACID Naturally occurring in grapes, giving wine its attractive and refreshing sharpness.

ADEGA (Portuguese) Winery.

AFTERTASTE The flavour of a wine that lingers in the mouth and may even develop after swallowing.

APPELLATION (French) The name of a geographical area, such as a region, village or vineyard, by which a winemaker is authorized to identify and sell a wine grown there, under regulations specific to the country of production.

AROMA The smell of a wine, particularly the pleasant, distinctive aromas arising from the grapes used.

BARREL Wooden cask (usually of oak) used for the fermentation and/or maturing of wine prior to bottling. An oak barrel has the greatest impact on wine when new, as tannins and flavours leach out; over time, the barrel becomes more neutral.

BARREL AGEING A wine matured in barrel for some years before bottling picks up additional flavours from the wood and is granted gentle oxidation.

BARRIQUE (French) Traditional Bordeaux oak barrel with a capacity of 225 litres.

BIODYNAMICS The growing of vines biodynamically is ruled by the influences of the planets and other cosmic forces, coupled with strict adherence to the purity of organic and inorganic materials applied to the vines. The biodynamic timetable also governs all processes in the making of the wine and its subsequent development.

BODEGA (Spanish) Winery.

BOTRYTIS The fungus *Botrytis cinerea*, also known as noble rot, which shrivels grapes, concentrating the sugar and adding a slightly burnt flavour. It is a vital factor in the making of many of the world's greatest sweet wines.

BOTTE (Italian) Large oak barrel, between 1000–15,000 litres in capacity. Exposure to oxygen is proportionately less than in a smaller barrique, and because botti are used for many years they impart little or no additional flavour to the wine.

BOTTLE AGEING The period after bottling and before opening, during which the constituents develop together influenced by the small amount of air in the bottle. Great wines, mostly reds but some whites, may benefit from 10–20 years' bottle ageing, but many wines are now made to mature earlier.

BRUT (French) Dry, generally used when describing sparkling wines and Champagne.

CALCAREOUS Of soil, containing calcium carbonate.

CANOPY The foliage of the vine that shades the grapes beneath it and also acts as the sugar factory of the plant.

CANOPY MANAGEMENT Use and appropriate pruning of vine leaves, either to allow the grapes maximum exposure to the sun, or to shelter them from it.

CARBONIC MACERATION Whole bunches of grapes, uncrushed, are fermented under a blanket of carbon dioxide to maximize colour and fruit and release a little tannin.

CHAI (French) A building in which wine is stored and matured (used mostly in Bordeaux).

CHAPTALIZATION The addition of sugar to a fermenting wine to raise its alcohol level. It is used mostly in cool regions, and is forbidden in many quality wine-producing areas.

CHÂTEAU (French) Literally a castle, but in wine terms mostly used to describe an estate (which may or may not have a castle).

CLASSED GROWTH *See* Cru classé.

CLIMAT (French) An individual vineyard (or part of one) with its own microclimate.

CLONE A particular strain of a grape variety selected and propagated, often for its resistance to specific diseases or tolerance of climatic problems.

CLOS (French) Specifically a walled vineyard, but often used in the name of an estate whether or not it is walled.

COMMUNE (French) A village and the vineyards that belong to it.

CONCENTRATION A higher level of flavour or extract than usual.

COOPERATIVE A group of growers who share winemaking premises, usually vinifying their grapes together and marketing their wine collectively.

CORKED Descriptive of wine that is stale or musty smelling as a result of a faulty cork.

COSECHA (Spanish) Vintage.

CÔTE (French) A slope or hillside, often used to denote a superior vineyard.

CRIANZA (Spanish) Wine that has spent two years maturing, with at least 12 months in oak.

CRU (French) Literally a 'growth', in wine terms generally used to describe a specific vineyard.

CRU CLASSÉ (French) Originally, one of the wines of Bordeaux (Médoc, Barsac and Sauternes) that were classified in 1855 as being those that fetched the highest prices at the Exposition Universelle in Paris. The wines of St-Émilion and Graves were classified later. The term is occasionally used elsewhere.

CUVÉE (French) A blend, either from a variety of sources or from a specific single source.

DECANTING Pouring the wine from the bottle to another container, either to remove it from sediments or simply to allow it to develop increased flavours and aromas by passing it through air.

DOMAINE (French) An estate or property. The term is sometimes used in the name of a specific vineyard, and often in the name of a wine company.

DOSAGE A mixture of sugar and wine added to sparkling wine, which determines its final sweetness.

EISWEIN (German) Wine made from grapes that have been frozen before harvesting, thereby concentrating the sugar. Called Icewine in Canada.

ÉLEVAGE (French) Literally 'breeding': the raising and maturing of a wine from fermentation to bottling.

EN PRIMEUR (French) Wine bought before it is bottled, generally giving favourable prices to the buyer and cash flow to the grower.

EXTRACTION The development of flavours, colour and minerals by leaving juice in contact with the grapes' solid matter (skins, pips, stalks) before and after fermentation.

FERMENTATION The conversion of grape sugars into alcohol through the action of yeast.

FILTRATION The removal of yeasts and other unwanted particles from wine before bottling.

FINING The removal of soluble particles such as proteins and tannins using a coagulant.

FINISH Residual flavours detected just after swallowing, giving lasting impressions of sweetness, dryness or particular flavours.

FLOR (Spanish) A film of yeast that develops on the surface of dry sherries (and a few other wines), protecting them from oxidation.

FORTIFIED WINE A wine to which grape spirit has been added, to increase alcohol content and in some cases arrest fermentation, retaining residual sugars.

GENERIC A wine named for its region of origin or a particular style rather than being named after a grape variety or a more specific origin.

GRAFTING The process by which a vine variety is joined to a supporting rootstock, particularly a phylloxera-resistant rootstock.

GRAND CRU (French) Literally 'great growth', a term used to distinguish the finest vineyards from the rest (particularly in Burgundy and Champagne).

GRIS (French) Literally 'grey'; in wine terms pale pink.

HYBRID A grape variety that is the result of a cross between two different vine species.

ICEWINE See Eiswein.

LAY DOWN To store, or 'cellar', wine in a cool, dark place for some years to allow it to mature.

LATE HARVEST A wine made from grapes left on the vine longer than usual, for greater sugar levels.

LEES Sediment at the bottom of a wine barrel.

LENGTH The amount of time flavours remain on the palate after swallowing a wine.

MALOLACTIC FERMENTATION The action of bacteria on naturally occurring malic acid, clean and crisp, converting it into softer lactic acid. This may be prevented for more aromatic varietals such as Sauvignon Blanc and wines with low natural acidity.

MÉTHODE TRADITIONELLE (French) Method of making sparkling wines in which bubbles are produced by secondary fermentation in bottle.

MOELLEUX (French) Literally 'mellow', a term applied to some sweet or semi-sweet wines.

MOUTHFEEL Impressions of texture on the palate.

MUST The juice of a grape after pressing and before fermentation.

NÉGOCIANT (French) A wine merchant or broker that buys in grapes or wine from other growers, completing the winemaking and selling the result under its own name.

NOBLE ROT See Botrytis.

NON-VINTAGE Mainly applied to sparkling wines, especially Champagne, to indicate a wine that is blended from several different vintages.

NOSE The smell of a wine, including aromas arising from chemical reactions during fermentation, ageing, exposure to oak etc; also described as the 'bouquet'.

OAKED Descriptive of wine that has been given an oaky flavour, either through maturation in oak barrels or by the introduction of oak chips.

OENOLOGY The science of winemaking.

OLD VINES Though the age at which they can be so described is not defined, old vines produce a lower yield, which should imply higher quality wine.

PÉTILLANT (French) Lightly sparkling.

PHYLLOXERA Destructive American sap-sucking insect, related to aphids.

PREMIER CRU (French) First growth, a superior vineyard, especially in Burgundy and Champagne.

PUNT Indentation in the bottom of most wine bottles.

QUINTA (Portuguese) Farm or estate.

RACKING Transferring a wine to a different container to take it off its lees and to allow it to oxygenate.

RESIDUAL SUGAR The sugar remaining in a wine after fermentation, which determines how sweet or dry it is.

ROOTSTOCK Vine root on to which a wine-producing variety is grafted.

SECOND WINE Wine that is not considered good enough for inclusion in the principal wine of a vineyard or estate, often from younger vines; it is cheaper and very likely good value.

SEDIMENT Small particles that settle from a wine stored in bottle for many years.

SOLERA (Spanish) System of stacked barrels used for blending wines, especially sherry, from several different vintages.

STRUCTURE The balance of acids, tannins and fruit in a wine.

SUR LIE (French) Describes a wine that has been aged on its lees to increase flavour.

TANNINS Bitter phenolics derived from grape skins, pips and stalks (and from oak barrels), necessary to preserve wine.

TERRA ROSSA Red earth found over well-drained limestone in areas with Mediterranean climate, particularly Coonawarra in South Australia.

TERROIR (French) The particular combination of soil, microclimate and exposure to the sun that gives an individual vineyard its unique characteristics.

TIRAGE (French) The process of leaving a sparkling wine on its lees for added flavour.

TOASTY Slightly burnt taste characteristic of certain white wines, often derived from the toasting of the barrel in which it was either fermented or aged.

VARIETAL A wine made from a single, specified grape variety.

VENDANGE TARDIVE (French) See Late harvest.

VIEILLES VIGNES (French) See Old vines.

VIGNERON (French) Vine grower.

VIN DE PAILLE (French) Literally 'straw wine' – made from sweet grapes, originally dried on straw mats.

VIN DOUX NATUREL (French) Fortified wine whose sweetness is provided by natural residual sugars.

VINIFICATION Winemaking.

VIN SANTO (Italian) Literally 'holy wine' – dessert wine made from dried grapes.

VINTAGE The process of gathering the grapes, and the year in which the grapes were harvested.

VITICULTURE Vine growing and vineyard practice.

VITIS VINIFERA The European grapevine.

WINERY Where wine is made.

YIELD Quantity of fruit produced in a vineyard.

Index

ACKNOWLEDGEMENTS

We are grateful to the many producers who have supplied images of their wines for inclusion in this book, and to those listed below for permission to reproduce their photographs. We apologize for any unintentional omissions and would be happy to insert an appropriate acknowledgement in future editions. Key: a = above, b = below, c = centre, cl = centre left, cr = centre right, l = left, r = right, t = top.

Alta Vista, pp 206–207.

Angelus, Château, p 9bl.

Australian Wine and Brandy Corporation/Matt Turner, pp 214–15, 221.

Beck Wines, Graham, p 169.

BIVB/D. Gadenne, p 13a; G. Monamy, p 9tl; /J.P. Muzard, p 9tr, 11ccl.

Bouchard Finlayson, pp 9bcr, 159b, 166–67.

Burge Wines, Grant p 208b.

Cape Mentelle, pp 7b, 212tl.

Carlisle Winery/Mike Officer, pp 8b, 11tcr.

Castello di Fonterutoli, pp 9br.

Cephas/Nigel Blythe, pp 27a, 30, 53, 100–101, 105, 131, 132, 134–35, 140, 143; /Fernando Briones, p 114–15; /Andy Christodolo, pp 79, 80, 81, 196, 199, 202; /Steve Elphick, p 181; /Dario Fusaro, p 74; /Mike Herringshaw, p 24; /Kevin Judd, pp 182, 204, 208a, 209b, 226b, 227, 228–29, 231, 232–33; /Kjell Karlsson, p 9cl; /Herbert Lehmann, pp 88, 125, 156; /Diana Mews, p 109; /Janis Miglavs, p 186; /Steven Morris, p 223; /Karen Muschenetz, pp 170a, 184–85; /R. and K. Muschenetz, pp 142, 194a; /Alain Proust, pp 7a,

160, 164–65, 168; /Mick Rock, pp 2, 6b, 9bcl, 10, 13b, 17a, 18–19, 20b, 20–21, 28–29, 32–33, 34–35, 37, 38–39, 42–43, 44–45, 46, 49, 50, 51, 56, 57, 58, 59, 61, 62, 64, 65, 67, 68, 70a, 73, 76–77, 82, 83, 84–85, 86–87, 91, 92, 95, 96, 97, 98a, 98b, 99b, 103, 104, 106, 111, 112, 113, 116, 117, 118, 119, 120, 121, 122–23, 126, 127, 141, 145a, 148, 149, 153, 154, 155, 172–73, 175, 178–79, 182, 189, 210, 220, 225a, 225b; /Ian Shaw, pp 9cr, 15a, 24, 26, 52, 54; / Matt Wilson, pp 195a, 200, 201.

Chalone Vineyard, pp 171a, 183.

Climens, Château, p 29.

Cono Sur, p 194b.

Corbis/Diego Giudice, p 206.

Domaines Barons de Rothschild (Lafite) 17b.

Deutsches Weininstitut (DWI), pp 128a, 129a, 130b, 138a, 138–39.

Domaine Clarence Dillon/Château Haut-Brion, pp 6b, 9ccl, 9ccr, 12a, 22.

Dow's, p 122a.

Fattoria Lavacchio, p 10cr.

Figeac, Château, p 25.

Freixenet, p 108b.

Getty Images/Thomas Northcut, pp 102b, 232b; /Lew Robertson, pp 39a, 108a; /Paul Taylor, pp 8a, 20a, 130a; /TS Photography, pp 86, 134a, 226a, 234.

Golan Heights Winery/Rina Nagila, pp 144a, 157.

Groot Constantia Estate, p 158a.

Grünhaus, Maximin, pp 128b, 129b.

Henschke, pp 10tr, 11tl, 11tcl, 11tc, 11cc, 11ccr, 11bcl, 11bc, 11bcr, 209a, 217.

Hugel & Fils/www.hugel.com, pp 9tcl, 10br, 11br, 40, 41.

Klein Constantia, pp 158b, 159a, 162–63.

La Chablisienne/Daniel Chaslerie, p 47.

La Crema, p 177.

La Rioja Alta, p 99a.

Lavaque Winery, Felix, p 203.

Leeuwin Estate/Frances Andrjich, pp 212–13.

Margaux, Château, p 9tcr.

Montevetrano/Rafaelle Venturini, p 71a.

Napa Valley Vintners/Jason Tinacci, pp 170b, 171b, 173r, 174.

Palmer, Château, pp 12b, 14.

Pulenta Estate, p 195b.

Reschke, Dru/Koonara Wines, p 218.

Schloss Vollrads, p 137.

Sierra Cantabria, p 11tr.

Sipp Mack, p 11bl.

Stanlake Park, p 151.

Tenuta dell'Ornellaia, pp 70b, 71b.

Weingut Nittnaus, p 145b.

Weingut Stadlmann/Lammerhuber, p 146.